❧ History ❦

MAKING SENSE OF HISTORY
Studies in Historical Cultures
General Editor: Jörn Rüsen, in Association with Christian Geulen

Western Historical Thinking: An Intercultural Debate
   Edited by Jörn Rüsen

Identities: Time, Difference, and Boundaries
   Edited by Heidrun Friese

Narration, Identity and Historical Consciousness
   Edited by Jürgen Straub

The Meaning of History
   Edited by Jörn Rüsen and Klaus E. Müller

History: Narration—Interpretation—Orientation
   Jörn Rüsen

Thinking Utopia: Steps Into Other Worlds
   Edited by Jörn Rüsen, Michael Fehr and Thomas W. Rieger

HISTORY

Narration—Interpretation—Orientation

Jörn Rüsen

Berghahn Books
New York • Oxford

Published in 2005 by

Berghahn Books
www.berghahnbooks.com

Copyright © 2005 Jörn Rüsen
First paperback edition published in 2005
Reprinted in 2006

All rights reserved. Except for the quotation of short passages for the purpose of criticism and review, no part of this book may be reproduced in any form or by any means, electronic or mechanical, including photocopying, recording, or any information storage and retrieval system now known or to be invented, without written permission of the publisher.

Library of Congress Cataloguing-in-Publication Data

Rüsen, Jörn.
   History : narration--interpretation--orientation / Jörn Rüsen.
     p. cm. -- (Making sense of history ; vol. 2)
   ISBN 1-57181-624-0 (alk. paper)
    1. History--Philosophy. 2. Historiography. I. Title. II. Series.

D16.8.R915 2004
907'2--dc22   2004049099

British Library Cataloguing in Publication Data

A catalogue record for this book is available from the British Library.

Printed in the United States on acid-free paper.

Contents

List of Tables and Figures — vii

Preface — ix

Introduction: How to Understand Historical Thinking — 1

I: Narration

Chapter 1
Historical Narration: Foundation, Types, Reason — 9

Chapter 2
Narrative Competence: The Ontogeny of Historical and Moral Consciousness — 21

Chapter 3
Rhetoric and Aesthetics of History: Leopold von Ranke — 41

Chapter 4
Narrativity and Objectivity in Historical Studies — 59

II: Interpretation

Chapter 5
What is Historical Theory? — 77

Chapter 6
New History: Paradigms of Interpretation — 93

Chapter 7
Theoretical Approaches to an Intercultural Comparison of Historiography — 109

Chapter 8
Loosening the Order of History: Modernity, Postmodernity, Memory   129

III: Orientation

Chapter 9
Historical Thinking as *Trauerarbeit*: Burckhardt's Answer to a
    Question of our Time   147

Chapter 10
Historizing Nazi-Time: Metahistorical Reflections on the Debate
    Between Friedländer and Broszat   163

Chapter 11
Holocaust-Memory and German Identity   189

Bibliography   205

Index   221

List of Tables

1.1	Typology of Historical Narration	12
2.1	The Four Types of Historical Consciousness	29
7.1	Schema for a Universal Periodization of Historical Thinking	124

List of Figures

8.1	Schema of Historical Thinking	133
11.1	The Past Conditions the Present	196
11.2	The Present Conditions the Past	198

Preface

This book is a completely revised version of my "Studies in Metahistory," which was published in 1993 in the Series of the Human Sciences Research Council at Pretoria.[1] The editor of the series, Johan Mouton, had the idea to publish a collection of my articles which cover essential issues of metahistory. It should thematize principles of historical thinking in general, present some investigations in the history of historiography, and reflect the logic and function of historical studies as an academic discipline.

Our discussions took place in a political situation where the work of the humanities had become part of a general intellectual effort to strengthen the spirit of critical thinking and the awareness of the factual and moral participation of the humanities in the political culture of its time. We shared the widespread opinion that reflections of metahistory could not only sharpen the insight of professional historians and scholars of the other humanities into the logic of historical thinking, but at the same time contribute to the struggle of overcoming apartheid at the academic level.

I would like to thank Johan Mouton again for his initiation of the book. I am grateful to Peter Duvenage who took care of the collection, edited the translations and wrote an introduction. I thank Christina Landmann for her translations. The new version of the book was realized with the help of Nicole Pavenstädt and Christian Geulen, who made the first check of the texts. Trygve Tholfsen gave me a lot of useful hints to improve the text. He will not be content with my corrections, but I am very grateful for his careful and critical reading. I would like to give my special thanks to Angelika Wulff for her critical reading and her intensive effort to bring the book into good order. I owe a deep gratitude to Inge Rüsen for her intensive work to improve my English. Another special thank goes to Annelie Ramsbrock; without her enduring and careful help the manuscript would not have been completed. At Berghahn Books it gives me a great pleasure to thank Mark Stanton, who attentively followed every phase of this project and Veronica Smith, who copyedited the manuscript. Finally, I would like to thank Marion Berghahn for her never ending interest in getting this book published.

Note

1. Jörn Rüsen, *Studies in Metahistory* (Pretoria, 1993).

Introduction:
How to Understand Historical Thinking

> Lasset uns unser Ziel so rein, so hell, so schlackenfrei
> annehmen, als wir's können; denn wir laufen
> in Irrlicht und Dämmerung und Nebel.
> Herder[1]

History is much more than only a matter of historical studies. It is an essential cultural factor in everybody's life, since human life needs an orientation in the course of time which has to be brought about by remembering the past. Historical studies are a systematic way of performing this function of orientation. In order to understand what historians do one should start with this fundamental and general function.

Human life has its very specific time order. Nietzsche has described it at the beginning of his "Second Untimely Meditation:"

> Consider the herds that are feeding yonder: they know not the meaning of yesterday or today; they graze and ruminate, move or rest, from morning to night, from day to day, taken up with their little loves and hates and the mercy of the moment, feeling neither melancholy nor satiety. Man cannot see them without regret, for even in the pride of his humanity he looks enviously on the beast's happiness. He wishes simply to live without satiety or pain, like the beast; yet it is all in vain, for he will not change places with it. ... He wonders also about himself—that he cannot learn to forget, but hangs on the past: however far or fast he runs, that chain runs with him.[2]

The burdening chain of memory has become a fundamental condition of human life, because human beings have lost their guidance by natural instincts and are forced to replace instincts with a self-created cultural framework of orientation. The loss of instincts has opened up a new realm for experiencing time—it appears no longer in the pregiven order of a biological system but as a change of the world which has to be brought into a cultural order of significance and meaning. It appears as a challenge for interpretation. As such it has

---

Notes for this section begin on page 5.

the character of contingency: A permanent irritation to be deliberately brought into an order of insight and understanding. Contingency means that things happen in a way that forces people to move their own mind to come to terms with them. Compared with the determination of instincts this movement of the human mind can be called freedom, and time as contingency can be understood as a shadow of freedom. Human beings have lost the natural guidance of animals in pursuing life, they are "thrown" into the freedom of culturally creating the guidance of their lives by themselves.[3]

This freedom is a matter of hard work. Time has to be made intelligible by reflecting its experience as a matter of interpretation. By interpretation time gets a sense and aquires a significant feature: it becomes history.[4]

What is history? In respect to the anthropologically universal function of orientating human life by culture the answer is very simple: history is time which has gained sense and meaning. History is meaningful and sense-bearing time. It combines past, present and future in a way that human beings can live in the tense intersection of remembered past and expected future. History is a process of reflecting the time order of human life, grounded on experience and moved by outlooks on the future.

Across the huge variety in which this cultural feature of time we call history has been realized, all its variations share a common mental practice and form: narration.[5] By narration time gains sense. Narratives transform the past into history; they combine experience and expectation—the two main time dimensions of human life. As a synthesis of experience and expectation it includes a relationship to the human subject as well—its identity as a coherence of the self in the changes of time. Narratives create the field where history lives its cultural life in the minds of the people, telling them who they are and what the temporal change of themselves and their world is about.

The chapters of this book try to survey this field. They follow different coordinates which intersect and meet at knots of significance, bringing about what we call the sense of history. One coordinate is the procedure and logic of historical narration; a second one is cognitive principles of rationality and truth claims in historical thinking; and a third is the practical function of historical thinking in human life. By these three lines of inquiry and analysis three different modes of understanding history are integrated that used to be presented as conflicting if not contradictory.

Truth claims and rationality constitute historical studies as an academic discipline or as a "science" in a broader sense. History is a well-established academic discipline with a long and stable tradition and with a deeply rooted self-confidence of its professionals. Historical representations have always claimed for truth, but in the course of the modernisation of history toward an academic discipline of professionals, historical truth more and more became alienated from its traditional version as a matter of the morality of the historians. It was presented and reflected as a matter of research which followed its own specific method. This method defined historical thinking as a "science," which needs professionalism in the form of a trained and skilled practice in dealing with source material.

Even today scholarly professionalism in history and claims for historical truth are closely interrelated. Academic training still furnishes historians with cognitive skills that make them feel superior in telling "how it really was" (Ranke)[6] to all others who also deal with the past (for example, novelists, filmmakers, educationists, politicians etc.). Nevertheless, there has always been an uncomfortable feeling for professional historians when they thought about the relationship of their discipline to the natural sciences, and made attempts to declare their discipline a science. These frequent attempts have never really been convincing.[7] There has always remained an awareness of a fundamental difference between the natural sciences and history as a part of the humanities. Historical studies traditionally tried to maintain truth claims and a capacity for scientific objectivity, but at the same time they tried to mark a difference from the natural sciences by stating their own logic.[8]

For more than four decades *narrativity* has gradually become the most convincing answer to the question for this distinctive nature of history.[9] Historians tell stories, and story-telling follows the rules of narration; and these rules essentially differ from all modes of scientific argumentation which are based upon and aiming at general laws, if possible in a mathematical form. The disclosure of its narrative form has more and more turned history away from reflecting and explicating truth claims and methodical procedures of getting valid knowledge about the past. It moved away from the sciences and came closer to literature, as narration is a linguistic procedure for creating meaning, of which the fine arts and (mainly) literature are paradigmatic. Historical sense does not have the logical feature of a law of nature, but of a pattern of significance in which norms and human subjectivity play an important role. This is one of the main results of the so called "linguistic turn" in history or, more precisely, in understanding the work of the historians.

In its scientific meaning historical truth was understood as "objectivity"— an overcoming of all subjective particularity in interpreting the human world. Historical narration, instead, is focussed on this subjective particularity.[10] It discloses and represents human subjectivity in making sense of the world. 'Identity' is a key word of this ascription of subjectivity to history. History is a specific intellectual procedure (and its manifestation) of interpreting the past in a mode that the people of today understand their own world and their difference from others. This understanding includes a future perspective of their world and themselves; it is committed to the value system of their cultural orientation. In understanding temporal change history combines experiences and values in the indivisible whole of a narration.

But the linguistic turn in reflection on history failed in addressing the truth claims in dealing with the past, which were still moving the minds of the historians. Even when professional historians presented the history of their own discipline as full of partiality and political and moral commitment, they could not but claim for truth.[11] What they said about the nonobjectivity of history, its essential subjectivity, can still be confronted with the question of whether what is said about the past "really was the case" or not, and historians made a lot of efforts to convince the reader with a positive answer. What about this truth? Historical narrative has to be analyzed in respect to its distinctive nature, its difference from fictional literature, its specific interest in empirical evidence. This brings about a new awareness of *historical interpretation* as an argumentative mode of putting the facts of the past into a coherent historical order. The emphasis on narrative has led to new knowledge of the poetical and rhetorical means of a symbolic (mainly linguistic) representation of the past.[12] Historiography was analyzed as a symbolic order, as a text, which is structured according to the rules of aesthetics. This emphasis caused interpretation as a cognitive procedure and its methodical rules of research to disappear.[13]

Representation or interpretation? This alternative is not at all convincing. History is both, and it is high time to distinguish them and analyze their different legitimacy on the one hand and their close and principal interrelationship with each other on the other hand. This brings theory back into the reflection on the historian's work, since theory is a specific ("scientific") logical means of historical argumentation in the procedure of interpretation. Representing the result of it is another part of the same activity of doing history and should be clearly distinguished from interpretation.

Representation and interpretation depend upon each other. Decisive for this mutual dependence is the practical function of historical thinking in human life. Can we understand its power on the human mind without its claims for truth? But what underlies this truth? Is it only the factual evidence of the past? As such it has no power since its factuality is only a consequence of its having passed away. As a fact of the past ("what really was the case") history is dead—but does it live only by fiction of the present? As a simple fiction with no reference to something "real," nobody would listen to historical narratives when dealing with the difficult questions of historical identity and future perspectives of human activity derived from the past.

In order to find out how and why history is both—factual and fictional, empirical and meaningful—one has systematically to take into account its narrative character. As a narration history is a part of the cultural orientation that human activity and suffering require. Historical narration is a part of social communication within which it gains and unfolds its mental power. "Historical culture" is the very field of human life where history is a part of social reality and not only a reflection on it.

History is a narrative construction of the human mind. It uses cognitive means of creating sense of the experience of the past and it uses poetical and rhetorical means of bringing this sense into the effective cultural framework of human life. But at the same time those who do this construction and negotiate it in their social context are constructed themselves. They have been shaped by the same past which they are historically dealing with.

This double nature can be disclosed and brought into view if the practical function of history is considered. This function includes both the need for history as cultural orientation in human life and the potentials of fulfilling this need in the human mind.

The following chapters are constituted by the systematic interrelationship of narration, interpretation and orientation in and by history. History is treated as a mode of thinking, but that does not mean a narrow perspective privileging the cognitive dimension of dealing with the past. On the contrary, the political and the aesthetical dimensions are systematically taken into account. The emphasis on addressing sense criteria is committed to the attempt of broadening the perspective in which history appears as an essential element of human culture. This is supported by a threefold mode of argument: Case studies put the issue of history into a historical perspective. Here the emphasis is on classical authors, modern developments and current debates. Systematic argument is the second strategy for reflecting on history. Here the emphasis is on fundamental problems such as theory, objectivity, typology, comparison etc. Finally, there is an attempt to reflect on history in a pragmatic way. Here the emphasis is on developing historical consciousness, and learning history as a process of gaining narrative competence.

The mixture of these three modes of argument should bring history into a complex perspective with a variety of outlooks—meeting the power and fascination history has in our lives.

Notes

1. Johann Gottfried Herder, "Auch eine Philosophie der Geschichte zur Bildung der Menschheit," in idem *Zur Philosophie der Geschichte. Eine Auswahl in zwei Bänden*, vol. 1, *Abhandlungen, Fragmente, Notizen*, Berlin, 1952, 522 (Let us take up our aim as clean, as bright, as free of slag, as we can, since we walk in twilight, dusk, and fog).
2. Friedrich Nietzsche, *The Use and Abuse of History,* trans. Adrian Collins, New York, 1985, 5.
3. Immanuel Kant has expressed this cultural quality of human nature, this constitutive "being thrown" into freedom in the third sentence of his "Idee zu einer allgemeinen Geschichte in weltbürgerlicher Absicht" (1784): "Die Natur hat gewollt: daß der Mensch alles, was über die mechanische Anordnung seines tierischen Daseins geht, gänzlich aus sich selbst herausbringe" [Nature has intended that man develop everything that transcends the mechanical ordering of his animal existence, entirely by himself] (A 390—trans. T.M. Greene and H. Hudson); I quote it according to the 1st edn (A); Immanuel Kant, *Schriften zur Anthropologie, Geschichtsphilosophie, Politik und Pädagogik*. 1. Teil (Werke in 10 Bänden, ed. Wilhelm Weischedel, vol. 9), Darmstadt, 1968, 31–61.

4. Cf. Jörn Rüsen, "History: Overview," in *International Encyclopedia of the Social & Behavioral Sciences*, eds. Neil J. Smelser and Paul B. Baltes, Amsterdam, 2001, pp. 6857–64.
5. Cf. Chap. 1.
6. "Wie es eigentlich gewesen," in Leopold Ranke, *Geschichten der romanischen und germanischen Voelker von 1494–1514*, Sämtliche Werke vol. 33, Leipzig, 1855, viii.
7. Cf. Isaiah Berlin, "The Concept of Scientific History," in W.H. Dray, ed., *Philosophical Analysis and History*, New York, 1966, 5–53.
8. Cf. e.g., *Philosophical Analysis and History*, ed. W.H. Dray; *A New Philosophy of History*, eds. Frank R. Ankersmit and Hans Kellner, Chicago, 1995.
9. A breakthrough to narration in the discourse on explanation as a mode of "scientific" argumentation was brought about by Arthur C. Danto, *Analytical Philosophy of History*, Cambridge, 1965; the difference from the traditional understanding of "scientific" explanation (called "rational") is evident, if one compares Danto's philosophy with the classical text of a positivistic understanding of history by C.G. Hempel, "The Function of General laws in history," *Journal of Philosophy*, 39 (1942), 35–48.
10. Cf. chap. 4.
11. An excellent example is Peter Novick, *That Noble Dream. The "Objectivity-Question" and the American Historical Profession*, New York and Cambridge, 1988.
12. Cf. Hayden White, *Metahistory: The Historical Imagination in Nineteenth Century Europe*, Baltimore, 1973.
13. Cf. The polemic by Keith Windschuttle, *The Killing of History: How Literary Critics and Social Theorists are Murdering our past*, New York, 2000.

I: Narration

Chapter 1

Historical Narration: Foundation, Types, Reason

> Queen: ... no dancing, girl
>   – some other Sport.
> Lady: Madam, we'll tell tales.
> Queen: Of sorrow or of joy?
> Lady: Of either, madam.
> Queen: Of neither, girl.
>   Shakespeare[1]

What is historical narration? Most historians will feel bored when they hear this question. They will probably think: 'Leave this matter to the people in the literature and philosophy departments', but in fact this question impacts on the fundamentals of their own work and brings philosophy and linguistics much nearer than usual to historical studies.

    Hayden White, with elaborate sagacity, labored to convince historians of this fact when he treated "the historical work as what it most manifestly is," that is to say, "a verbal structure in the form of a narrative prose discourse." But since he explicated this discourse of historians as "generally poetic, and specially linguistic, in nature,"[2] he shocked most historians. They felt consigned to the uncomfortable and ambiguous vicinity of poetry and robbed of their hard-earned dignity as scholars of a highly rationalized, methodologically confirmed discipline. Nevertheless, it is worthwhile to enter the poetical sphere. The didactical term "poetical" should be understood in the original sense of poesies, which simply means making or producing something. Indeed, no historian could deny the fact that there is a creative activity of the human mind working in the process of historical thinking and recognition. Narration is the way this activity is being performed and "history"—more precisely, a history—is the product of it.

    I will not enter into a complex epistemological discussion of the narrative structure of historical knowledge.[3] Instead, I want to point to the narrative

---

Notes for this section begin on page 19.

fundamentals of historical consciousness by quoting an inconspicuous argument. Despite the prejudice against locating poetry within the fundamentals of historical studies, I want to quote a brief dialogue between King Henry IV and his noble counselor Warwick:

> KING HENRY
> O God! that one might read the book of fate,
> And see the revolution of the times ...
> ... how chances mock,
> And changes fill the cup of alteration
> With divers liquors! O, if this were seen,
> The happiest youth, viewing his progress through,
> What peril past, what crosses to endure,
> Would shut the book, and sit him down and die.
> WARWICK
> There is a history in all men's lives,
> Figuring the nature of the times deceased;
> KING HENRY
> Are these things then necessities?
> Then let us meet them like necessities[4]

From this small but profound dialogue we can learn what historical narration is: it is a system of mental operations defining the field of historical consciousness. Here time is seen as a threat to normal human relations, casting them into the abyss of uncertainty. The most radical experience of time is death. History is a response to this challenge: it is an interpretation of the threatening experience of time. It overcomes uncertainty by seeing a meaningful pattern in the course of time, a pattern responding to human hopes and intentions. This pattern gives a sense to history. Narration therefore is the process of making sense of the experience of time.

I understand Hayden White's statement about narration in this way as a poetical act constituting historical knowledge.[5] Narration is a process of poesies, of making or producing a fabric of temporal experience woven according to the need to orient oneself in the course of time. The product of this process of narration, the fabric capable of such orienting, is "a history." With respect to the threat of death, narration transcends the limits of mortality into a broader horizon of meaningful temporal occurrences. This is one of the essential truths of the tales of *A Thousand and One Nights*. Scheherazade knows that to narrate is to overcome death; narration is an act of demortalizing human life.[6]

But the Shakespearean answer to the question "What is historical narration?" is as ambiguous as poetry itself. It tells enough about narration for us to understand it as a fundamental operation in the depths of historical consciousness; but since not all narration is historical, it tells too little about this difference. And this is also very often the case in the topical discussion of the philosophy of history when it stresses the narrative procedures of historiography.

So we need the help of more theoretical arguments to complement Shakespeare. The traditional argument would be to differentiate between factual and fictional narratives. Historical narration is usually defined as dealing only with facts and not with fictions. This differentiation is very problematic and finally unconvincing, because the all-important sense of a history lies beyond the distinction between fiction and fact. In fact it is absolutely misleading—and arises from a good deal of hidden and suppressed positivism—to call everything in historiography fiction, if it is not a fact in the sense of hard data.

I think that the peculiarity of a historical narration lies in the following three qualities and their systematic relationship:[7]

1. A historical narrative is tied to the medium of memory. It mobilizes the experience of past time, which is engraved in the archives of memory, so that the experience of present time becomes understandable and the expectation of future time is possible.
2. A historical narrative organizes the internal unity of these three dimensions of time by a concept of continuity. This concept adjusts the real experience of time to human intentions and expectations. By doing so it makes the experience of the past become relevant for present life and influences the shaping of the future.
3. A historical narrative serves to establish the identity of its authors and listeners. Dependent upon this function is whether a concept of continuity is plausible or not. This concept of continuity must be capable of convincing the listeners of the permanence and stability of themselves in the temporal change of their world and of themselves.

By these three qualities historical narration brings about the orientation of practical life in time—an orientation without which it is impossible for humans to find their way.

Until now I have given only a rough outline of the wide and manifold field of historical narration. It is necessary first to establish a general theoretical model of the structure, process and function of historical narration before one considers the varieties of historiography. Only with such a model can we adequately distinguish historiography from other forms of understanding in our own and all other cultures.

But the proof of the pudding is in the eating, and so the proof of the abstract description is in the understanding of concrete phenomena. Therefore the question is inevitably: how can we develop understanding of the narrative fundamentals of historical knowledge into the cognition of the manifold manifestations of historiography? To paraphrase Karl Marx: How can we ascend from the abstract to the concrete? We can do this by means of typology.

And so we have come to the second point of this chapter, in which I would like to give an outline of a general typology of historical narration, which should disclose the wide and manifold field of historiography. In this typology I try to stress the specific historical character of making sense of the experience of time by narration. With this intention, similar to that of Johann Gustav Droysen and Friedrich Nietzsche, the following typology differs substantially from that of Hayden White, which interprets historiography as literature and does not at all recognize its specificity.

The point I start from is the function of historical narration. As I have already mentioned, historical narration has the general function of orienting practical life in time by mobilizing the memory of temporal experience, by developing a concept of continuity and by stabilizing identity. This general function can be realized in four different ways. I think, that these four ways are grounded in anthropological universals: one can distinguish four necessary conditions which must be fulfilled so that human life can go on in the course of time: affirmation, regularity, negation, transformation. According to these relationships of human life to time I can see four different functional types of historical narration with corresponding forms of historiography.

I would like to illustrate the types by examples drawn from the field of women's history; a subject matter which has focused the discussion on the fundamentals of historical studies for a long time.[8]

TABLE 1.1 TYPOLOGY OF HISTORICAL NARRATION

	Memory of	Continuity as	Identity by	Sense of time
traditional narrative	origins constituting present forms of life	permanence of originally constituted forms of life	affirming pregiven cultural patterns of self-understanding	time gains the sense of eternity
exemplary narrative	cases demonstrating applications of general rules of conduct	validity of rules covering temporally different systems of life	generalizing experiences of time to rules of conduct	time gains the sense of spacial extension
critical narrative	deviations problematizing present form of life	alteration of given ideas of continuity	denying given patterns of identity	time gains the sense of being an object of judgment
genetical narrative	transformations of alien forms of life into proper ones	development in which forms of of life change in order to establish their permanence dynamically	mediating permanence and change to a process of self-definition	time gains the sense of temporalization

SOURCE: Jörn Rüsen, 2004

Example One

Every form of human life is necessarily organized by traditions. They cannot be denied totally, otherwise people would lose the ground under their feet. The first type takes this into account. Traditional narrative articulates traditions as necessary conditions for humans to find their way. Traditional narratives in the field of women's history are very rare, but monuments are a traditional way of historically making sense of the experience of time. I found a good example in Grahamstown (South Africa) in the main street leading from Rhodes University to the cathedral. There is a monument which is dedicated "to Pioneer women" and inscribed as follows, representing historical meaning as traditional narratives do: Keep their memory green and sweet/they smoothed the thorns with bleeding feet. To put it in the generalizing manner of theory: traditional narratives remind one of the origins constituting present systems of life; they construct continuity as the permanence of originally constituted systems of life, and they form identity by affirming given—or more precisely, pre-given—cultural patterns of self-understanding. Other examples are: stories which tell about the origin and the genealogy of rulers, in order to legitimate their domination; within religious communities, stories of their foundation; stories which are told at the occasion of centennials and other jubilees (in Boston [U.S.] you can even *walk* a traditional narrative following the Freedom Trail painted as a red line on the sidewalk). In all these stories time gains the sense of eternity.

Example Two

Traditions alone are not sufficient as forms of orientation because they are very limited in their empirical content. Furthermore, they are manifold and heterogeneous, and call for an integration by rules or principles. These rules and principles are abstract because they are general and cover a wide range of diverse experiences of time. They therefore require relation to this diversity: it is exemplary narratives which bring about this relation. They concretize abstract rules and principles, telling stories which demonstrate the validity of the rules and principles in single cases. To use our example: one can look back at an early period of women's studies. In order to demonstrate the abstract principle of women's equality, female historians preferred stories which told a lot about the accomplishments, capacities, importance, and efficiency of women of the past. This approach had the effect that many important women and their works in art, handicraft, science and religion and their learning in economics and politics were saved from oblivion.

To put it in the generalizing way of theory again: exemplary narratives remind one of cases which demonstrate applications of general rules of conduct; they impose continuity as the supertemporal validity of rules which cover temporally different systems of life; and they form identity by generalizing experiences of time to rules of conduct. Other examples of this type of historical narration are stories which present models of virtues or vices. In the newspapers we can always find allusions to historical occurrences, and these allusions follow the logic of exemplary narration. An example is the following part of an article in the *Cape Times* of 17 February 1987:

> Will we say: "We did not know?" The recent address in Parliament by the Minister of Finance ... where he admitted that he ... did not know what was going on in the black townships is cause for concern.
> We all know that the German people were not informed about the terrible conditions in the ghettos and prisoner of war camps or the extermination horror ... and at the end, their answer to all this was: "we did not know." Some terrible parallels can be formed which could apply in the South African context; and will we, at the end of the day, also say "we did not know?"

The core of the logic of exemplary narration is formulated by the old phrase: *historia vitae magistra* [history is the teacher of life]. Stories of the exemplary type open up the field of temporal experience beyond the limits of tradition: time gains the sense of spatial extension.

Example Three

The third type is critical narration. It is based on people's ability to say no to traditions, rules and principles which have been handed down to them. This "no" stands before each intended alteration of the cultural patterns of historical understanding. It opens up the space for new patterns.

In women's history this type of narration is abundant. Well known are the stories relating the suffering of women in the long history of patriarchal domination. By these stories feminist historians shake the validity of traditional patterns of womanhood, thus opening minds for alternatives.

In theoretical terms critical narratives remind one of deviations which make the present conditions of life problematic; they schematize continuity only indirectly, namely by dissolving or destroying culturally effective ideas of continuity. As far as continuity is concerned these stories live on what they destroy. They form identity by denying given patterns of selfunderstanding: it is the identity of obstinacy.

Other examples of this type are the historical works which follow Voltaire's motto: "When reading history it is but the only business of a healthy mind to refute it."[9] Critical narratives are anti-stories. These stories call temporal experience before the tribunal of the human mind: time gains the sense of being an object of judgment.

Example Four

But critical narrative is not the last word of historical consciousness. Its dynamic of negation is not sufficient; it only replaces one pattern with another. The pattern that finds the change itself meaningful and significant is still missing. This pattern defines the fourth type: that of the genetical narrative. Stories of this type give direction to the temporal change of humans and the world, to which the listeners must accordingly adjust their lives in order to cope with the challenging alterations of time.

In women's history, stories of this type of narrative overcome the alternative of affirmation or negation, of defining or refusing given traditions and principles of womanhood. They replace the abstract antithesis by stressing the element of dynamic structural change, and use gender as a historical category. It is this element of structural development which mediates the anticipation of alternatives with the experience of the hitherto achieved alterations of the state of womanhood and of gender relations.

In the concepts of theory genetical narratives remind one of transformations which lead from alien forms of life into proper ones. They present continuity as development, in which the alteration of forms of life is necessary for their permanence. And they form identity by mediating permanence and change to a process of self-definition (in German this is called *Bildung*). Stories of this type represent the forces of change as factors of steadiness; they take away the threat of losing oneself in the temporal movement of human subjectivity, interpreting it rather as a chance of gaining oneself. They organize human self-understanding as a temporally dynamic process: time gains the sense of temporality.

Now one may ask, what is won by discerning these four types? It is impossible to answer this question before we have looked into the complex relationships between them. Each type corresponds to one necessary condition which must be fulfilled if human life is to find its way in the course of time. Therefore, the four types do not exclude one another but are closely connected, although each is clearly distinguished from the others. The complexity of this connection is too wide to explicate here in full, so I will just summarize the two main points: first, all four elements are found in every historical text, one necessarily implies the others. Second, there is a logical progression from the traditional to the exemplary and from the exemplary to the genetical narrative. Critical narrative serves as the necessary catalyst in this transformation.

To realize the whole fabric of relations between the types we have to combine the quality of implication with that of transformation. The result will not be a muddle or a higgledy-piggledy mess, but a systematically ordered texture, the logic of which can be called dialectic. By this structure the typology enables us to analyze concrete works of historiography in a clear-cut conceptual framework. As Max Weber has demonstrated, it is the systematic, abstract, and strictly conceptualized form of theory which makes typologies useful for empirical research. And it is about this usefulness or function of the typology of historical narration that I now consider.

The first and most simple use of the typology is to classify historical works. So we can characterize Jacob Burckhardt's *History of the Greek Culture* or George Bancroft's *History of the United States* as a traditional narrative,

Machiavelli's *History of Florence* as exemplary, Voltaire's *Essai sur les moeurs et l'Esprit des nations* as critical, and Theodor Mommsen's *History of Rome* as genetical. But such classification does not take us very far. Only when we take into account the internal relationship among the types can they disclose much more about historical works. In every historical work it is the composition of these four narrative elements that constitutes its peculiarity. The typology allows one to disclose this peculiarity: it furnishes the conceptual means of discerning different elements of historical narrative and of reconstructing their composition into a whole. Thus we can exactly identify a historical narrative with respect to those qualities which fulfill the specifically historical function. To give a small example: in the historiography of historicism the genetical type prevails. Turning to the first work of Ranke, one of its leading representatives, in *Geschichten der romanisch-germanischen Völker von 1494 bis 1514* (1824) the typologically sophisticated eye nevertheless finds distinctly exemplary forms which are not sufficiently integrated into the prevailing genetical sense of the book. This is even more surprising since, as is well known, in the foreword Ranke wrote the famous denial of exemplary history: he said he did not want to judge the past; his history just wanted to show how it actually had been ("er will bloß zeigen, wie es eigentlich gewesen"). By detecting this quality of Ranke's first book, the typology opens a new way to understand it.

Just as we can characterize the peculiarity of a single historical work by using concepts of historical narration in general, so can we apply the typology for comparative analysis. It offers us the criteria of comparison, aiming at the deep structure of historical narration, and it also offers us a procedure of differentiation concerning the specifically historical quality of the compared works. Furthermore we can employ the typology to open up historical perspectives on historiography.

Historical perspectives are drawn from leading ideas of temporal change: in the light of such ideas temporal changes gain the quality of historical development.[10] Concerning historiography, leading ideas of its development can be drawn from the internal tendencies of the types of historical narration. The types can be arranged according to a certain logical order. Each genetical narration has exemplary and traditional forms and functions of historical narration as its preconditions; likewise each exemplary narration has traditional ones. The traditional one itself is original. The critical narration is defined by its negation of the other three types.

If we now give a temporal sense to this logical order, we achieve a conceptual framework for the historical development of historiography. Historically, historiography can be seen in the light of a general tendency leading from traditional narratives to exemplary, and from exemplary to genetical narratives; the critical narratives are catalysts. I would like to call this tendency, in the words of the Enlightenment, a "theoretical" or "hypothetical history." By this I do not want to attribute to the tendency a metaphysical meaning, but rather the quality of a rational order of historical experience. Therefore, the tendencies do not separate the temporal change of historiography from general history and do not form an autonomous sphere of *Geistesgeschichte;* its conception serves as if it were a mirror, showing how the challenge of temporal change is met by a structural change of historical narration.

The conception of the internal dynamic tendencies in the relationship of the four types can be used to periodize the history of historiography. In this periodization the three types mark the three main steps in the evolution of the historical consciousness from early pre-Neolithic cultures to pre-industrial cultures and to modern societies.

In this evolution the acceptance and significance of time itself is transformed. In the first period the course of time became arrested in eternity; in the second period, which in our culture can be traced from Herodotus to Voltaire, this eternity acquired the quality of supertemporally valid principles, and the course of time widened to a multitude of experiences; in the third period, which began in the second half of the eighteenth century, time is temporalized: human self-understanding is no longer seen as a rejection of variety and change, but rather as defined by change and variety. The sphere of real historical experience becomes infinite.[11]

The typology not only gives us a general periodization of the history of historical thinking, it also gives special periodizations within particular epochs. As I have said, the four types are always present in historical texts; one is dominant, the others secondary. The dominant form establishes a general epoch; the relationship among the secondary ones, and between them and the dominant, may define subperiods.

These theoretical considerations can lead to conceptual frameworks of empirical research and interpretation. The epoch of the late Enlightenment, for instance, can typologically be described as a structure shift from exemplary to genetical narration as dominant forms in the deep structure of historical narration. Reinhart Koselleck depicted this shift as a dissolution of the topos *historia magistra vitae* at the outset of the move toward modern history.[12] It would be worthwhile to look for the analogous shift from traditional to exemplary narration as a founding form of historical thinking. I assume that this shift took place during the rise of ancient civilizations.

There is another use of the typology which I would like to point without dealing with it in detail; it is still a hypothetical one. We scarcely know anything about the structural development of historical consciousness in the process of individualization and socialization. But the temporal interpretation of the logical order of the four types would lead to a hypothesis about this development. It seems worthwhile for further differentiation and empirical investigation to conceptualize the ontogenetical development of historical consciousness as a structural process which brings about narrative competence in a sequence of the four types, along with the stages of development in other fields we know much more about—as, for instance, the stages of moral development according to Piaget and Kohlberg.[13]

After this quick excursion into the history of historical thinking, and after an even quicker glimpse of the psychology of historical learning, I would like to conclude my considerations on historical narration with a glance at its most elaborate forms: that is modern historical studies and modern historiography. I will just raise one question: in which way do modern historical studies and historiography fit into the typology of the four functions of historical narration?

Modern historical studies and historiography are distinguished from other forms of historical narration by the achievements of theoretically- and methodologically-organized empirical research. Can one of the four types be applied to this research? Or do we have to ask for a new, fifth type? Both questions are inappropriate, because the peculiarity of modern historical studies with respect to the structure and function of historical narration lies across the four types. This peculiarity is based on the special manner of realizing the fabric of historical narration woven by elements of all types. It is the manner of reasoning and arguing theoretically and methodically in the process of making sense of the experience of time. In each historical narrative we can find elements of reasoning and arguing; they have to make the stories credible. Historical studies are nothing but an elaboration and institutionalization of this reasoning and arguing,[14] which most historians identify in their discipline as the methodical rationality of empirical research.

But this self-understanding of historians as scholars lacks insight into the fundamental practical function of historical narration. As I have shown, this is the function of formulating human identity by mobilizing the forces of historical memory; or, to put it briefly, orienting human life in the course of time. If professional historians recognized this function as a function of their own work, maybe their work would have a little bit more relevance to practical life.

To stress this aspect of historiography is one of the main purposes of the theory of history in general and the typology of historical narration in particular.[15] But it is not the task of the theoretician to prescribe historiography. He or she can only try to elucidate the structure of historical narration, and discuss aspects of reasoning and arguing in it. So, finally, I would like to raise one point concerning the historiographical representation of continuity. As I have already said, continuity is the leading idea of a history connecting the experience of the past with the expectation of the future, thus realizing the unity of time. Historians have presented this idea in different ways. In the good old times of so-called narrative historiography, they presented it by the stream of events as seen by a godlike omniscient author. In modern times of structural and social history, historians often present their idea of continuity in the form of a theory (e.g., theory of modernization). This means a progress in reasoning, for in such form concepts of continuity are matters for discussion; but nevertheless, the reader is exposed to a finished process of making sense of temporal experience.

I can imagine a further progress in reasoning. This might happen if historians presented history to readers in such a way that by reading it they would have to create the sense-making idea of continuity themselves, using their own reason. Then historiography would gain a form which does lie in the vicinity of modern literature.

Notes

First published in: *History and Theory*, Beiheft 26 (1987), "The Representation of Historcal Events", pp.87–97.

1. Shakespeare, *Richard III*, Act 3, Scene 4, v. 9sqq.
2. Hayden White, *Metahistory: The Historical Imagination in Nineteenth Century Europe*, Baltimore, 1973, ix.
3. Arthur Danto, *Analytical Philosophy of History,* Cambridge, 1968; Hans Michael Baumgartner, *Kontinuität und Geschichte. Zur Kritik und Metakritik der historischen Vernunf,* Frankfurt am Main, 1972; Frank Ankersmit, *Narrative Logic. A Semantic Analysis of the Historian's Language*, The Hague, 1983; Paul Ricoeur, *Time and Narrative*, 3 vols. Chicago, 1984–1988; Jürgen Kocka, "Theory Orientation and the New Quest for Narrative: Some Trends and Debates in West Germany," *Storia della Storiographia,* 10 (1986), 170–81; Alan Megill, "Recounting the Past: Description, Explanation and Narrative in Historiography," *American Historical Review,* 94 (1989), 627–53; David Carr, *Time, Narrative and History: Studies in Phenomenology and Existential Philosophy*, Bloomington, 1986, 2nd edn 1991; Jerzy Topolski, ed., *Narration and Explanation: Contributions to the Methodology of Historical Research*, Amsterdam, 1990.
4. Shakespeare, *King Henry IV*, Act 2, Scene 1, v. 45–56.
5. Cf. also White, *Content of the Form*.
6. This is emphasized by Volker Klotz, "Erzählen als Enttöten. Notizen zu zyklischem, instrumentalem und praktischem Erzählen," in Eberhard Lämmert, ed., *Erzählforschung. Ein Symposion*, Stuttgart, 1972, 319–34.
7. For a more detailed argument see Rüsen, "Die vier Typen des historischen Erzählens," 153–230.
8. Cf. e.g., Ursula A.J. Becher, Jörn Rüsen, eds., *Weiblichkeit in geschichtlicher Perspektive*, Frankfurt am Main, 1988.
9. Voltaire, *Oeuvres complètes*, ed., L. Moland, vol. 11, (Paris, 1878), p. 427.
10. The logic of theoretical perspective is described in Rüsen, *Rekonstruktion der Vergangenheit*.
11. Peter Reill illuminated the German part of this beginning: Peter Reill, *The German Enlightenment and the Rise of Historicism,* Berkeley, 1975. Cf. Horst Walter Blanke and Jörn Rüsen, eds., *Von der Aufklärung zum Historismus. Zum Strukturwandel des historischen Denkens, Historisch-politische Diskurse*, vol. 1, Paderborn, 1984.
12. Koselleck, "Historia magistra vitae", 38–66. Cf. Rüsen, *Konfigurationen des Historismus*, 29–94.
13. See below, chapt. 2.
14. Rüsen, *Historische Vernunft*, 85 sqq.
15. Cf. Jörn Rüsen, "The Didactics of History in West Germany: Towards a New Self-Awareness of Historical Studies," *History and Theory,* 26 (1987), 275–86.

Chapter 2

Narrative Competence: The Ontogeny of Historical and Moral Consciousness

---

Question: What comes immediately into your mind, when you think history?
Answer: Today will tomorrow be yesterday.[1]

A narrative in four variations

The ancient castle of Col is located in the Highlands of Scotland. It is the ancestral residence of the chiefs of the Maclean clan and is still in the possession of a member of the Maclean family, who lives in the castle. On the wall is a stone engraved with the following inscription: "*If any man of the clan of Maclonich shall appear before this castle, though he come at midnight, with a man's head in his hand, he shall find here safety and protection against all.*"

This text is from an old Highlands treaty concluded upon a highly memorable occasion. In the distant past, one of the Maclean forefathers obtained a grant of the lands of the Maclonich clan from the Scottish king; that clan had forfeited its land by giving offence to the king. Maclean proceeded with an armed force of men to take possession of his new lands, accompanied by his wife. In the ensuing confrontation and battle with the other clan, Maclean was defeated and lost his life. His wife fell into the hands of the victors, and was found to be with child. The chief of the victorious clan transferred the pregnant Lady Maclean to the custody of the Maclonich family with a specific stipulation: if the baby born should be a boy, it was to be killed immediately; if a girl, the baby should be allowed to live. Maclonich's wife, who also was pregnant, gave birth to a girl at about the same time Lady Maclean gave birth to a boy. They then switched the children. The young boy Maclean, having by this ruse of transposition survived the death sentence passed on him before birth, in

---

Notes for this section begin on page 38.

time regained his original patrimony. In gratitude to the Maclonich clan, he designated his castle a place of refuge for any member of the Maclonich family who felt himself in danger.

This narrative is contained in Samuel Johnson's *Journey to the Western Islands of Scotland,* first published in 1775.[2] It is my intention in this chapter to utilize this story in order to demonstrate the nature of narrative competence and its various forms, and the importance of such competence for moral consciousness. To approach this demonstration in a concrete manner, let us envisage this narrative within the context of an actual situation in which moral values are challenged, and where their use and legitimation require historically based argument.

Imagine you are a member of the Maclean clan living now in the ancestral castle: one dark night a member of the Maclonich clan—let us call him Ian—knocks at your door asking for help. He tells you he is being sought by the police because of a crime he is alleged to have committed. How would you react? Would you help hide him from the police, or decide on some other course of action? Imagine that later on you find it necessary to explain what is going on to a friend who chances by and is unfamiliar with the ancient clan narrative. Whatever your action in respect to Ian Maclonich, you are obliged to narrate to your friend the tale about the switched infants in order to make plausible to him (and thus interpretable) the situation in which you find yourself and the decision you have made. Your narration of this clan legend will probably differ depending on the nature of that decision. Moreover, your original decision itself depends on your interpretation of the ancient clan legend about the transposed infants. I suggest that there are four principal possibilities for such an interpretation:

1. You can hide Ian Maclonich because you feel there is a *binding obligation* on your part to honor the ancient Highland agreement. In this case, you will tell your friend that you—as a Maclean—feel obliged to assist Ian because you regard as binding the ancient and still existent ties between the two clans. You then proceed to narrate the legend of the transposed infants, with the conclusion that you will hide Ian Maclonich from the police in keeping with the ancient clan treaty, thus renewing and continuing its long validity in the relationship between the two clans.
2. You hide Ian Maclonich, yet do so for a variety of other reasons. Thus, you can say that you have helped Ian because in the past a Maclonich aided a member of the Maclean clan, and you now feel obliged to reciprocate on the basis of a *general principle* of reciprocity of favors. Or you can say that you are coming to his aid in order to fulfill the obligation of a treaty between clans: because treaties have to be kept as such, that is, they are binding qua treaty. You go on to narrate the legend, concluding with a remark that mutual aid or the keeping of a treaty between clans is a guiding and important moral principle for you, as proven previously when the baby was rescued.

3. You can refuse to hide Ian Maclonich. Then you first have to explain his request for help by narrating the tale of the infants and the stone with its inscription. But you will comment on this story by stating that you do not believe it, that it is merely a "myth" or "legend" devoid of any evidence or binding validity, and that it does not obligate you morally in any way. Or you can argue that since the introduction of modern Scottish law, those old clan treaties have lost the validity they once had, and are outdated. In this case, you present a series or combination of *critical historical arguments* to relieve yourself of the obligation to keep the ancient treaty. You argue historically in order to sever any bonds between you and the Maclonich clan which may have been valid and binding in the past.
4. You can decide to convince Ian Maclonich that it is fruitless to hide from the police and that it would be better for him to surrender himself to the authorities. You, in turn, promise to do whatever you can to assist him, for example, by hiring the best lawyer available. In this case, you narrate the tale of the infants but circumscribe it by adding the following argument: the legal system has gone through an enormous transformation from the clan law of the premodern age to our modern period. You still feel obliged to help someone from the Maclonich clan, but wish to do so in a way based on *modem considerations,* and not as the ancient treaty prescribes.

This ancient clan narrative dealing with the Macleans, the Maclonichs and the exchanged infants in its four variations provides the point of departure for my arguments here. The tale indicates the need for historical consciousness in order to deal with moral values and moral reasoning. Its four variants, I hope to demonstrate, reflect four stages of development by learning.

The relationship between historical consciousness and moral values and reasoning

In the situation depicted in our narrative, we must decide upon a course of action. Such a decision is dependent on values. These values are general principles, guidelines for behavior, key ideas or perspectives which suggest what should be done in a given situation where various options exist. Such values function as a source of arbitration in conflicts and as objectives guiding us when we act.

What meaning does it have to term these values "moral?" Our perspectives shape action systematically, acknowledge the social relationship within which we live and have to decide upon a course of action to be taken. They express this social relationship as an obligation for us, addressing us at the core of our subjectivity, calling upon our sense of responsibility and conscience. How does history enter into this moral relationship between our action, our self and our value orientations? The narrative sketched at the outset of this chapter can serve to furnish an answer: when moral values are supposed to guide the actions we take in a given situation, we must relate them to this situation, and interpret the values and their moral content in respect to the actuality in which we apply them, and evaluate the situation in terms of our code of applicable moral values. For such a mediation between values and action-oriented actuality, historical consciousness is a necessary prerequisite. Without that consciousness, we would not be able to understand why Ian Maclonich has asked us to hide him from the police. Without such consciousness as a prerequisite to action, we would be unable to deal with the situation and arrive at a decision which appears plausible to all parties involved—Ian, the visiting friend, and yourself as a Maclean.

But why should historical consciousness be a necessary prerequisite for orientation in a present situation requiring action? After all, such consciousness by definition is pointed toward events in the past. The simple answer is that historical consciousness functions as a specific orientational mode in actual situations of life in the present: it functions to aid us in comprehending past actuality in order to grasp present actuality. Without narrating the ancient story of the exchanged infants, it would be impossible to explain to your visiting friend the "actual situation" and justify—which is to say legitimate—your decision. Moreover, the narrative's explanatory power serves to ground the situation not only for the uninformed outsider, but also for yourself as an involved party, a Maclean clansman.

What, then, is specifically "historical" in this explanation, this interpretation of the situation and its legitimation? In its temporal orientation, historical consciousness ties the past to the present in a manner which bestows on present actuality a future perspective. This implied reference to future time is contained in the historical interpretation of the present, because such interpretation must enable us to act—that is, it must facilitate the direction of our intentions within a temporal matrix. When we say we feel bound or obligated by the ancient treaty, we define a future perspective on our relationship to the Maclonich clan. The same is true of all other historical explanations and legitimations associated with our decision.

I wish to derive a general characteristic of historical consciousness and its function in practical life from the narrative example given.[3] Historical consciousness serves as a key orientational element, giving practical life a temporal frame and matrix, a conception of the "course of time" flowing through the mundane affairs of daily life. That conception functions as an element in the intentions guiding human activity, our "course of action." Historical consciousness evokes the past as a mirror of experience within which life in the present is reflected, and its temporal features revealed. Stated succinctly, history is the mirror of past actuality into which the present peers in order to learn something about its future. Historical consciousness should be conceptualized as an operation of human intellection rendering present actuality intelligible while fashioning its future perspectives. Historical consciousness deals with the past qua experience; it reveals to us the web of temporal change within which our lives are caught up, and (at least indirectly) the future perspectives toward which that change is flowing.

History is a meaningful nexus between past, present and future—not merely a perspective on what has been, *wie es eigentlich gewesen*. It is a translation of past into present, an interpretation of past actuality via a conception of temporal change which encompasses past, present and the expectation of future events. This conception moulds moral values into a "body of time" (e.g., the body of the continuing validity of an ancient treaty). History clothes values in temporal experience. Historical consciousness transforms moral values into temporal wholes: traditions, timeless rules of conduct, concepts of development or other forms of comprehension of time. Values and experiences are mediated by and synthesized in such conceptions of temporal change.

Thus, the historical consciousness of a contemporary member of the Maclean clan translates the moral idea that treaties are binding and must be fulfilled into the concrete form of an actual treaty valid over time. Historical consciousness amalgamates "is" and "ought" into a meaningful narrative which informs about past events to help render the present intelligible, and to bestow upon present activity a future perspective. In so doing historical consciousness makes an essential contribution to moral–ethical consciousness. The sense-creating procedures of historical consciousness are necessary for moral values and for moral reasoning as well if the plausibility of moral values is at stake. The reference here is not to logical plausibility of values (in respect to their coherence, for example); rather, it is to plausibility in the sense that values must have an acceptable relationship to reality.

Historical consciousness has a practical function:[4] it bestows upon actuality a temporal direction, an orientation which can guide action intentionally by the agency of historical memory. This function can be termed "temporal orientation." Such orientation occurs in two spheres of life, involving firstly external practical life and, secondly, the internal subjectivity of the actors. Temporal orientation of life has two aspects, one external, the other internal. The external aspect of orientation via history discloses the temporal dimension of practical life, uncovering the temporality of circumstances as shaped by human activity. The internal aspect of orientation via history discloses the temporal dimension of human subjectivity, giving selfunderstanding and awareness a temporal feature within which they take on the form of historical identity, that is, a constitutive consistency of the temporal dimensions of the human self.

By means of historical identity, the human self expands its temporal extension beyond the limits of birth and death, beyond mere mortality. Via this historical identity a person becomes part of a temporal whole larger than that of his/her personal life. Thus, the role of a member of the Maclean clan of today presupposes a historical family identity which extends back to the ancient time when clans battled over a king's gift of territory. By giving Ian Maclonich assistance today, we affirm this identity of what it means to be a Maclean in respect to the future. A more familiar example of such "temporal immortality" (as historical identity can be characterized) is national identity. Nations often locate their wellsprings in a hoary and ancient past, and project an unlimited future perspective embodying national self-assertion and development.

The narrative competence of historical consciousness

The linguistic form within which historical consciousness realizes its function of orientation is that of the narrative. In this view, the operations by which the human mind realizes the historical synthesis of the dimensions of time simultaneous with those of value and experience lie in narration: the telling of a story.[5] Once the narrative form of the procedures of historical consciousness and its function as a means of temporal orientation are clear, it is possible to characterize the specific and essential competence of historical consciousness as "narrative competence."[6] Such competence can be defined as the ability of human consciousness to carry out procedures which make sense of the past, effecting a temporal orientation in present practical life by means of the recollection of past actuality.

This general competence concerned with "making sense of the past" can be divided into three subcompetencies. These can be best defined in terms of the three elements which together constitute a historical narrative: form, content and function. With respect to content, one can speak of the "competence for historical experience;" with respect to form, the "competence for historical interpretation;" and with respect to function, the "competence for historical orientation."[7]

Historical consciousness is characterized by the "competence of experience." This competence entails an ability to have temporal experience. It involves the capacity of learning how to look at the past and grasp its specific temporal quality, differentiating it from the present. A more elaborate form of such competence is "historical sensitivity." In terms of our narrative, it is the competence to understand the stone in the wall of the Maclean castle and the need to take note of its inscription: that is, that it bears information important for the members of the Maclean family.

Historical consciousness is further characterized by the "competence of interpretation." This competence is the ability to bridge time differences between past, present and future by a conception of a meaningful temporal whole comprising all time dimensions. The temporality of human life functions as the principal instrument of this interpretation, this translation of experience of past actuality into an understanding of the present and expectations regarding the future. Such a conception lies at the core of the meaning-creating activity of historical consciousness. It is the fundamental "philosophy of history" active within the meaning-creating activities of historical consciousness, shaping every historical thought. In terms of our narrative, it entails the competence to integrate the event of the exchange of infants into a concept of time which links that ancient period with the present, giving this complex a historically weighty significance for the Macleans in their relationship with the Maclonichs. Such a concept could be embodied either in the notion of the unbroken validity of the treaty, or the evolution of law from a premodern form to its modern manifestation.

Finally, historical consciousness is characterized by the "competence of orientation." Such a competence entails being able to utilize the temporal whole with its experiential content, for the purposes of life-orientation. It involves guiding action by means of notions of temporal change, articulating human identity with historical knowledge, interweaving one's own identity into the concrete warp and woof of historical knowledge. In terms of the Highlands narrative, it entails the ability to utilize the interpretation of the treaty in order to deal with the current situation and determine a course of action: to decide whether or not to hide Ian, or assist him in some other way, and to legitimate this decision—in each instance using a "good historical reason" related to the identity of a member of the Maclean clan.

Four types of historical consciousness

In the preceding section, an attempt has been made to explicate the basic operations of historical consciousness, its relationship to moral consciousness and its main competencies. The concluding section of this chapter deals with the question of development.

The various incisive theories on the development of moral consciousness worked out and empirically confirmed by such thinkers as Piaget, Kohlberg and others are familiar from the literature on cognitive development.[8] My intention here is to propose an analogous theory of development concerning the narrative competence of historical consciousness, so crucial for relating values to actuality or morality to activity by a narrative act: the telling of a story about past events.

In order to find stages of structural development in historical consciousness, it is necessary, first of all, to distinguish basic structures within the procedures involved in making historical sense of the past. I propose to explicate such basic structures in the form of a general typology of historical thinking. This typology conceptually encompasses the entire field of its empirical manifestations, and can therefore be utilized for comparative work in historiography, including intercultural comparisons.[9]

The typology is already implicit in the four different modes of historical argument briefly alluded to above in connection with the request by Ian Maclonich to seek refuge from the police. What then is the typological meaning of these four modes?

My starting point is the function of historical narration. As already mentioned, such narration has the general function of serving to orient practical life within time. It mobilizes the memory of temporal experience, developing the notion of an embracing temporal whole, and bestows on practical life an external and internal temporal perspective. Historical consciousness realizes this general function in four different ways, based on four different principles for temporal orientation of life: (a) affirmation of given orientations, (b) regularity of cultural patterns and life-patterns (*Lebensformen*), (c) negation and (d) transformation of topical orientating patterns. These are all brought about via the agency of historical memory.

There are six elements and factors of historical consciousness in terms of which these types can be described:

1. its content—the dominant experience of time, drawn from the past;
2. the patterns of historical significance, or the forms of temporal wholes;
3. the mode of external orientation, especially in respect to the communicative forms of social life;
4. the mode of internal orientation, particularly in respect to historical identity as the core of historicity in human self-awareness and self-understanding;
5. the relation of historical orientation to moral values
6. its relation to moral reasoning (see Table 2.1).

The traditional type

Traditions are indispensable elements of orientation within practical life, and their total denial leads to a sense of massive disorientation. Historical consciousness functions in part to keep such traditions alive.

When historical consciousness furnishes us with traditions, it reminds us of origins and repetition of obligations, doing so in the form of concrete, factual, past occurrences which demonstrate the validity and binding quality of values and value systems. Such is the case when, for example, in our role as a member of the Maclean clan, we feel an obligating link to an ancient treaty. In such an approach, both our interpretation of what occurred in the past and our justification for hiding Ian Maclonich are "traditional." Some other examples of "traditionality" are commemorative public speeches, public monuments, or even private stories narrated by individuals to each other with the purpose of confirming their personal relationship. Thus, both you and your spouse will indeed be "enamored" of the narrative describing how you first fell in love—

TABLE 2.1 THE FOUR TYPES OF HISTORICAL CONSCIOUSNESS

	Traditional	Exemplary	Critical	Genetic
Experience of time	repetition of an obligatory form of life	representing general rules of conduct or value systems	problematizing actual forms of life and value systems	change of alien forms of life into proper ones
Patterns of historical significance	permanence of an obligatory life form in temporal change	timeless rules of social life, timeless validity of values	break of patterns of historical significance by denying their validity	developments in which forms of life change in order to maintain their permanence
Orientation of external life	affirmation of pregiven orders by consent about a valid common life	relating peculiar situations to regularities of what had happened and should happen	delimitation of one's own standpoint against pregiven obligations	acceptance of different standpoints within a comprising perspective of common develoment
Orientation of internal life	internalization of pregiven life forms by limitation—role taking	relating self-concepts to general rules and principles —role legitimation by generalization	self-reliance by refutation of obligations from outside—role making	change and transformation of selfconcepts as necessary conditions of permanence and self-reliance—balance of roles
Relation to moral values	morality is pre-givenness of obligatory orders; moral validity as unquestionable stability by tradition	morality is the generality of obligation in values and value-systems	breaking the moral power of values by denying their validity	temporalization of morality-chances of further development become a condition of morality
Relation to moral reasoning	the reason of values is their effective pregivenness enabling consent in moral questions	arguing by generalization, referring to regularities and principles	establishing value-criticism and ideology-critique as important strategies of moral discourses	temporal change becomes a decisive argument for the validity of moral values

SOURCE: Jörn Rüsen, 2004

if indeed you still love each other. Traditional orientations present the temporal whole which makes the past significant and relevant to present actuality and its future extension as a continuity of obligatory cultural- and life-patterns over time. Traditional orientations guide human life externally by means of an affirmation of obligations requiring consent. Such traditional orientations define the "togetherness" of social groups or whole societies in the terms of maintenance of a sense of common origin. In regard to internal orientation, such traditions define historical identity, the affirmation of predetermined cultural patterns of self-reliance and self-understanding. They shape identity formation as a process in which roles are assumed and played out.

The importance of tradition for moral values is clear. Traditional historical orientation defines morality as tradition. Traditions embody morality as an unquestioned stability of *Lebensformen,* cultural- and life-patterns over time and its vicissitudes. In respect to moral reasoning, traditions are reasons upholding and under-pinning the moral obligation of values. If practical life is orientated predominantly in terms of traditions, the reason informing values lies in the permanence of their actuality in social life, a permanence which history serves to bring to our recollection.

The exemplary type

It is not traditions we utilize here as argument—but rather rules. The story of the struggles between the clans and the transposition of the two infants stands here for a general timeless rule: it teaches us what course of action to take, and what to refrain from doing.

Here, historical consciousness deals with the experience of the past in the form of cases representing and embodying rules of temporal change and human conduct. The horizon of time-experience is significantly expanded in this mode of historical thought. Tradition moves within a rather narrow frame of empirical reference, but historical memory structured in terms of exempla is able to process an infinite number of past events, as they do not possess any specific significance in themselves, but only in relation to an abstract idea of temporal change and human conduct, valid for all times, or whose validity is at least not limited to a specific event.

The pattern of significance involved here has the form of timeless rules. History in this conception is viewed as a past recollected with a message or lesson for the present, as didactic: *historia vitae magistra* is a time-honored apothegm in the Western historiographical tradition.[10] It teaches rules, their derivation from specific cases, and their application. The mode of orientation realized by historical consciousness in this exemplary type is rule-focused: it entails the application of historically derived and proven rules to actual situations.

Many classical examples of historiography in a variety of differing cultures reflect this type of historical significance. In the ancient Chinese tradition, the best example is the classic by Suma-Kuang *Tzu-chih t'ung-chien (A Mirror for Government)*. Its very title indicates how it conceives of the past as exemplum: political morality is taught in the form of cases of governments which have succeeded or failed.

In respect to the internal orientation of life, exemplary historical thinking relates life roles and principles, and functions to legitimate such roles by abstract reasoning. Historical identity is here constituted in the form of assuming competence for the regularity of actual cultural- and life-patterns. Historical identity is given the shape of prudence (*prudentia*). Its subject is given competence for deriving general rules from specific cases and applying them to other cases.

Proceeding in this way, such a mode of historical consciousness makes a significant contribution to moral reasoning. Exemplary historical thought discloses the morality of a value or valuesystem culturally embodied in social and personal life by proving its generality: it has a validity extending beyond its immediate concrete eventfulness, a validity extending to a gamut of situations. Morality is conceptualized as having timeless validity.

The contribution of this mode of historical interpretation to moral reasoning is clear: history teaches moral argument by means of the application of principles to specific and concrete situations—such as a knock on the door by a member of the Maclonich clan in the dead of night.

The critical type

The decisive argument in the critical version of our narrative is that as a member of the Maclean clan, we feel no obligation whatsoever to its presumed "binding" quality. For us, it is an ancient tale which has lost any relevance for present action and actuality. Yet this is not automatically so: as a Maclean, we are still somehow a part of this story, the ancient stone indeed bears its inscription upon our wall. Thus, we must discredit the story if we do not wish to help Ian in his distress. We must present a new interpretation which—by means of historical reasoning—denies the validity of the treaty.

The easiest way to do this is to state that the story is untrue. In order to be convincing we must muster evidence, and that requires us to engage in critical historical argument, establishing the plausibility of the contention that there are no historical reasons which could motivate us to offer help to Ian Maclonich.

We can develop an ideological critique, stating that there was a ruse involved: a trick by the Maclonichs to trap the Macleans into a kind of moral dependence on them. We can argue that even in that ancient period, it was prohibited to murder infants, which is the pivotal motif on which the narrative turns. Such argument is based on offering elements of a counter-narrative to the one behind the stone engraving. By means of such a counter-narrative, we can unmask a given story as a betrayal, debunk it as misinformation. We can also argue critically in another way, contending that the treaty engraved on the stone has lost its current validity, since new forms of law have since emerged. Then we can narrate a brief "counter-story:" the story of how laws have changed over time.

What are the general characteristics of such a mode of historical interpretation? Here, historical consciousness searches for and mobilizes a specific kind of experience of the past: evidence provided by counter-narratives, deviations which render problematic present value systems and *Lebensformen*.

The concept of an embracing temporal totality including past, present and future is transformed in this mode into something negative: the notion of a rupture in continuity still operative in consciousness. History functions as the tool by which such continuity is ruptured, deconstructed, decoded—so that it loses its power as a source for present-day orientation. Narratives of this type formulate historical standpoints by demarcation, distinguishing them from the historical orientation entertained by others. By means of such critical stories, we say *no* to pregiven temporal orientations of our life.

In regard to ourselves and our own historical identity, such critical stories express a negativity—what we do not want to be. They afford us an opportunity to define ourselves unentangled by role determinations and prescribed, predefined patterns of self-understanding. Critical historical thinking clears a path toward constituting identity by the force of negation.

Its contribution to moral values lies in its critique of values. It challenges morality by presenting its contrary. Critical narratives confront moral values with historical evidence of their immoral origins or consequences. For example, modern feminists criticize the principle of moral universality. They claim it channels us into overlooking the nature of "otherness" in social relations in favor of an abstract universalization of values as a sufficient condition of their morality. They contend that such "universalization" is highly biased and ideological, serving to establish the male norm as the general human norm and disregarding the uniqueness qua gender of men and women as a necessary condition of humanity.[11]

Critical historical thinking injects elements of critical argument into moral reasoning. It calls morality into question by pointing to cultural relativity in values contrasted with a presumed and specious universality, by uncovering temporal conditioning factors as contrasted with a bogus "timeless" validity. It confronts claims for validity with evidence based on temporal change: to the power of relativization of historical conditions and consequences. In its most elaborate variant, it presents moral reasoning as an ideology critique of morality. Two classic examples of such an enterprise are Marx's critique of bourgeois values[12] and Nietzsche's *Genealogie der Moral*.[13]

The genetic type

At the core of procedures to make sense of the past lies change itself. In this framework, our argument is that "times have changed:" we thus deny both the option of hiding Ian due to traditional or exemplary reasons and of critically negating the obligation to this old story as a reason for refusing to hide him. In contrast, we accept the story, but place it in a framework of interpretation within which the type of obligation to past events has itself changed from a premodern to modern form of morality. Here change is of the essence, and is what gives history its sense. Thus, the old treaty has lost its former validity and taken on a new one; consequently, our behavior necessarily differs now from what it would have been in the distant past. It is construed within a process of dynamic evolvement.

We therefore choose to help Ian Maclonich, but in a way different from that prefigured in the treaty preserved in stone on the wall of our castle. We allow the story to become part of the past; at the same time, however, we bestow upon it another future. It is change itself which gives history its meaning. Temporal change sheds its threatening aspect, instead becoming the path upon which options are opened up for human activity to create a new world. The future surpasses, indeed "outbids," the past in its claims on the present—a present conceptualized as an intersection, an intensely temporalized mode, a dynamic transition. This is the quintessential form of a kind of modern historical thought shaped by the category of progress, though it has been thrown into radical doubt by the intimations of postmodernity mused upon by a certain segment of the contemporary intellectual elite.

Historical memory in this mode prefers to represent experience of past actuality as transformational events, in which alien cultural- and life-patterns evolve into more positive "modern" configurations. The dominant pattern of historical signification here is that of development, where patterns change in order, paradoxically, to maintain their very permanence. Thus, permanence takes on an internal temporality, becoming dynamic. In contrast, permanence by tradition, by timeless exemplary rules, by critical negation—the rupture of continuity—is in essence static in nature.

This mode of historical thinking views social life in all the profuse complexity of its sheer temporality. Differing standpoints are acceptable because they can be integrated into an embracing perspective of temporal change. Returning to our narrative, we, as the modern Maclean, are eager to persuade the modern Maclonich that it would be wisest for him to turn himself over to the police, and then accept our aid. His expectations and our reaction must intersect, and we believe that this intersection is part of the historical interpretation within which we deal with the actual situation. This mutual acknowledgment is part of the future perspective we derive from the past through our decision in the present not to offer him refuge, but rather to help him in a way we believe is more in keeping with the tenor of our times: "I know a good lawyer."

In respect to our self-understanding and self-reliance, this type of historical consciousness imbues historical identity with an essential temporalization. We define ourselves as being a cross-point, an interface of time and events, permanently in transition. To remain what we are, not to change and evolve, appears to us as a mode of self-loss, a threat to identity.[14] Our identity lies in our ceaseless changing.

Within the horizon of this kind of historical consciousness moral values become temporalized, morality shedding its static nature. Development and change belong to the morality of values conceptualized in terms of a pluralism of viewpoints and the acceptance of the concrete "otherness" of the other, and mutual acknowledgment of that "otherness" as the dominant notion of moral valuation.

According to this temporalization as a principle, moral reasoning relies here essentially on the argument of temporal change as necessary or decisive for establishing the validity of moral values. Thus one can move on from the final stage in the Kohlbergian scheme of the development of moral consciousness to a higher stage: moral principles include their transformation within a process of communication. It is here that they are realized concretely and individually, engendering differences; those differences, in turn, activate procedures of mutual acknowledgment, changing the original moral form. One fascinating illustration of this stage of moral argument, which cannot be elaborated on in the context of this chapter, is the example of the relations between the sexes. The idea of universal human rights is another key example demonstrating the plausibility of this genetic mode of argument in reference to moral values.[15]

This typology is meant as a methodological and heuristic tool for comparative research. Insofar as morality is connected with historical consciousness, we can utilize the typological matrix to help categorize and characterize cultural peculiarities and unique features of moral values and modes of moral reasoning in different times and places. Since elements of all four types are operatively intermixed in the procedure which gives practical life a historical orientation in time, we can reconstruct complex relations among these elements in order to pinpoint and define the structural specificity of empirical manifestations of historical consciousness and their relationship to moral values.[16]

The development of narrative competencies

It is not my intention here to focus on the comparative method in historiography. Instead, I wish to make use of the typology in order to construct a theory of the ontogenetic development of historical consciousness. Such a theory is familiar from psychological studies on cognitive development,[17] but to my knowledge there has been no serious attempt to date to widen this psychological perspective by investigating historical consciousness and its cognitive competencies. Since historical consciousness can be conceptualized as a synthesis of moral and temporal consciousness, it might appear to be a relatively simple matter to develop a genetic theory of historical consciousness. Unfortunately, however, we find that Piaget and his followers have pursued the category of time only within the framework of the natural sciences,[18] so that their work remains basically silent on questions of historical consciousness.

To embark upon an investigation of historical consciousness and its essential relationship with moral consciousness it is first necessary to clear the ground, as it were: a theoretical framework must be constructed which defines the field and explicates in conceptual terms what the basic questions are. It is my view that such a typology can effectively serve this purpose. It defines fundamentally and discloses the procedures of historical consciousness, even affording some basic notions as to what the development of historical consciousness might entail.

What conceptions of development can indeed be derived from the typology? We can come closer to answering this by logically ordering the types in a sequence defined by the "principle of precondition."

The traditional type is primary, and does not presuppose other forms of historical consciousness, yet it constitutes the condition for all other types. It is the font, the beginning of historical consciousness. The logical sequence of types, each the precondition for the next is as follows: traditional, exemplary, critical, genetic. Though this sequence is based on logical criteria, it may have empirical applications, and there is reason to assume it is also a structural sequence in the development of historical consciousness.

1. First, the sequence entails increasing complexity. Stages in human evolution can also be described in terms of increasing capacity to digest complexity.
2. Growth in complexity can be specified and differentiated following the logical ordering of preconditions. Thus, the extent of experience and knowledge of past actuality expands enormously as one moves from the traditional to the exemplary. The critical type requires a new qualification of temporal experience based on the distinction between "my own time" and the "time of the others." Finally, the genetic type goes even beyond this quality by temporalization of time itself: "my own time" is dynamic, altering, undergoing change, as is that "of the others" as well.
3. There is also a growth in complexity with regard to the patterns of historical significance. There is no relevant difference between fact and meaning in the form of traditional historical consciousness. They diverge in exemplary historical consciousness. In the critical form, meaning itself undergoes differentiation, intensified into even more complex differentiation in the genetic form.
4. This is likewise true when it comes to the degree of abstraction and complexity of logical operations.

5. There is also an increasing complexity of external and internal orientation. In external orientation, this can be demonstrated by the manner in which historical consciousness characterizes social life: traditions are exclusivistic, they present one own's cultural- and life-patterns as the only acceptable *Lebensformen*. Exemplary thinking enlarges upon this by generalization, while critical thought elaborates definite, critique-based standpoints and delimitations. Genetic thought clears the temporal ground for a pluralism of standpoints.
6. Moving through the typological series, there is growing complexity in relation to historical identity. It begins with the unquestioned form of historical self-understanding imprinted by tradition and extends on to the fragile balance engendered by multidimensional, multiperspectival genetic forms. My arguments here have been principally theoretical, but there appears to me to be a certain amount of empirical evidence as well to substantiate the hypothesis that historical consciousness follows the typological order sketched here in its evolution.
7. Everyday observations demonstrate that the traditional and exemplary modes of historical consciousness are widespread and frequently encountered; critical and genetic modes, in contrast, are far more rare. This fact correlates with degree of education and knowledge, and with the progress of human intellect toward more complex capacities.
8. Experience in the teaching of history in schools indicates that traditional forms of thought are easiest to learn, that the exemplary form dominates most history curricula, and that critical abilities, and genetic abilities even more so, require enormous amounts of effort by both teacher and pupil.

Observations on historical learning and empirical research

In conclusion, I would like to turn to the question of historical learning. Learning can be conceptualized as a process of digesting experience, absorbing it into competencies. Historical learning is a process of digesting the experience of time into narrative competencies.[19] "Narrative competence" here is understood as the ability to narrate a story by means of which practical life is given an orientational locus in time. This competence consists of three principal abilities:

1. The ability to experience, related to past actuality.
2. The ability to interpret, related to the temporal whole which combines (a) experience of the past with (b) understanding of the present and (c) expectations regarding the future.
3. The ability to orient, related to the practical need to find a path through the straits and eddies of temporal change.

In theoretical terms, it is not difficult to explicate the development of historical consciousness as a process of learning. Learning is conceptualized in this framework as a specific quality of the mental procedures of historical consciousness. Such procedures are termed "learning" when competencies are acquired to (a) experience past time, (b) interpret it in the form of history, and (c) utilize that interpretation for the practical purpose of orientation in life.

Using the typology, historical learning can be explained as a process of structural change in historical consciousness. Historical learning entails far more than simply acquiring knowledge of the past and expanding the stock of that knowledge. Seen as a process by which competencies are progressively acquired, it emerges as a process of changing the structural forms by which we deal with and utilize the experience and knowledge of past actuality, progressing from traditional forms of thought on through—and up—to genetic modes. Thus, the typology offers a basis for a usefully differentiated theory of historical learning. Such a theory combines three central elements of narrative competence (experience, interpretation, orientation) and four stages of their development. A theory of historical learning of this kind can be of some significance for the theory of the development of moral consciousness and moral learning.

Unfortunately, theory alone does not suffice for dealing with the knotty questions of historical and moral consciousness. The proof of theory lies in amassing empirical evidence substantiating its theses, and here research still needs to be done. There have been empirical on historical consciousness and historical learning,[20] but there is still a comprehensive psychology of historical learning lacking. No further study on the relationship between historical and moral consciousness and learning seems to exist.

An investigation of this nature faces formidable obstacles; principal among these is the intricate complexity of historical consciousness and its competencies. The four types presented here are not strict alternatives, permitting any simple count of their distribution in manifestations of historical consciousness. Normally, the types appear in complex admixtures, and it is necessary to discover their hierarchical ordering and relationship in any empirically given manifestation of historical consciousness. Nonetheless, the typology can direct our sights, and function heuristically in defining questions and preparing strategies for use in empirical studies. Such a typology impresses on investigators that what is important to discover in regard to historical consciousness is not the extent of knowledge involved, but rather the framework and effective principles operative in making sense of the past.

How can these be found in empirical evidence? There is one very basic, elicitation-oriented approach: let persons relate narratives which are relevant for the temporal orientation of their own personal lives, and then analyze the narrative structures of such stories. Such an investigative tack seeks to establish answers to questions such as these: what type (in the typology) do these elicited narratives seem to follow? Is there any relation between the dominant type and the age of the narrator? Or his/her level of education?

Empirical experiments were recently undertaken using our approach in connection with the Highlands story.[21] Pupils and students were told the clan tale of Maclean and Maclonich in a highly "neutral" version. They were confronted with the current situation of Maclean and asked to decide what he should do in regard to Ian Maclonich's request for assistance, and write a short justification of their decision containing a specific reference to the motif of the transposed infants. These texts were then analyzed in regard to the patterns of historical interpretation they utilized. Empirically, the four types were indeed distinguishable, and it even proved possible to differentiate more sensitively between these basic types of the typology. It was established that there are significant correlations between narrative patterns used, age of the respondent and stage of education and learning.

This constitutes only one limited example of empirical research, and questions were not explored regarding the moral component of historical consciousness. Nonetheless, I would contend that any discussion of moral values and moral reasoning should also attempt to relate to the associated dimensions of historical consciousness and learning.

Notes

This chapter was first published in *History and Memory*, 1.2 (1989), 35–60.

1. Answer of a student on a questionnaire concerning historical conscience, February 1987 (cf. Jörn Rüsen et al., "Untersuchungen zum Geschichtsbewußtsein von Abiturienten im Ruhrgebiet," in *Geschichtsbewußtsein empirisch*, eds. B. von Borries, H.-J. Pandel, J. Rüsen, Pfaffenweiler, 1991, 221–344.)
2. Samuel Johnson, *A Journey to the Western Islands of Scotland*, Haven and London, 1971, 133 sqq. The tale presented here is a simplified version.
3. A summarizing description is given by K.-E. Jeisman, "Geschichtsbewusstsein," in *Handbuch der Geschichtsdidaktik*, eds. K. Bergman, A. Kuhn, J. Rüsen, G. Schneider, Düsseldorf, 1985, 40–44; cf. idem, *Geschichte als Horizont der Gegenwart. Über den Zusammenhang von Vergangenheitsdeutung, Gegenwartsverständnis und Zukunftsperspektive*, Paderborn, 1985, pp. 43 sqq.
4. This question is discussed principally from the narrow perspective of the function of historical studies in social life, for example, by J. Kocka, *Sozialgeschichte. Begriff—Entwicklung—Probleme*, 2nd edn, Göttingen, 1986, 112–31. Cf. Rüsen, *Lebendige Geschichte*.
5. Cf. White, *Metahistory*; Rüsen, *Historische Vernunft*; Paul Ricoeur, *Time and Narrative*, 3 vols, Chicago, 1984–1988; David Carr, *Time, Narrative and History*, Bloomington, 1986.
6. I have sketched an outline of a theory of narrative competence in respect to the question of the main objectives of historical learning in Jörn Rüsen, "Historisches Lernen. Grundriß einer Theorie," in idem, *Historisches Lernen. Grundlagen und Paradigmen*, Köln, 1994, 74–121.
7. For a more detailed explication see chap. 12.

8. Jean Piaget, *Das moralische Bewußtsein beim Kinde*, Frankfurt am Main, 1973; Lawrence Kohlberg, *Zur kognitiven Entwicklung des Kindes*, Frankfurt am Main, 1974; cf. R.N. Hallam, "Piaget and Thinking in History," in Marin Ballard, ed., *New Movements in the Study and Teaching of History*, London, 1970, 162–78.
9. For a more detailed explanation of this typology, see Rüsen, "Die vier Typen des historischen Erzählens," 153–230; Rüsen, *Lebendige Geschichte*, part 1. In the previous chapter I have outlined my typology. I repeat it here with other examples and with a systematic enlargement to the question of moral consciousness.
10. Cf. Koselleck, "Historia magistra vitae," 38–66.
11. Cf. Seyla Benhabib, "The Generalized and the Concrete Other: Visions of the Autonomous Self," *Praxis International*, 5(4) (1986), 402–24.
12. E.g., human and civil rights in his essay "Zur Judenfrage," in K. Marx and F. Engels, *Werke 1*, Berlin, 1964.
13. Friedrich Nietzsche, "Zur Genealogie der Moral (1887)," in idem, *Sämtliche Werke. Kritische Studienausgabe*, in 15 vols., eds. G. Colli and M. Montanari, Munich, 1988, vol. 5, 245–412.
14. One of Bertolt Brecht's "Stories of Mr Keuner" illustrates this beautifully: "A man who hadn't seen Mr Keuner for a long time greeted him with the remark: 'You don't look any different at all.' 'Oh', said Mr Keuner, and turned pale." Bertholt Brecht, *Gesammelte Werke*, 12, Frankfurt am Main, 1967, 383 (trans. Rüsen).
15. Cf. Ludger Kühnhardt, *Die Universalität der Menschenrechte. Studie zur Ideengeschichtlichen Schlüsselbestimmung eines politischen Schlüsselbegriffs*, Munich, 1987; Jörn Rüsen, "Menschen- und Bürgerrechte als historische Orientierung," in Jörn Rüsen, *Historisches Lernen. Grundlagen und Paradigmen*, Köln, 1994, 204–35.
16. An interesting contribution to such comparison with special respect to Chinese historiography is Changtze Hu, *Deutsche Ideologie und politische Kultur Chinas. Eine Studie zum Sonderwegsgedanken der chinesischen Bildungselite 1920–1940*, Bochum, 1983.
17. Cf. Jörn Rüsen, 'Historisches Lernen. Grundriß einer Theorie', in idem, *Historisches Lernen. Grundlagen und Paradigmen*, Köln, 1994, 74–121. In addition, see Hans G. Furth, *Piaget and Knowledge. Theoretical Foundations*, Englewood Cliffs, NJ, 1969.
18. Cf. Jean Piaget, *Die Bildung des Zeitbewußtseins beim Kinde*, Frankfurt am Main, 1974.
19. Cf. Jörn Rüsen, *Historisches Lernen. Grundlagen und Paradigmen*, Köln, 1994, passim.
20. Recent publications in this field in Germany include: Bodo von Borries; Hans-Jürgen Pandel and Jörn Rüsen, eds., *Geschichtsbewußtsein empirisch*, Pfaffenweiler, 1991; Bodo von Borries, Hans-Jürgen Pandel and Jörn Rüsen, eds., *Geschichtsbewußtsein im interkulturellen Vergleich. Zwei empirische Pilotstudien*, Pfaffenweiler, 1994; Magne Angvik and Bodo von Borries, eds., *Youth and History. A Comparative European Survey on Historical Consciousness and Political Attitudes among Adolescent*, 2 vols., Hamburg, 1997; Bodo von Borries, *Jugend und Geschichte. Ein europäischer Kulturvergleich aus deutscher Sich*, Opladen, 1999; Bodo von Borries, *Das Geschichtsbewußtsein Jugendlicher. Eine repräsentative Untersuchung über Vergangenheitsdeutungen, Gegenwartswahrnehmungen und Zukunftserwartungen von Schülerinnen und Schülern in Ost- und Westdeutschland*, Weinheim, 1995; Bodo von Borries, "Forschungsprobleme einer Theorie des Geschichtsbewußtseins. Am Beispiel einer Studie zum empirischen Kulturvergleich," in Horst-Walter Blanke, Friedrich Jaeger and Thomas Sandkühler, eds., *Dimensionen der Historik. Geschichtstheorie, Wissenschaftsgeschichte und Geschichtskultur heute, Jörn Rüsen zum 60. Geburtstag*, Köln, 1998, 139–152; Bodo von Borries and Hans-Jürgen Pandel, eds., *Zur Genese historischer Denkformen. Qualitative und quantitative Zugänge*, Jahrbuch für Geschichtsdidaktik 4, 1993/94, Pfaffenweiler, 1994.
21. Hans-Günter Schmidt, "'Eine Geschichte zum Nachdenken'. Erzähltypologie, narrative Kompetenz und Geschichtsbewußtsein: Bericht über einen Versuch der empirischen Erforschung des Geschichtsbewußtseins von Schülern der Sekundarstufe I (Unter- und Mittelstufe)," *Geschichtsdidaktik*, 12 (1987), 28–35.

Chapter 3

Rhetoric and Aesthetics of History: Leopold von Ranke

> Vivre, c'est interpréter, c'est donner un sens aux choses et aux événements par rapport à nous-mêmes.
> Bernard Groethuysen[1]

The question

Current discussions on the theory of history stress the poetical and rhetorical character of historiography; yet it is precisely this character that is generally neglected in the self-awareness and self-understanding of most professional historians. There is a good deal of postmodernism in the quest for rhetoric and aesthetics in modern historiography because the modernism of historiography is defined by it's academic or, in a broader sense of the word, its scientific character. The widespread and deeply rooted opinion of academic historians, as well as of postmodernist theorists of history, is that this scientific character stands in opposition to rhetoric and aesthetics. In the argument that follows I will demonstrate that the contrast between the postmodernist understanding of historiography, as being rhetorical, and the modernist scientific approach to historical knowledge leads us to one-sided views of historiography.[2]

Leopold von Ranke's work is a good example of the fact that rhetoric and aesthetics can be mediated with a rationality that defines the academic or scientific character of historical studies. Ranke manifests both aspects of historiography: his work represents the new academic standards that have emerged as a result of a process of "scientification" (*Verwissenschaftlichung*) in the humanities since the late eighteenth century, while exemplifying a new literary quality of history writing which makes it an integral part of the prose literature

---

Notes for this section begin on page 55.

of the nineteenth century. We can look at Ranke's work as a document of scientific (*verwissenschaftlichte*) historiography and, at the same time, as an important part of the so-called narrative realism. Therefore, it seems worthwhile, on the one hand, to confront Ranke's historiography with the postmodern quest for the rhetorical principles of historiography and, on the other hand, to take account of the modernist view that historical studies, with their systematic rationality, represent.

The antirhetorical turn of history toward science

From a historical perspective, modern historical studies have laid claim to a systematic rationality by emphasizing antirhetorical arguments, constituting thus the academic or scientific character of history and moulding its status as a discipline in its own right within the humanities. The noted and influential document that claimed a new standard for historical studies, and asserted their antirhetorical turn, was Ranke's first book, *Histories of the Latin and Germanic Nations 1494 to 1514,* first published in 1824.[3] Here he made his famous declaration that history does not have the responsibility to judge the past in order to teach the present for the sake of the future. As Ranke stated, his study "only wants to show how it really had been."[4] This claim of objectivism reflects the new self-understanding of historical studies as an empirical science with a special set of methodological rules constituting historical knowledge as a process of research.[5] After the publication of his book, Ranke received a chair in history in Berlin, and one of the main reasons for his advancement was the appendix of the book containing a critical analysis of the historiography of his time.[6] Here Ranke presented the historical method he used in obtaining valid knowledge about the past from the sources. Research entailed the analysis of the documentary reports of the past in an attempt to arrive at an understanding of what really had been.

To emphasize this new scientific approach in historiography, Ranke contrasted the way he thought history should be written with the traditional rhetorical attitude taken by historiography. He referred to Guicciardini's historiography as an example of this rhetorical attitude whereby the agents in the historical events explain their intentions through their speeches. In the text, these speeches have a rational function insofar as they explain the historically important actions by illuminating the leading intentions of the actors. The explicatory model used here is that of elucidating actions by their intentions.[7] Ranke did not argue against this mode of explanation but against the fictional character of the speeches, for they are not documented by sources. The actors say what the historian imagines they would have said had they been asked for the reasons for their actions. For Ranke it was the fictional character of the speeches which prohibited the historian from integrating them into a sequence of events, despite their explanatory function; he did not, however, discuss this function.

What the intellectuals of Ranke's time meant by rhetoric was that fictional speeches were used in a historiographical text which pretended to say what "really had been" in the past. They understood rhetoric to be a strategy of speaking or writing that was characterized by the use of persuasion and by the absence of truth claims, or—one could also say—by the use of language tricks instead of convincing arguments. Rhetoric connoted the use of language for strategic purposes—that is, to influence strategically the mind of the audience—whereas scientific historiography used language to articulate the results of empirical research; to put it simply, truth instead of tricks. Ranke directed these words against Guicciardini's presentation of fictional speeches: "We on our side have another concept of history. Naked truth without any embellishment; painstaking research into the particular; the rest lies in the hands of God; let us reject all fiction even in the smallest matter and reject any fantasy whatsoever."[8]

Ranke thus confronted fantasy with truth. For him, rhetoric in historiography endangers truth; it covers over the boundary separating truth from fiction. This danger can be prevented by research: namely, by the systematic uncovering of the empirical evidence provided by the sources. Research, according to Ranke, guarantees truth for it enables historians to describe what has been and permits them to respect the boundary between empirical evidence or truth, on the one hand, and fantasy or fiction, on the other. This dichotomy has become part and parcel of the basic arguments by which historians have gained—and are defending—their image as experts whose knowledge is indispensable for rendering a convincing and respectable representation of the past.

Ranke's work represents a turning point in the development of historiography: it separated history writing from literature and tied it to science. Traditionally, the skill of historians had been their ability to reach the mind of their audience by the persuasive force of language. The past became alive by speaking the language of common sense and by teaching a practical competence in mastering the typical problems of everyday life.[9] Historiography was oriented toward the practical needs of its audience. It was guided by the principle of addressing an audience, by speaking to someone. It was indeed rhetorical. Ranke, however, oriented historiography toward research and empiricism. It claimed to speak the truth regardless of all expectations and prejudices of its audience. It no longer taught practical competence but claimed to provide empirical knowledge, simply to show how it really had been.

After this turning point, which signaled the writing of history in the form of an academic discipline, most historians presented—and still present—their vision of what historiography is, and must be, in a way that is remarkably narrow minded. They see research as their main task; historiography is basically nothing more than a comprehensive summary of research results. They consider the literary forms in presenting these results to be of secondary importance and functionally dependent on the methodological principles of gaining from the sources a solid knowledge of the past.

The unenlightened synthesis of art and science

The fact that Ranke did not share this narrow-mindedness is further testimony to his importance. Besides emphasizing research as the basis for historiography, he also acknowledged the fact that writing history—the shaping of the research results into an acceptable story—was based on principles other than research. While the principles of research are essentially scientific and belong to the realm of modern systematic rationality, the principles of writing history are essentially artistic or poetic and belong to the realm of literature. In Ranke's words, "History is distinguished from all other sciences in that it is also an art because it recreates and portrays that which it has found and recognized. Other sciences are satisfied simply with recording what has been found; history requires the ability to recreate."[10]

What did Ranke mean by saying that history as a science (*Wissenschaft*) is "also" an art? What is the relationship between the scientific and the poetic principles? Is it characterized by a hierarchical order or is it mediated? Ranke did not give a clear answer grounded in theory. He explicated the scientific character of historiography by pointing to philosophy which represents the decisive element, namely, "discovering causality and conceptualizing the core of existence."[11] History, Ranke states, does this "discovering" and "conceptualizing" by working with the sources which provide the empirical evidence for what has really happened in the past. The mode of "discovering causality and conceptualizing the core of existence," making its appearance in the course of past human affairs, is the historical method, the set of rules guiding historical research as a process of knowledge. Ranke described these rules only briefly but very precisely as "collecting, finding, penetrating," and thus indicated the three main operations of historical research: heuristics, critique and interpretation.[12] Aside from this, he simply described the artistic or poetic character of historiography as "reproducing the life as it appeared."[13] This reproduction, as Ranke claimed, is achieved by activating the "ability to recreate."[14] The question is, how does this ability operate in historiography and how is it related to the methodological principles of research?

Ranke did not provide a clear answer. He simply stated that there are two forces of the mind in operation: the intellectual force, its most representative manifestation being philosophy, and the poetical force, its most representative manifestation being art. Both forces are mediated in history, because, as Ranke states, "History brings both together in a third element peculiar only to itself."[15] What is, one must ask, this "third element?" It constitutes the peculiarity of historical studies, includes historical research and, at the same time, mediates it with historical writing in order to make a whole called "history." This is a decisive question, at least for my argument, because it is related to the modernist character of history as a science, as well as to the postmodern view of history as a rhetorical language game. Ranke himself rejected the dichotomy between science and art in history by underscoring the fact of their mediation in history. It is important, therefore, to understand what Ranke meant by the "third element," mediating between the "conceptualizing" and the "reproducing" forces of the mind.

It is unfortunate that Ranke's explanation is not very clear. He described this element as a characteristic of the human mind and of the tendency of historical consciousness toward the real. This drive toward reality distinguishes it from philosophy and art which are directed toward the ideal. This argument leads us back to Ranke's famous dictum that he only wanted to show how it "really had been." Hence our question should be reformulated to read: what factor leads to the objectivity of what "really had been?" On this matter, Ranke's answer is clear: it is research. If this is true, then the basic role of art is negated, because research cannot mediate between itself and art. To quote Ranke again: "History is never the one without the other ..."[16] Therefore, the question as to what constitutes the third element still remains open. In other words, what actualizes the peculiar historical realism combining art and science?

Ranke did not deal with this question theoretically. For him the simple act of writing history based on the results of empirical research was sufficient proof that a synthesis of art and science did occur in historiography. Art simply takes place in the act of writing history. It differs from science insofar as science requires conceptual and methodological clarity in the process of gaining knowledge. By contrast, art does not require rules or reflected principles. "Art rests on itself: its existence proves its validity. Science, in contrast, must be totally worked out to its very concept and must be clear to its core."[17] Apparently Ranke did not think that the artistic or poetic side of history necessitated the kind of professional skill historians needed as researchers. "The rest lies in the hands of God," were his words, and we can read them as an allusion to a nonrational—or better, a superrational—procedure that is generated in that realm of the human mind where cognitive principles and methodological rules have no place. Here is where rhetoric was formerly located.

What happened to rhetoric when Ranke placed it into God's hands? Let me dwell on these words for a moment. If taken literally, they lead to the following answer: rhetoric must have been spiritualized. This, indeed, was the case because rhetoric assumed an aesthetical substance or, at least, elements of an aesthetics, which changed its character to align it with the modern rationalization of historiography based on scientific research. The antirhetorical turn of historiography did not simply abolish rhetoric, but changed it, gave it a new character, a new form of speaking to its audience.

Ranke represented this novelty on both the practical and the theoretical levels. As far as the former is concerned, Ranke's main works have an undeniable aesthetic quality; they belong to the great prose literature of realism. This aesthetical quality, however, was not unique to Ranke; it was representative of nineteenth-century European historiography in general. One need think only of Thomas B. Macaulay, Jules Michelet or Theodor Mommsen, who received the Nobel prize for literature for his *History of Rome*.

On the level of theory, Ranke speaks of art in history in a way that can easily be understood as classical aesthetics.[18] It sees art as a precognitive procedure by which an image of life is produced without being subjected to rules. The procedure itself generates its own rules, and the more original they are—that is, the less they are already formulated—the more successful and the more effective the artifacts become. This idea of art is fundamentally antirhetorical because rhetoric supplies the rules for linguistic procedures, and the rules stand for their success as well as their effect. This antirhetorical idea of art was the reason why Ranke let art in history "rest on itself," and, with respect to historical knowledge, to concentrate his efforts on research rather than on linguistic forms.

Up to this point, I have not only not answered the question concerning the peculiar historical element in the human mind that mediates between science and art, but by pointing to the aesthetic effect of the antirhetorical turn of history in Ranke's time, I have complicated the question even further. Nevertheless, this complication provides a way of answering the question posed. For Ranke, rhetoric was negated by scientific research, and only a remnant of rhetoric in a fundamentally changed form was left, namely, the aesthetics of historiography. The mediating element in question comes into view as soon as we ask whether Ranke's assertion that rhetoric has completely vanished in aesthetics is convincing. I do not think that this is the case. Hence, I will inquire into the hidden rhetoric in Ranke's historiography in order to find an answer to the question of what it is that combines the conceptualizing forces of the mind with those of the imagination, and imparts to them their specific historical character.

Back to rhetoric

From the current discussions on the theory of history we can learn that the concept of rhetoric, underlying the antirhetorical turn of historical studies in the direction of science (*Wissenschaft*), and still dominant in the minds of professional historians, is too narrow.[19] Its wider meaning becomes apparent when we look at Ranke's arguments on science and art in history. As "active forces of the human mind" (*tätige Geisteskräfte*), both science and art deal with the same subject matter, which Ranke calls *Leben*—life, in the sense of human life—or *Existenz*.[20] The subject matter of history is the appearance of life in time. As a science, historical studies recognize life by conceptualizing the information of the source materials; as an art they reproduce life by means of imagining the past as vivid, temporal events in the realm of human affairs. Both operations of historical consciousness are guided by underlying patterns of significance which give events and their temporal connection the character of life or existence; in Ranke's words, they gain the character of being something which "really had been."

What tells the historian what "really had been" in the temporal course of past human affairs? Although many historians—and perhaps even Ranke himself—thought, and think, that this reality is an objective fact as told by the sources, it is something else. It is something even more "objective"—in the sense of being alive, effective, and constitutive of human existence—than a dead fact, the positive information of what is or what was the case. History represents this fundamental liveliness in linguistic form; it is the liveliness of language as a form of human existence.

The past thus presented by historiography becomes alive in the language of historians by which they present, via memory, their image of the past in such a way that it captures the liveliness of the present. In what sphere is history alive in this fundamental, existential way? Where is it part of a "real," that is, practical life? It is located within the framework of the cultural orientation guiding human activity and human suffering in social praxis. History is an essential feature for interpreting the self and the world without which human action is impossible.

What is the connection between this general argument and rhetoric? I have already spoken of rhetoric in history as being nothing but a set of linguistic forms within which historical knowledge acquires its elementary and basic liveliness in practical human life. The patterns of significance making sense of the facts of the past and giving meaning to the contemporary life-praxis are the linguistic forms of the historical narrative, which can be further described as *topoi* of the historiographical discourse.[21]

The rhetoric of history consists of a set of *topoi*—that is, basic patterns of significance that must be used when, through narrative presentation, the past is to play a vivid role in life-praxis. Presented in such topical patterns, historical knowledge becomes part of practical life guiding the meaningful orientation of human activity and of suffering in time. Rhetoric furnishes historical knowledge with ideas of temporal processes that connect past, present, and future in a pattern of meaning and significance, providing the potential for orientation in interpreting the self and the world which is essential for guiding human action.

Of course, the concept of rhetoric includes much more than the mere insertion of fictional elements in narratives of factual occurrences; it constitutes much more than a mere set of linguistic tricks to be used in the strategy of persuasion. It has to be seen as a necessary condition for a historical understanding of the past in that the liveliness and vitality of language give the past significance in present life-praxis. How is this achieved by Ranke? My intention here is not to describe his network of rhetorical forms which, from past occurrences as he discovered them by research, results in a vivid historical narration. I can only hint at some of the most important rhetorical structures as the inherent, shaping principles of Ranke's historiography. Before doing so, however, I will distinguish between different levels and aspects of rhetorical structures in historiography in general.

The basic rhetorical structure of every historiographical text is constituted of a mixture of four fundamental and elementary *topoi* of historical narration: the traditional, the exemplary, the critical and the genetic mode of making sense out of the empirical facts of the past.[22] This basic structure can be filled and made concrete with the political aspirations toward the intended orientation of practical life in its temporal dimension by means of historical knowledge. Here we can easily distinguish between left and right, moderate and radical, feminist and patriarchal, and such like intentions. In short, it is possible to locate every political position in historiography shaping the design of the past. Besides the political rhetoric, we can also find all other factors shaping the liveliness of historiography through rhetorical patterns, such as ethics, religion, world views, and ideologies. We can analyze these factors by means of typologies, and we can transform every typology into a set of rhetorical *topoi* in historiography.

As far as Ranke is concerned, I shall describe the rhetoric of his historiography by merely pointing to two levels or aspects: namely, the basically historical, and the political, *topoi*. Both are well known as characterizing the peculiarity of Ranke's mode of history writing: he provides history with meaning by a predominant use of the *topos* of genetical narration, and his political attitude is historiographically visible as moderate conservatism.

The genetical *topos* is present in the often used category of "development" (*Entwicklung*) and in a multitude of metaphors of movement expressing the thoroughgoing historical sense of the past occurrences Ranke presented. The following quotation of his *History of the Popes* is characteristic of this rhetoric of the genetical type of historical orientation in time: "We are forced irresistibly to the conviction that all the purposes and efforts of humanity are subjected to the silent and often imperceptible, but invincible and ceaseless march of events."[23] Ranke presents this "march of events" as a historical process leading to the political constellation of modern states in Europe that he thought to be the predominant force of his time. In the context of our quotation, Ranke expresses this genetical perspective, prevalent of modern history, as "a spirit of community in the modern world which has always been regarded as the basis of its entire development, whether in politics, religion, manners, social life, or literature."[24]

Politically, Ranke shaped this perspective by presenting primarily the interactions of the leading personalities, thus underlining the fundamental importance and competence of governments in arriving at essential decisions, without relating to any great extent to the people who were being governed or to their ordinary lives. Ranke's political ideas and his political positions are well known,[25] as are their manifestations in his historiography. Less known, however, is the way he transformed them into rhetorical modes and strategies of historical writing.

We can describe these modes and strategies by referring to perspectives on acts of government and to attributes that characterize political actions and actors. Such perspectives often entail a view from above, favoring state politics as the main force of historical development, and it can be found in Ranke's characterization of mass movements (for example, the Peasant Wars in Reformation Germany) as being driven by blind natural forces rather than by reflected and culturally legitimized intentions.[26]

All of these rhetorical strategies are present in Ranke's historiography as well as in nineteenth-century historiography in general. But where does this leave the antirhetorical turn of historiography toward its modern scientific form? Recognizing the unbroken force of rhetoric in historiography, one could easily take the position that all antirhetorical statements of historiography based on research are nothing but rhetoric itself. The antirhetorical posture seems to hide the rhetorical character of historiography in order to participate in the cultural prestige of science and to legitimize the professional skill of historians who have been cultivating an image of academic seriousness. This postmodern view on the modernism, which historiography has gained by its scientific methods, is seductive. It takes the literary character of historiography seriously into consideration and lifts the veil of ignorance which academic self-understanding has imposed on the writing of history as the main task of the historian. Unfortunately, however, the new awareness of historiography as a working process of writing produces a new veil over what historians do, now obscuring an important part of the work of the historian, the research process. I think it is worthwhile, therefore, to ask what are the consequences of the antirhetorical input of research into historiography. Do they have any effect, signalizing a new, a specifically "modern," quality in the art of writing history? The answer lies in looking at Ranke's work: it is aesthetics.

Forward to aesthetics

What is the difference between rhetoric and aesthetics?[27] It is by its rhetoric that historiography realizes its practical function of orienting the practical life of its audience to a temporal frame. It transforms the necessity of action into the linguistic forms of its temporal orientation via historical memory. By doing so, it follows the logic of practical needs in the interpretation of the world and the self. Aesthetics introduces an element of freedom into this constraint of practical needs shaping historiography; it unburdens historical memories that guide human action from the dominance of practical interests; it opens up a space for the free self-reflection in the temporal orientation of human activity. Its brilliance lies in freely dealing with historical knowledge, while using it rhetorically in the cultural struggle of life.

We become aware of this radiance of freedom, and acknowledge it, as we appreciate and enjoy Ranke's historiography as an extraordinary, well written work of a high literary standard, without the need to accept its particular standpoints on society and politics. Historiography shares this aesthetic quality with literature as *poesies*. Thus it seems to be a quality which has nothing to do with the antirhetorical turn which Ranke and all academic historians are so eager to underline and make claims for.

But I do not think that this is true. For me the aesthetic glow of the classical historiography of the nineteenth century is more than just a consequence of the personal capability of historians. It is a reflection of the process of the inner rationalization of historiography. It is the glow of reason within the artistic or poetic dimension of historiography. For us the linguistic articulation of scholarly skills in historiography are footnotes.[28] The more footnotes, the deeper the academic concern. Ranke's words do not have many footnotes. Their academic or scientific concern is much more internalized. This becomes evident as his claim for objectivity grounded in historical research is the principle of shaping historical knowledge via linguistic presentation.

It is often said that Ranke demonstrated historical objectivity in his historiography by avoiding speaking of himself. In his words, he wanted to "extinguish my person and only let the matter speak, to make apparent the powerful forces."[29] This is well known and seems to underline the attitude of authoritative narration. Nevertheless, he does speak of himself. I found the word "I" in the first volume of the *History of the Popes* thirteen times within a hundred pages. This "I" is the historian wondering how he should understand an event or an action,[30] explicating his source for a certain occurrence,[31] complaining about the impossibility of describing the multitude of Renaissance art works, etc. This "I" in fact never reflects his concept of holistic interpretation, the encompassing perspective within which Ranke presented the great march of events. It deals with singularity and not with the whole. Ranke conceives of the whole as a meaningful story which shows the internal order and connectedness of events, occurrences and actions in time; these temporal patterns are presented in narrative form to provide significance to temporal change of human life. Here lies the reason for the aesthetic quality of Ranke's historiography: it is his conception of temporal patterns and their narrative presentation that shows the sequence and connectedness of occurrences (mainly events) in time.

Ranke avoided speaking of himself while he presented his conception of integrative temporal patterns that form the basis of his historiography. He was convinced that this whole was essentially more than only the subjective construct of historians generated in their poetic mind. It represented the actual great temporal chain of human events, defining their historical order. Although this great temporal chain can be found in the source material, it first must be brought to light by the work of the historical researcher.

This basic notion of the objectively pre-established existence of temporal patterns in the course of past events destroys rhetoric; it is the main argument against the rhetorical tradition of historiography. In rhetoric it is the linguistic procedure of writing history which presents the past in such a way that the knowledge of it plays an active role in solving problems of orientation in current life-praxis. In Ranke's view it is the temporal patterns of history itself which form this tight connection between past and present time so that memory can function as an integral part in contemporary activities. Historiography does not mediate rhetorically between present day practical life and the knowledge of the past, but it explicates scientifically an internal connection, objectively pre-established, between past and present.

The temporal patterns bringing about this connection are constituted of the moving forces of temporal change in the human world. Ranke and the classical historicists of the nineteenth century saw these forces as operating in the intentions of the human mind, guiding and moving actions, which they defined as "idea" (*Idee*). For Ranke it was the spirit of mankind, present in every word and deed of all members of the human race, which shaped the temporal patterns, giving historical meaning to the course of events in the past, and joined this past course to the changes of the world that were occurring in present actions and in human suffering.

For Ranke, therefore, an idealistic philosophy of history replaced rhetoric.[32] This philosophy allowed the historian to find, by research, an underlying structure of temporal change that is shaped by the forces of the human mind, and this underlying structure comprises the actual occurrences of present-day life. In this way historical knowledge of what really happened in the past expresses what is really happening today. Past and present are joined by mental forces (*Ideen*) which place them into an intelligible order of time. The knowledge of this order is objective and theoretical (in the sense of being intelligible), because it is empirically evident in the events of the past and can be discerned in sources by means of research. At the same time, it is subjective and practical (in the sense of orienting practical life or actions by means of an idea of the temporal direction of the change to be effected in practice), because it enlightens the intentions guiding present-day activity and suffering. Therefore, the scientific mode of historical interpretation already represents, in principle, a sufficient condition for the actualization of historical knowledge in practical life. As a result, rhetoric as a strategy is no longer necessary.

As far as the philosophical basis of historicist historiography is concerned, we understand the antirhetorical turn of historical studies as a theorization of rhetoric: that is, as an application of essential principles of reasoning concerning the temporal sequence of human events by means of linguistic procedures which make the historical knowledge of the past meaningful for current life-praxis.

It is this reason which lends Ranke's historiography its remarkable aesthetic glow. Ranke did not conceptualize a basic philosophy of history, because in his time this was a form of historical knowledge competing with historical studies and incompatible with its strategies of empirical research. Hence he kept his conception of history in a pretheoretical status, which he called presentiment (*Ahnung*). In this status, his philosophy of history could function as an aesthetic element of historiography. The aesthetic glow of Ranke's historiography is the reflection (*Wiederschein*) of reason. For it is reason which makes it possible to recognize the temporal patterns of the underlying structure of events in the past. At the same time, reason provides for a rational procedure for historical research in explicating these patterns by "collecting, finding and penetrating" the source material.

Explaining the character of aesthetics and its difference from rhetoric, I have stated that aesthetics break through the practical constraints of historiography and liberates the audience in the way it relates to historical experience and its orientational potential in practical life. It is by aesthetics that historiography lightens the burden of history in the determination of human activity. It introduces the chance of autonomy within the framework of historical determinism. How does Ranke accomplish this? His pretheoretical theory of history guides the historian through the empirical evidence of the sources toward the forces of the human mind, the agents of temporal change in human life. It makes these forces comprehensible as moving forces, operating in the depths of one's own subjectivity where they fashion historical identity or the "self." Thus, by looking into the past, one can find the self, the spirit of one's own life by gaining consciousness of the temporal patterns or the direction of history. In Ranke's words, the historian explicates, by means of historical experience, "the plans of God in his government of the world" and "the forces that are in action for the education of the human race."[33] By its aesthetics, therefore, historiography addresses its audience in a way that makes visible the mental forces forming its identity in the temporal course of their lives. Gaining this consciousness of oneself is the freedom introduced by historiography to the orientational function in life-praxis.

Thus far I have spoken only about Ranke's aesthetics on a theoretical level. There remains the question of the meaning of aesthetics with respect to the political intentions and viewpoints that are rhetorically woven into the fabric of historiography, as well as the question of how the liberating and aestheticizing concept, or vision of temporal patterns, is presented historiographically.

How does one—historiographically—break through the constraints of one's point of view, grounded in one's standpoint toward political and social life? It would be wrong to say that the objectivity of historical insight into the mental forces moving temporal change neutralizes points of view. Neutrality is not freedom. Neutrality would simply deprive historiography of the significance and importance of historical knowledge for practical life. Ranke's claim of objectivism should be understood quite differently: it does not avoid points of view on social and political affairs, but offers a mode of dealing with them by gaining a deeper and broader temporal perspective of current life-praxis. It offers a comprehensive, mediating and reconciling historical perspective that can break the constraints of one-sided or exclusive points of view without negating the practical needs for historical orientation. Historiography transcends the contemporary constraints of partiality with a vision of temporal processes. As Ranke put it, historiography is guided by the intention "to let people share divine liberty"[34] in their practical life. How is this done in the practice of writing history?

This question leads us to Ranke's technique of historical composition. Its main principle is the narrative synthesis of general tendencies, structures and particular events. Ranke presents the temporal sequence of events as manifestations of the fundamental forces of temporal change in the human world. He writes, so to speak, a structural history of the human mind in the form of a history of, above all, political events.[35] This is done quite artfully, integrating various levels of events into a whole.[36]

The most profound level refers to the principle of historical time in general. Ranke called it the "great world-governing necessities"[37] or the "invincible and ceaseless march of events."[38] In his historical writing, this appears only in very short passages that encompass important occurrences and bridge different sectors of the text. It never appears in the form of a theoretical digression or explanation but as a rather casual, accidental and arbitrary remark.

The next level pertains to the abstract appearance of the abovementioned principle in the form of modes of temporal movements. Ranke spoke of tendencies of universalization and of tendencies of particularization, fighting with each other, both constituting the complexity of directions of temporal change. In Ranke's text, this level becomes evident as summary passages that signal particular developments comprising the temporal patterns.

Next comes the level of actions of individuals—mainly of persons who represent a political system, such as kings and queens, popes and ministers. Their activity appears as the surface of historical events; it supplies the main thread of the narrative. Events thus constitute the body of empirical evidence supported by the framework of principles. By narrating events, the underlying mental structure of temporal patterns appears at the surface of what happened as reported in the surviving documents. Ranke narrated the temporal sequence of events in such a way that it appears to emanate from "noneventual" or, as we call them, structural processes, such as nation building, the formation of political relations between states, the emergence of political cultures, and so on. The events provide the locus and actualize the underlying structures of temporal processes in their unifying tendencies. In this manner, the significance of events becomes a distinct formative element of Ranke's historiography. He speaks of "great moments,"[39] in which the general course of history is concentrated, and he characterizes and describes those moments in a dramatizing fashion. He enlarges the description of them by considering alternative developments, conflicting forces, flashbacks, and projections, and thus elucidates the historical role of events as emanating from temporal patterns, giving the course of events a historical meaning that has a senseful direction. Finally, these "moments" point to the temporal change in present-day life.

Ranke presents events as symbols; they appear in their narrative connection as units of both singular occurrence and general significance, as a mediation of facts and meanings taking place in time. This is the way reason, as the knowledge of temporal patterns, appears historiographically as the aesthetic reflection on the surface of the history of events. Ranke seems to follow Hegel's philosophy of art, which defines beauty, the essential aesthetic quality of a human product, as the "sensual appearance of the idea."[40]

Outlook of the present discussion

It is not my intention to praise Ranke's Hegelianism or to suggest that his mode of historiography is necessarily relevant to contemporary history writing. I simply wanted to remind us all of the historical importance of the introduction of reason into historiography, through which it adopted a certain aesthetic quality. Unfortunately, this aesthetic quality of modern history has been neglected in historical studies. It has been banished from the self-awareness of the professional historian. While losing its internal relationship with the systematic rationality of historical research, aesthetics became an extradisciplinary feature. It has also been forgotten in the postmodern turn of the theory of history, which has been rediscovering the rhetorical principles and procedures of historiography. It will remain forgotten as long as we do not distinguish between rhetoric and aesthetics, and as long as we fail to ask ourselves how we can make the liberating forces of reason function within the restraints of practical needs that become effective in historical narration. We know we cannot do this in the mode of Ranke and his contemporary historiographers as we have lost their confidence in an idealistic philosophy of history. This, however, is no argument against reason in history; on the contrary, it is an argument to strengthen our pursuit of it. The postmodern recognition of rhetoric in historiography should not lead us back to a premodern rhetoric, but toward a rhetoric of historiography which preserves the necessity of liberating reason in historiography and, at the same time, views this reason not simply as a technique for research. Such a broad and more profound vision would make it possible to approach historical studies without neglecting the question of the aesthetics of historiography.

Notes

This chapter was first published in, *History and Theory*, 29 (1990), 190–204.
1. (Life is interpretation, it is giving things and events a meaning by telling them to ourselves.) Bernard Groethuysen, "Introduction à la pensée philosophique allemande depuis Nietzsche", in idem *Philosophie et histoire*, ed., B. Danois, Paris, 1995, 91–143, quotation 96.
2. See Jörn Rüsen, "New Directions in Historical Studies," in *Miedzy Historia a Teoria. Refleksje nad Problematyka Dziejow Historycznej*, ed. Marian Drozdowski, Warsaw, 1988, 340–55; Rüsen, "Historische Aufklärung im Angesicht der Post-Moderne: Geschichte im Zeitalter der 'Neuen Unübersichtlichkeit'," in Jörn Rüsen, *Zeit und Sinn. Strategien historischen Denken*s, Frankfurt am Main, 1990, 231–51 (a shortened English version is: Jörn Rüsen, "Historical Enlightenment in the light of Postmodernism: History in the Age of the 'New Unintelligibility'," *History and Memory*, 1 (1989), 109–29.
3. Ranke, *Geschichten*.
4. Ranke, *Geschichten*, VII, "zeigen, wie es eigentlich gewesen."
5. See Jörn Rüsen, "Von der Aufklärung zum Historismus. Idealtypische Perspektiven eines Strukturwandels," in Rüsen, *Konfigurationen des Historismus*, 29–94.
6. Leopold von Ranke, *Zur Kritik neuerer Geschichtsschreiber*, Sämtliche Werke, vols 33–34, Leipzig, 1874. See also Ernst Schulin, "Rankes Erstlingswerk oder Der Beginn der kritischen Geschichtsschreibung über die Neuzeit," in idem *Traditionskritik und Rekonstruktionsversuch. Studien zur Entwicklung von Geschichtswissenschaft und historischem Denken*, Göttingen, 1979, 44–46.
7. The logic of this mode of explanation is discussed in Rüsen, *Rekonstruktion der Vergangenheit*, 30ff.
8. von Ranke, *Zur Kritik neuerer Geschichtsschreiber,* 24, "Wir unsers Orts haben einen anderen Begriff von Geschichte. Nackte Wahrheit ohne allen Schmuck; gründliche Erforschung des Einzelnen: das übrige Gott befohlen; nur kein Erdichten, auch nicht im Kleinsten, nur kein Hirngespinst."
9. A clear analysis of this can be found in Eckard Kessler, "Geschichte: Menschliche Praxis oder kritische Wissenschaft?" in idem *Theoretiker humanistischer Geschichtsschreibung*, Munich, 1971. See also, Eckard Kessler, *Das rhetorische Modell der Historiographie. Formen der Geschichtsschreibung*, eds., Reinhart Koselleck, Heinrich Lutz, Jörn Rüsen, Beiträge zur Historik, vol. 4, Munich, 1982, 37–85.
10. Ranke, "On the character" in G.G. Iggers and K. von Moltke, eds., *Theory and Practice*, 33–46. See also, Ranke's "Idee der Universalgeschichte," 72, "Die Historie unterscheidet sich dadurch von anderen Wissenschaften, daß sie zugleich Kunst ist. Wissenschaft ist sie: indem sie sammelt, findet, durchdringt; Kunst, indem sie das Gefundene, Erkannte wieder gestaltet, darstellt. Andere Wissenschaften begnügen sich, das Gefundene schlechthin als solches aufzuzeichnen: bei der Historie gehört das Vermögen der Wiederhervorbringung dazu".

11. Ranke, "On the character," 33; see also, Ranke, "Idee der Universalgeschichte," 72, "Die Kausalität zu ergründen, den Kern des Daseins in den Begriff zu fassen."
12. It was Droysen, who in 1857 first explained the main operations in this manner. See Droysen, *Historik*, 67 ff.
13. Ranke, "On the character," 34; see also, Ranke, "Idee der Universalgeschichte," 72, "das erschienene Leben zu reproduzieren".
14. Ranke, "On the character;" see also, Ranke, "Idee der Universalgeschichte," 72, "Vermögen der Wiederhervorbringung".
15. Ranke, "On the character," 34; see also, Ranke, "Idee der Universalgeschichte," 72, "Sie verbindet sie beide in einem dritten, nur ihr eigentümlichen Element."
16. Ranke, "On the character," 34. see also, Ranke, "Idee der Universalgeschichte," 72.
17. Ranke, "Idee der Universalgeschichte," 72, "Die Kunst beruht auf sich selber: ihr Dasein beweist ihre Gültigkeit, dagegen vollkommen durchgearbeitet sein bis zu ihrem Begriff und über Eigenstes klar muß die Wissenschaft sein."
18. Jörn Rüsen, *Ästhetik und Geschichte. Geschichtstheoretische Untersuchungen zum Begründungszusammenhang von Kunst, Gesellschaft und Wissenschaft*, Stuttgart, 1976, 14.
19. White, *Metahistory*; idem, *Tropics of Discourse. Essays in Cultural Criticism*, Baltimore, 1978; Idem, *Content of the Form*; Dominick LaCapra, *History and Criticism*, Ithaca, 1985; Jörn Rüsen, "Geschichtsschreibung als Theorieproblem der Geschichtswissenschaft. Skizze zum historischen Hintergrund der gegenwärtigen Diskussion," in Jörn Rüsen, *Zeit und Sinn. Strategien historischen Denkens*, Frankfurt am Main, 1990, 135–52.
20. Ranke, "On the character," 33ff. See also, Ranke, "Idee der Universalgeschichte," 72.
21. Rüsen, *Lebendige Geschichte*.
22. Cf. chaps. 1 and 2.
23. Ranke, *Theory and Practice*, 185. See also, Ranke, *Die römischen Päpste*, 23, "Es ist nicht anders, als daß alles menschliche Tun und Treiben dem leisen und der Bemerkung oft entzogenen, aber gewaltigen und unaufhaltsamen Gange der Dinge unterworfen ist."
24. Ranke, *Die römischen Päpste*, 23, "Es gibt eine Gemeinschaftlichkeit der modernen Welt, welche immer als eine Hauptgrundlage der gesamten Ausbildung derselben in Staat und Kirche, Sitte, Leben und Literatur betrachtet worden ist."
25. See Helmut Berding, "Leopold von Ranke," in H.-U. Wehler, ed., *Deutsche Historiker*, vol. 1, Göttingen, 1971, 7–14.
26. As Ranke writes in his *Deutsche Geschichte im Zeitalter der Reformation*, 143, "Unaufhörlich vernimmt man dies dumpfe Brausen eines unbändigen Elementes in dem Innern des Bodens, auf dem man steht."
27. For more detailed argument see Rüsen, *Lebendige Geschichte*.
28. See Peter Rieß, *Footnotologie: Towards a theory of the footnote*, Berlin, 1985.
29. Leopold von Ranke, *Englische Geschichte vornehmlich im 17. Jahrhundert*, vol. 2, Sämtliche Werke, vol. 15, Leipzig, 1877, 103, "Ich wünschte mein Selbst gleichsam auszulöschen, und nur die Dinge reden, die mächtigen Kräfte erscheinen zu lassen."
30. Ranke, *Die römischen Päpste*, 37.
31. Ibid., 39.
32. See Michael-Joachim Zemlin, *Geschichte zwischen Theorie und Theoria. Untersuchungen zur Geschichtsphilosophie Rankes*, Würzburg, 1988.
33. Ranke, *Theory and Practice*, 184. See also, Ranke, *Die römischen Päpste*, 22, "den Plänen der göttlichen Weltregierung, den Momenten der Erziehung des Menschengeschlechtes nachzuforschen."
34. See Leopold von Ranke, *Über die Verwandtschaft und den Unterschied der Historie und der Politik*, Sämtliche Werke, vol. 24, Leipzig, 1877, 290, "*De historiae et politices cognatione atque discrimine*" (On the relationship and difference between history and politics), inaugural lecture 1836.

35. See Hans Schleier, "Narrative und Strukturgeschichte im Historismus;" Georg G. Iggers, "Historicism (A Comment)," and Jörn Rüsen, "Narrative und Strukturgeschichte im Historismus," all in *Storia della Storiografia*; 10 (1986), 112–52.
36. The following remarks agree in large part with the observations made by Hermann von der Dunk, "Die historische Darstellung bei Ranke: Literatur und Wissenschaft," in: Wolfgang J. Mommsen, ed., *Leopold von Ranke und die moderne Geschichtswissenschaft*, Stuttgart, 1988), 131–65, mainly 151ff.
37. Ranke, *Die römischen Päpste*, 64, "große weltbeherrschende Notwendigkeiten." See also, Ranke, *Theory and Practice*, 185; Ranke, *Die römischen Päpste*, 23.
38. Ranke, *Theory and Practice*, 185; Ranke, *Die römischen Päpste*, 23.
39. See, for example, Ranke, *Die römischen Päpste*, 57 and 129.
40. Georg Wilhelm Hegel, *Ästhetik*, ed. Friedrich Bassenge, Berlin, 1955, 146.

Chapter 4

Narrativity and Objectivity in Historical Studies

>
> Scientific truth is precisely what is valid for all who seek the truth.
> Max Weber[1]

The problem

"Narrativity" and "objectivity" seem to be contradictory characterizations of historical studies. The category of narrativity brings historical studies close to literature; it discloses the literary character of historiography, and the linguistic procedures and principles which constitute "history" as a meaningful and sensible representation of the past in the cultural practices of historical memory. Objectivity, on the other hand, is a category that discloses a certain kind of historical knowledge, gained through the methodically-ruled procedures of research and that has furnished it with a solid validity jutting over the field of arbitrary meaning.

The metahistorical discourse[2] on the principles of historical thinking and historiography, like objectivity and narrativity, can historically be organized according to the following juxtapositions: (a) in the premodern tradition of rhetorics the historians' work was discussed as a literary practice of narration guided by truth claims; (b) in the modernizing process of rationalization which made history into an academic discipline, these truth claims became elaborated to a set of rules which constitute historical research as a warrant of objectivity. "Objectivity" meant a general validity of historical knowledge, based on its relationship to the experience of the past and on the rationality of the cognitive treatment of this experience. The postmodern discourse has criticized this attitude as false consciousness hiding the linguistic procedures of narration that constitute the distinctive nature of history as a mental construct of representing the past for the cultural purposes of present-day life.

Notes for this section begin on page 72.

The premodern discourse emphasized the relationship between the historians and their audience. It concentrated on moral principles which made the past important for the present, and moulded its representation into a moral message which enabled its addressees to understand and to handle the rules of practical human life. The modern discourse on history criticized this moral attitude and emphasized the relationship between the historians and the experience of the past given in source material. The historians explicated their competence as professionals to disclose the historical experience by the rationality of method. Ranke's famous words indicate this change of interest in the self-awareness of historical studies: "To history has been given the function of judging the past, of instructing men for the profit of future years. The present attempt does not aspire to such a lofty undertaking. It merely wants to show how, essentially, things happened."[3]

With the establishment of historical studies as an academic discipline, and with its claim for scientific standards of historical knowledge, metahistory had a two-fold function: it had to legitimize the academic character of the historians' profession by emphasizing the "scientific" nature of historical knowledge brought about by research and, at the same time, to stress the distinctive nature of this discipline which distinguishes it from other disciplines, mainly from the natural sciences. Despite many approaches to reshape historical studies according to the paradigm of natural sciences, most historians have cultivated a self-understanding as scholars and an awareness of their discipline which underlines the peculiarity of historical thinking. The principle of narrativity got its favorable conjuncture in metahistory as a criterion for this distinctiveness and peculiarity. With the principle of narrativity it can be made clear that historical thinking follows a different strategy of explaining than the modes of thought, the logic of which is centred on conformity to laws (*Gesetzmäßigkeit*).

The consequence of this new reflection of historical thinking according to the narrativity of its form, has brought about a radical loss of the traditional modern objectivistic attitude of historical studies. This is the reason why professional historians have always felt uneasy vis-à-vis the metahistorical reflection on the narrativity of their cognitive representations. Although they have been unable to replace this distinctive principle by another one that could legitimize, at the same time, a scientific approach to history and the methodical specifics of historical thinking and cognition, they have not been convinced that the cognitive advancements of their academic work are sufficiently realized by the metahistorical treatment of historical narration.

So the *present situation of historical studies* is characterized by an unclear relationship: on the one hand, there is the metahistorical strictness of narrativity as a principle of historical thinking, which logically prevents any scientific objectivity in representing the past as history; on the other hand, there are still well-established academic attitudes and procedures of professional historians, that enable them to pursue their work of research and historiography with a strong commitment to a methodical rationality. It is this rationality of method which furnishes the knowledge, gained by research and presented as historiography, with the claim for objectivity.

In this chapter I will try to reconcile these two attitudes. Doing so I will first follow the argument which emphasizes the narrative structure of historical knowledge and which uses it to criticize inadequate conceptions of historical objectivity. In a second step I will try to show that there exists something like historical objectivity and that it can be explicated and legitimated in the framework of a narrativistic theory of historical studies.

What is objectivity?

Objectivity[4] is a criterion of validity which renders historical thinking and historiography plausible; that is, it is a certain form of a truth claim, closely related to the rationalization of historical thinking and its academic—not to say scientific—character. Truth has always been a commitment of historiography. In the premodern, rhetorical, tradition of metahistory truth was conceptualized and prescribed for the historians as a moral attitude of historiographers and a rhetorical principle of their historiography. Truth was directed against prejudices and deformations of historical perspectives due to one-sided partiality, in favor of one faction or actor, in the presented past, and it was directed against the use of fictional elements in presenting the past. To tell the truth about the past was mainly seen to be a simple deliberation of the historiographers. The limits of interpretation were set by moral rules as guidelines for the historiographical work as well as guidelines for understanding the past and applying the knowledge of it to current affairs of human life and its future perspective. In his book, *How to write history*, Lukian of Samosata says that history has only one task and one purpose, namely to be useful, and that the historian can only realize this objective by writing the truth.[5] This "usefulness" of history brought about by commitment to truth, is a moral one: *historia vitae magistra*. History teaches the rules of human life by accumulating experience beyond the horizon of one single life. Historical representation has to bring about prudential (φρονησις, σωφροσυνη), that is, the competence of organizing practical life according to general rules which were derived by accumulated experience (in two words: rule competence). History is able to and committed to bringing about this pragmatic and moral competence by organizing the experience of the past in the form of a narrative which has a message in the form of generalized rules and principles of human activity. The truth claim is necessary in order to realize this relationship to experience.

The paradigm of this relationship is the wisdom of old people: as they have embodied in their minds an amount of experience due to the length of their lives, they are qualified to direct and orient the present-day life of their social group. To orient means to understand and handle practical problems with a knowledge of human affairs accumulated in life-long experience. History is seen as such an orienting force in human life, and the historian is the expert of the experience accumulated in the archives of collective memory. So history could be defined (Viperano in the humanistic discourse) as "rerum gestarum ad docendum usum rerum syncera illustrisque narratio" (authentic and enlightening narrative of human activities with the purpose to teach the handling of them).[6]

Objectivity is something quite different. It means a certain relationship of historical representation to the experience of the past. Ranke's already quoted dictum clearly states that this relationship is not primarily organized by the moral principle of prudentia (rule competence), but by the methodical principle of research as a cognitive procedure. This fundamental change in conceptualizing the basic truth claims of historiography is part of a structural shift in historical thinking which took place in the second half of the eighteenth century.[7] Here its modernization started, and it was brought about mainly by two principles: (a) a new category of history, now understood as the comprehensive temporal change of the human world, virtually including present and future—this has been expressed by the term of "history" or (more artificially) "the history;"[8] and (b) the rationality of method as a strategy of cognition in dealing with the experience of the past. The new category of "the history" defines the subject matter of historical thinking and historiography as a specific realm of the real world: history is the real human world in the dimension of time.[9] It is more than only a narrative, it is a prefiguration of the world which enables the historians to present the past in the form of a narrative. Objectivity means, so to speak, that the prudentia which in premodern times was told by the true story of the historians, has now become a pregiven reality of the human world itself.

Ranke's dictum which expresses this claim for objectivity, presupposes a certain philosophy of history: history is a temporal reality of the human world, it is an inner connection of temporal changes, pregiven, in the mode of experience, to historians. The historian has to represent this pregiven historical structure of the human world in his historiography. It tells "how it really has been." This reality is more than the sequence of events and changes in the past as they are reported in source materials, it is an embodied sense in itself. This "real" history has to be disclosed in a cognitive procedure which can only be realized by professional historians: research as a methical treatment of sources.

The temporal sequence of events and changes in the past is a manifestation of the historical deep structure of the human world. This structure, called "the history," is brought about by so-called "moving forces of the temporal change of the human world;"[10] it is these moving forces which ontologically constitute the reality of history. And this reality, pregiven in historical experience, can be disclosed in the relicts of the past by methodical research. The category of history and the rationality of historical research are thus closely interrelated: the former is the ontological precondition of the cognitive procedure of the latter. The prestigious claim for objectivity with which historians could pursue their profession as priests of the nation,[11] was based on a quasi-religious and metaphysical confidence that, by certain rational procedures, the human mind is able to disclose history as a reality structure of the human world in the temporal course of events and changes in the past.[12]

A famous document of this claim for objectivity is Wilhelm von Humboldt's essay "*On the historians' task*" (1821).[13] Here he expresses the objectivity claim in its historicist conceptualization as a "fusion" of the inquiring intellect and the object of the inquiry.[14] "Fusion" means that history as the entire subject matter (object) of historical thinking—the temporal reality of the human world—is ontologically constituted by mental forces (ideas), working through the intentionality (*Sinnbestimmtheit*, sense directedness) of human activities. Yet it is the same mental force which, on the other hand, by its interests of cognition moves the human mind in its cognitive approach to the experience of the past. The mind of cognition, related to experience, therefore, is a part of the mind of reality, pregiven by experience. The interests of cognition are a part of the mental forces which constitute history as a subject matter of cognition. One can even say that history itself speaks through the historian, that historiography represents the inner reality of history as a pregiven comprehensive form of human life. That is what objectivity means. Its epistemological ground is, in Humboldt's words, "an original antecedent congruity between subject and object."[15] Research as a cognitive procedure is based on this congruity. It leads the historians in dealing with the experience of the past, which is present in its relicts, in the source materials, in such a way that "the reality of history" is disclosed by them.

Here we can see the philosophical implications of this kind of historical objectivity. It sets clear lines of interpretation in treating the source material according to the rules of methodical research, and at the same time applies the concept of history as a temporal movement of the human world constituted by mental forces of human activity. Historical knowledge furnished with this claim of objectivity could function as a cultural orientation of practical—mainly political—life. It brought about a future perspective along the line of the direction of temporal change of the past[16] and a collective identity of the people who it is addressed to as based on constitutive moving forces of human history.

Narrativity as an objection to objectivity

Even in the context of the objectivistic conception of historical cognition there has always been an awareness of constitutive elements of subjectivity, opposed to a simply reified character of history. Many historians were aware of the involvement of their academic work in politics, and they even deliberately participated in politics. They recognized this involvement not as an external addition of their scholarly commitment, but as a constitutive factor of their historiography itself, as a forming element of its internal cognitive structure, as inseparable from the methodical rationality of their discipline. The term under which this objection of poor objectivity was discussed was *"partiality."* Droysen polemicized against the "eunuchic objectivity"[17] of historical studies which tried to neutralize itself from the political struggle about collective (mainly national) identity, within which historiography was an important argument. The same was true for Sybel, Gervinus, and others.[18] They didn't see the involvement and partiality of historians in the political struggle of forming collective identity by historical commemoration as being opposed to objectivity but, on the contrary, as being a necessary condition of historical objectivity. It is the standpoint of the historian within the political struggle of his or her time which opens up a perspective within which the powerful mental forces constituting history as a specific form of human reality became available and visible, and thus were disclosed for a cognitive approach.

The idea that objectivity is constituted by partiality follows the idealistic philosophy of history, which identifies the moving mental forces in the historical interest of historians with the mental forces of human activity, that constitutes history as the temporal reality of human life. The Marxist–Leninist concept of objectivity by partiality follows a similar philosophy of history and epistemology. Partiality in the class struggle is a necessary condition for objective knowledge of human society in general and its historical development in particular. In both concepts of objectivity the point is however, that not every partiality leads to objectivity, but only a reflected one, in which the historian uses the cognitive abilities of the human mind in a specific way: he or she generalizes his or her standpoint in a way that can integrate the different conflicting interests in the political context into a comprehensive interest. Accordingly the different perspectives, derived from the different standpoints, were integrated into a comprehensive perspective. Within this perspective the change of the human world in the past indicates a direction toward the future. It is the insight into this comprehensive perspective and direction of development that enables historians to transgress the struggle for power and to settle it by a common orientation. For the classical historicist concept of historical studies this comprehensive standpoint and perspective was realized in nationalism, more or less moderated by an idea of humankind as a principle of international communication.

Historical cognition, therefore, could be seen as a mental procedure with two ends: an *objective* one, related to the experience of the past pregiven in its relicts, that is the source material, on the one hand, and a *subjective* one related to orientation problems of practical life on the other. The guarantee of objectivism is source critique, and the guarantee of subjectivism is the involvement of the historian in the political struggle for a collective identity in the field of historical commemoration. Both are mediated in the cognitive operation of historical interpretation. It is interpretation by which the solid information of empirical evidence of the past gains its specific historical feature and becomes integrated into the mental structure of a historical narration, within which it can function as a factor of cultural orientation. As a methodical procedure interpretation stands for objectivity. Realizing a historical perspective within which the evidence of the past is related to orientation problems of the present, interpretation brings subjectivity as a constitutive work of cognition into the formation of this narrative. This objectivity and this subjectivity are but two sides of the same coin.

Because of this function, historical interpretation, which is the decisive cognitive procedure of historical studies, has remained ambiguous. In the development of historical studies there have always been two attitudes to dissolve this ambiguity. First, an *objectivistic attitude* tries to structure historical interpretation by using a form of knowledge in which the subjectivity of the historian (his or her interest in the past) is transgressed by a certain concept of history. This concept categorizes the temporal change and development of the human world in the past as a pregiven entity, to be disclosed by a cognition which is true despite any practical interest, standpoint and partiality. Very often the historians borrowed the cognitive structures of this "objective" history from the social sciences, thus participating in the claim of these sciences for following the logic of the natural sciences and sharing their cultural prestige. They believed in an epistemologically solid ground for the scientific character of historical studies. Examples for this strategy are Karl Lamprecht's attempt to transgress historicism into a new concept of history as a social science, as well as related attempts of the early Annales-School, not to speak of Marxism and the various positivistic attempts to raise history into the status of a science ("Erhebung der Geschichte in den Rang einer Wissenschaft").[19]

The second attitude is an epistemological reconstruction of the patterns of historical interpretation which accepts its roots in practical involvement and interest, and with them an unavoidable element of subjectivity; but at the same time it emphasizes its methodical rules and theoretical means as guarantees of intersubjective validity of historical knowledge. The best known example of this strategy is Max Weber's interpretation of objectivity and his methodology of ideal types.[20]

The objective approach has lost its credibility. Its ideological impact could not be overlooked: subjective interest and political struggle for power could easily be discovered in the various ideas of reified history. The latest retreat of objectivity as a constitutive idea for historical studies as an academic discipline became apparent with the metahistorical rise of narrativity as the constitutive form of historical knowledge and as the mental procedure of doing history. Narrativity is a concept which explicates the constitutive relationship of historical thinking to the cultural practices of collective memory and identity. It shows that historical cognition realizes its specifying constitution in practical life by its narrative form. Historical interpretation is fundamentally committed to this form; it has to bring the empirically evident information of the past into a narrative. Only in this form is the information of the past specifically "historical," and only in this form can historical knowledge fulfill its cultural functions.

Historical knowledge brought about by the cognitive procedure of methodically ruled research owes to narrativity qualifications which are commonly understood as strong negations of objectivity: namely, retrospectivity, perspectivity, selectivity, and particularity.[21] By "retrospectivity" the approach to empirical evidence of the past is influenced by projections of the future which tend to transgress the horizon of the experience of the past. The retrospectivity of historical knowledge can be called the open door through which non-empirical elements, subjective interests, norms and values, desires, and threats enter the historical relationship between past and present, and even have an impact in its cognitive structure guided by methodical rationality. "Perspectivity" pertains to the constitutive relationship between past and present, it anchors the historical perspective in the practical orientation problems of the historian's time. It realizes the dependence of historical sense and meaning upon the standpoint of the historians in the social life of their time. "Selectivity" indicates the consequences of retrospectivity and perspectivity for the empirical content of historical knowledge. Only a certain kind of information from source material becomes relevant for research: that which meets the subjective input of sense, meaning and significance of the past for the orientation problems of the present. The selection criteria are norms and values which shape the past with historical sense, meaning, and significance. Only the features of this sense, meaning, and significance of the past can be recognized as history. Particularity reflects the limits of the approach of historical interpretation to the empirical evidence of the past. Essentially it relates historical knowledge to the purpose of identity building by historical memory. Since identity is logically particular—it is always different to others—historical knowledge as a creative mirror of identity formation is always particular, and therefore demands a plurality of approaches to the past. Thus it corresponds to the plurality of identities, dimensions of identity, and related interests and differentiation in practical life.

With its retrospectivity, perspectivity, selectivity, and particularity, historical knowledge is a part of a cultural discourse by which difference and distinction are brought about as an essential output of cultural orientation in the human world. This is especially true for social relations and political domination. One can speak of a principle of "communicativity," which constitutes historical knowledge as an element of this cultural discourse. It moulds the academic discourse as a part of the cultural struggle for power. It deals with power by realizing its principles in the perception and interpretation of the human world in the mirror of historical memory. In the context of this communication history as represented past gains the vividness and power of being a part of everyday life. Confronted with this unavoidable integration of history into life, historical objectivity appears as its contrary, as a cultural means in the political struggle for power in the symbolizing forces of culture. Every history of historiography is an empirical proof for this role of historical studies.[22]

There is one term in the recent discourse of metahistory which indicates the retreat of objectivity from the field of historical studies (at least in the perspective of the metahistorical reflection of its constitutive principles): "fictionality." Fictionality is a counter-concept of objectivity in the semantic context of a positivistic epistemology. Objectivity stands for the epistemological attribute of the empirical solidity of the information gained from source material by the research procedure of source critique. This information consists of the so-called "facts:" they state that at a certain time, at a certain place, something happened in a certain way for certain reasons. Facts are answers to the "when/where/what/how/why" questions. Such a fact doesn't have a specifically historical sense in itself, or a meaning and significance. It gets this historical sense only in a certain temporal and, at the same time, semantic relationship to other facts. This relationship is brought about by historical interpretation. In order to realize this "historization," historical interpretation makes use of principles of sense, meaning, and significance, which have a different ontological status from the facts themselves. Compared with the pure factuality of the information from the sources, there is something more than only the factual in the narrative temporal relationship which gives the facts their specifically "historical" quality. In order to indicate this difference, the term "fictionality" is used. Since interpretation brings the historical relationship between the facts into a narrative form, the procedure of interpretation is very closely related to the procedure of narrating a story. This is expressed also by the term "fictionality." The sense-generating process of historical interpretation appears under the domination of this category as "an essentially poetical act" of the same kind of sense generation as that in literature and fine art.[23]

Fictionality thus marks the ontological and epistemological status of those elements in historical knowledge and historiography which don't share the pure factuality of the information from the sources. This term makes sense under the unquestioned presupposition of a positivistic epistemology. Additionally, it confirms a widespread concept of historical method, in which it is narrowed to the mechanism and technology of source critique. The mental operation which transforms the source information into a sense and meaningful narrative sequence, into a historical narration, now becomes explicated as narration. Metahistory, which asks for its principles, transgresses the traditional methodology focussing on objectivity into the poetics and rhetorics of historiography and historical representation focussing on subjectivity. Now the constitutive principles of historical sense generation are of an aesthetic and a linguistic nature.

This *"poetization" of historical cognition* corresponded with a lack of methodology of historical interpretation. Metahistory eclipsed, historical studies still use a more or less theoretically explicated conceptual framework of interpretation when they mould the facts into a sense-bearing historical relationship.[24] The poetical act at least included cognitive procedures committed to the methodical rules of historical research. The new awareness of linguistic strategies of making sense of history turned the historians' attention back to the act of writing history. Historiography has never been completely neglected in the metahistorical reflection of historical studies which underlined its claim for objectivity and its self-understanding and prestige as a "science." But it has been connected with, and become dependent upon, the methodical rationality of historical research, and lost its constitutive role in sense-generation when dealing with the experience of the past. Now it is the other way around: the rational means of research, if they are thematized at all, seem to be dependent on basic linguistic procedures of sense generation when shaping the source information into a sense-bearing narrative. How can we escape this ambivalence?

Approaching a new concept of objectivity

In order to realize a return of truth claims to historical thinking first of all the meaning of objectivity has to be cleared up. This meaning can be seen in two ways. First, objectivity means a constitutive relationship of historical thought to experience: there is something in the narrative construction called "history" which cannot be invented, which is pregiven and has to be recognized by the historians. Rational procedures of historical research are based on this relationship of historical thinking to an object-like pregivenness of experience to historical interpretation. Experience is one of the limits of interpretation: historical interpretation cannot transgress the border of experience when it pretends to state what happened in the past, when, where, how and why something happened or was the case. This relationship to experience does not at all prevent constitutive subjective inputs of sense generation by the historian into his or her empirical approach to the past. In its second meaning, objectivity even covers this subjective side of historical interpretation: it means a mode of this subjectivity itself, that is, the intersubjective validity of a historical interpretation. In a simple understanding, this objectivity as intersubjectivity means that historical interpretation is not at all arbitrary or random concerning those subjective elements of historical sense which mould the information of the source material into a sense and meaningful historical narrative, and constitute "history" as a sense-bearing relationship between past and present (which is tendentially related to the future). This meaning of objectivity deals with the relationship of historical interpretation to cultural discourse and its social life, within which every historical narrative is constituted, to which every historical narrative is addressed, and within which every historical narrative plays a role of orienting practical life. Objectivity means that historical experience can be interpreted in respect to these three perspectives in such a way that there are good reasons to accept one historical narrative and to refuse another one. The term "reason" indicates the issue: there are principles of interpretation which every historian is committed to as long as he or she wants to realize a historical narrative, the validity of which is beyond poor subjectivity in the meaning of arbitrariness or being completely at random.

The claim for objectivity in the meaning of a constitutive relationship to historical experience can easily be legitimated by referring to the established research procedures of historical studies. One has to concede that historical method is influenced by and even dependent upon a heuristic approach to historical experience that includes constitutive elements of subjectivity, such as sense, meaning, and significance in the specifically historic relationship between past and present. But, nevertheless, the methodical rationality of research has got a validity which cannot be put into such doubt that the information from the sources loses its cognitive role as a limit of interpretation.[25]

In the case of subjectivity things are different: it is an open question whether there is a comparable, strict, methodical, rationality in the procedures by which the information from the source materials were moulded into a meaningful historical narrative. We should not overlook the point that there are at least some undeniable rational criteria of intersubjectivity which stand for the consistency of a historical narrative. This consistency has to be investigated concerning the principles of intersubjectivity as a necessary condition for the plausibility or the "truth" of a historical narrative.

It is useful to distinguish two dimensions of this consistency: theoretical coherence and practical coherence. Theoretical coherence is a matter of concepts and their relationship to the information from source materials. The postmodern discourse of metahistory has dealt mainly with metaphors as basic elements of historical sensegeneration in transforming the experience of the past into a meaningful history for the present.[26] The methodical rationality of historical studies has already brought about a transformation or, better, a transgression of metaphors into concepts. By this conceptualizing historical interpretation has a certain quality which contributes to its intersubjective validity: the quality which I would like to call "reconstructability." I see this in the sense that historical interpretation can have a transparency and clarity which makes it in principle possible to construct and corroborate and refute the argument which it has brought about. This is what is meant by the famous words of Max Weber: …" es ist und bleibt wahr, daß eine methodisch korrekte wissenschaftliche Beweisführung auf dem Gebiete der Sozialwissenschaften, wenn sie ihren Zweck erreicht haben will, auch von einem Chinesen als richtig anerkannt werden muß."[27] This transparency can be translated into a methodical rule of historical interpretation: it should be done within an explicit conceptual framework. By "explicit conceptual" it means that in a more or less theoretical form, historical interpretation has a certain kind of reflexibility which enforces the element of explanatory rationality in telling the story of the past, thus giving the sense of this story an argumentative form in which it is addressed to the rational competences of all those to whom it is told. The creative mental processes of historical narrativity gain the quality of an argumentative structure and bring the rational forces of control by empirical evidence, logical coherence, and explanatory force into the game of historical sense generation.

"Practical coherence" is a quality of the historical narrative by which it gains plausibility concerning the practical function it fulfills in the cultural orientation of practical life.[28] Is it possible to find and to identify coherence and intersubjectivity—that is an indication of reason—even in the abyss of life where interests, conflicts, will of power, and the overwhelming force of gaining self-esteem and social recognition play a decisive role in moulding the images of the past for the purposes of today and for the future perspective? The answer is simple and clear: without discursive elements of intersubjectivity, practical human life would be impossible. I think of all the cultural factors which enable human beings to settle their conflicts in a peaceful way: to come to terms with experience, to convince each other by arguments and not by force, to develop and to accept reasons for orientating practical life in cultural frameworks of activity.

These elements can be specified in respect to the most sensitive and practical function of historical thinking: its role in forming personal and social identity. Corresponding to the methodical rationality, which brings about theoretical coherence of a historical narrative, there is a universal practical reason and rationality in regulating the differences and tensions of identityforming. It is apparent in the political struggle for power and in conflicting strategies of getting a livable balance of self-esteem and social acknowledgement in respect to historical identity. It is a powerful cultural means for individuals and groups to find their social place in relationship to others. I think it is the category of equality and the related concept of humankind, that serve as cultural rules to deal with differences.

This category is the practical counterpart to the theoretical forces of sense generation that furnish historical narratives with the already-mentioned argumentative transparency. With the category of equality such a transparency can be brought about in the practical field of identity formation as well. The whole modern system of law is based on it. This sounds very theoretical concerning the real practical problems, but we can easily show how relevant this abstract argument is for practical life. What is a lack of intersubjectivity in the formation process of historical identity? It is lack of acknowledgement, marginalization, an asymmetrical moral relationship between togetherness and otherness. Equality is a regulative idea to overcome this lack of intersubjectivity.

But for the purposes of identity formation by historical memory this category of intersubjectivity is fundamentally insufficient. It states an abstract universality, which lies beyond the diversity of differences within which culture realizes human identity. We need a far more extended and deeper principle that meets this diversity. On the theoretical level of regulative ideas, one can easily transform the abstract universality of equality into a concrete universality, that meets the challenges of differentiation as a necessary cultural procedure in identity formation. Since every identity is particular, intersubjectivity in respect to the difference of particularities is a question of how to interrelate this particularity. It should be committed to the methodical rule that one has to accept one's difference from the others and the difference from the otherness within oneself. Here the regulative idea of intersubjectivity is mutual recognition and acknowledgement.[29]

This regulative idea can be applied to historical interpretation: it is related to the perspectiveness of every historical narrative. It commits historical interpretation to a perspective which either includes the difference of standpoints related to the different identities, or enforces other perspectives as complementary and are related to other standpoints. Plurality of standpoints and perspectives should not be considered as an objection to objectivity, but as its realization in respect to the necessities of practical coherence. But plurality can be realized in a two-fold way: it can be logically based on a strict negation of objectivity, discrediting it as a "noble dream," but then there would be no regulating principle vis-à-vis the conflicts and constraints among different perspectives, there would only be "a bellum omnium contra omnes" or a "clash of civilizations" fought with the weapons of narrativity. The other possibility is a concept of pluralism, guided by a comprehensive rule of complementarity, mutual criticism in the mode of transparent, reasonable argument, and mutual acknowledgement and recognition. I think that there is no doubt which kind of pluralism should be preferred.

Such a regulative idea of practical coherence has consequences for the heuristic approach to historical experience. This approach is always pushed forward by striving for norms and values that constitute historical sense. Practical inter-subjectivity is such a value, and it has its echo, its response in the experience of the past itself, as history can be conceptualized as a process of striving to realize this principle in human life forms, in constitutions, law systems, social behaviour etc.

This echo of historical experience furnishes intersubjectivity as theoretical and practical coherence of historical narratives with an additional quality of objectivity in the meaning of a truth-bearing relationship to experience. History as experience is not outside ourselves. Historical experience is not simply pregiven in the relicts of the past as the historians deal with them in the form of sources. History is also pregiven within ourselves, particularly as we ourselves are results of a long-lasting temporal development. Before we think of history, and before we commemorate, it we have already become history. Before we think of the past as past—and this is the necessary condition of the cultural construction of "history" as an element of cultural orientation—the past is present. In this presence of the past, intersubjectivity and objectivity in the sense of experience are the same. In this pregivenness the past has not yet become history; it has not yet even become the past; as history and past—we can say—it is invisible. To render it visible we have to distinguish between the three different time dimensions and have to pursue the mental procedures of historical consciousness. The result of their work is the historical representation of the past. It can only fulfill its orienting function if it has not lost the invisible history of ourselves. Only a historical representation of the past, which brings this history into our minds, has the quality of objectivity in which the aspect of experience and the aspect of intersubjectivity are synthesized, as well as the theoretical and practical dimension of generating historical sense in the relationship between past and present.

The claim for objectivity realized in the academic procedure of historical cognition is very often thought to bear a certain "smell of death." Many professional historians think that their service to the truth can only be realized if they neutralize their representation of the past against the life struggles of their time. This neutrality is a deceptive thing. No historical narrative is possible without a perspective and related criteria of historical sense. These criteria are derived from the cultural orientation of practical life. They may have got a conceptual form in which a good deal of the vigor of life has been lost but they still bear the feature of this life. So historical objectivity does not prevent the colourful features of practical life in historical representation; on the contrary, it is a principle which organizes this feature. Emotion, imagination, power, and will are necessary elements of historical sense generation. The claim for objectivity does not rob them of their vigor of life. Objectivity can be recognized as a form of their liveliness in which historical narratives enforce experience and intersubjectivity in cultural orientation, and by doing so it may help to render the burden of life a little more bearable.

Notes

1. Max Weber, *Sociological Writings*, ed. Wolf Heydebrand, New York, 1994, 259.
2. What I mean by "metahistorical" and by "metahistory" is explicated in chapt. 8.
3. Ranke, *Theory and Practice*, 137, "Man hat der Historie das Amt, die Vergangenheit zu richten, die Mitwelt zum Nutzen zukünftiger Jahre zu belehren, beigemessen: so hoher

Ämter unterwindet sich gegenwärtiger Versuch nicht: er will bloß zeigen, wie es eigentlich gewesen." (Ranke, *Geschichten*, VII.)
4. Cf. Rüsen, *Historische Vernunft*, pp. 85ff; idem *Studies in Metahistory*, 49ff.; Allan Megill, ed., *Rethinking Objectivity*, Durham, 1994 (originally appeared in Annals of Scholarship, vol. 8, no. 3–4 (1991), vol. 9, no. 1–2 (1992)).
5. Lukian, *Wie man Geschichte schreiben soll*, ed. H. Homeyer, Munich, 1965, §9, 107.
6. Eckhard Kessler, *Theoretiker humanistischer Geschichtsschreibung*, Munich, 1971, 19, footnote 57; G.A. Viperano, *De poetica libri tres*. (Poetiken des Cinquecento 10) I, 7 a; 13, pp. 10 sq. Munich, 1967. Cf. Kessler's excellent introduction: "Geschichte, menschliche Praxis oder kritische Wissenschaft? Zur Theorie humanistischer Geschichtsschreibung," in op.cit., 7–47; idem, "Das rhetorische Modell der Historiographie," in *Das rhetorische Modell der Historiographie. Formen der Geschichtsschreibung*, eds., Reinhart Koselleck, Heinrich Lutz, Jörn Rüsen (*Beiträge zur Historik*, vol. 4), Munich, 1982, 37–85.
7. Cf. Rüsen, *Konfigurationen des Historismus*, 45ff.; Koselleck, "Historia magistra vitae," 38; Horst Walter Blanke, *Historiographiegeschichte als Historik* (Fundamenta Historica, vol. 3), Stuttgart/ Bad Cannstatt, 1991; Wolfgang Küttler; Jörn Rüsen; Ernst Schulin, eds., *Geschichtsdiskurs*, vol. 2, *Anfänge modernen historischen Denkens*, Frankfurt am Main, 1994.
8. For logical reasons I prefer the term "the history," although it is scarcely used in English.
9. I prefer the term "the history" according to the German "die Geschichte." The word "History" (with capital H) might be misunderstood.
10. Cf. Wilhelm von Humboldt, "Betrachtungen über die bewegenden Ursachen der Weltgeschichte," in idem, *Schriften zur Anthropologie und Geschichte*, (Werke in fünf Bänden), ed., Andreas Flitner, Klaus Giel, Darmstadt, 1960, 578–84 (Akademieausgabe II, 360–66).
11. Wolfgang Weber, *Priester der Clio. Historisch-sozialwissenschaftliche Studien zur Herkunft und Karriere deutscher Historiker 1800–1970*. 2nd edn, Frankfurt am Main, 1987.
12. Cf. Jörn Rüsen, "Historische Methode und religiöser Sinn—Vorüberlegungen zu einer Dialektik der Rationalisierung des historischen Denkens in der Moderne," in Küttler, Rüsen, Schulin, eds. *Geschichtsdiskurs*, vol. 2, 344–80.
13. Wihelm von Humboldt, "Über die Aufgabe des Geschichtsschreibers," in idem *Werke in fünf Bänden*, eds. Andreas Flitner, Klaus Giel. Darmstadt, vol. 1: *Schriften zur Anthropologie und Geschichte*, Darmstadt, 1960, 585–606 (*Gesammelte Schriften* [Akademieausgabe] IV, 35–56); English translation in *History and Theory* 6 (1967), 57–71; furthermore in Ranke, *Theory and Practice*, 5–23.
14. Ranke, *Theory and Practice*, 8.
15. Ibid., 15 ("eine vorhergängige, ursprüngliche Übereinstimmung zwischen dem Subjekt und Objekt"), 596ff.
16. A key source of this practical function of historical objectivity (one may even speak of its ideological character) is Ranke's inaugural adress, *Über die Verwandtschaft und den Unterschied der Historie und der Politik* (Sämtliche Werke, vol. 24), Leipzig, 1877, 280–93.
17. Droysen, *Historik*, 236.
18. Heinrich von Sybel, "Über den Stand der neueren deutschen Geschichtsschreibung (1856)," in idem, *Kleine historische Schriften*, Munich, 1863, 343–59; Georg Gottfried Gervinus, "Grundzüge der Historik (1837)," in idem *Schriften zur Literatur*, ed. G. Erler, Berlin, 1962, 49–103; cf. Jörn Rüsen, "Der Historiker als 'Parteimann des Schicksals'—Georg Gottfried Gervinus," in Rüsen, *Konfigurationen des Historismus*, 157–225.
19. A famous formulation of Johann Gustav Droysen, title of his influential review of Thomas Buckles "History of Civilization in England" (Droysen, *Historik*, 451ff.).
20. Max Weber, "Die 'Objektivität' sozialwissenschaftlicher und sozialpolitischer Erkenntnis," in idem, *Gesammelte Aufsätze zur Wissenschaftslehre*, 3rd edn., ed., Johannes Winckelmann, Tübingen, 1968, 146–214. (English translation in, Max Weber, *The Methodology of the Social Sciences*, trans. and ed. by Edward A. Shils and Henry A. Finch, New York, 1949); partly in, Max Weber, "'Objectivity' in Social Science," in idem, *Sociological Writings*, ed. Wolf Heydebrand, New York, 1994, 248–59.

21. Cf. Klaus Füßmann, "Historische Formungen. Dimensionen der Geschichtsdarstellung," in Klaus Füßmann, Heinrich Theodor Grütter, Jörn Rüsen, eds., *Historische Faszination. Geschichtskultur heute*, Köln, 1994, 27–44, esp. 32–35.
22. Peter Novick, *That Noble Dream. The "Objectivity-Question" and the America Historical Profession*, New York and Cambridge, 1988.
23. White, *Metahistory*, x.
24. Cf. Rüsen, *Rekonstruktion der Vergangenheit*.
25. Joyce Appleby, Lynn Hunt, Margaret Jacob, *Telling the Truth about History*, New York, 1994; Mark Bevir, "Objectivity in History," *History and Theory*, 33 (1994), 328–44; Lionel Gossman, *Between History and Literature*, Cambridge, 1990; Jürgen Kocka, *Sozialgeschichte. Begriff—Entwicklung—Probleme*. 2nd edn., Göttingen, 1986, 40–47, "Objektivitätskriterien in der Geschichtswissenschaft;" Reinhart Koselleck, Wolfgang Mommsen, Jörn Rüsen, eds., *Objektivität und Parteilichkeit* (Beiträge zur Historik. vol. 1) Munich, 1977; Jörn Rüsen, ed., *Historische Objektivität. Aufsätze zur Geschichtstheorie*, Göttingen, 1975.
26. Cf. Frank R. Ankersmit, *History and Tropology: The Rise and Fall of Metaphor*, Berkeley, 1994.
27. Max Weber, "Die 'Objektivität' sozialwissenschaftlicher und sozialpolitischer Erkenntnis," in idem, *Gesammelte Aufsätze zur Wissenschaftslehre*, 3rd edn., ed. Johannes Winckelmann, Tübingen, 1968, 155. (It is and remains true, that a methodically correct argument in the field of the social sciences has to be accepted even by a Chinese, if it intends to reach its objective.)
28. Chris Lorenz adresses this dimension of objectivity in an epistemological perspective and connects it with theoretical intersubjectivity by his claim for "internal realism." Chris Lorenz, "Historical Knowledge and Historical Reality: A Plea for 'Internal Realism'," *History and Theory*, 33 (1994), 297–327.
29. Cf. Charles Taylor, *Multikulturalismus und die Politik der Anerkennung*, Frankfurt am Main, 1993; Jörn Rüsen, "Vom Umgang mit den Anderen—Zum Stand der Menschenrechte heute," *Internationale Schulbuchforschung*, 15 (1993), 167–78; idem, "Human Rights from the Perspective of a Universal History," in Wolfgang Schmale, ed., *Human Rights and Cultural Diversity. Europe—Arabic-Islamic World—Africa—China*, Frankfurt am Main, 1993, 28–46.

II: Interpretation

Chapter 5

What is Historical Theory?

> A noble mind is committed to foundation, and when established, Dao will be growing.
> Konfuzius[1]

The problem

Theories are statements which are, in a complex way, linked to each other and have a high degree of generalization. Theories undoubtedly play a decisive role in all sciences which claim to be scientific (as, for example, theoretical physics). The scientific nature of knowledge is often closely connected with the nature and scope of its ability to theorise.

For historical studies, however, this poses a problem. It is indeed significant that in antiquity, when a type of theoretical knowledge was developed as an element essential to Western culture, it was regarded as impossible to theorise in historical studies. Aristotle expressed this view that poetry is

> more philosophic and of greater importance than historiography, because poetry treats of the general and historiography of the particular. The general consists of describing the things which people regard as of high quality, and do so because it is reasonable and necessary; poetry occupies itself with the general and supplies it with the particular. The particular concentrates on reporting what Alcibiades did or experienced.[2]

Whether historical knowledge can be theoretical or not is still controversial. Closely connected to this problem is the question regarding the scientific nature of historical studies, its distinguishing characteristics, its methodology and what distinguishes it from all other sciences.

The problem of theory functions on two levels within historical studies. For clarity of the argument these two levels will be distinguished, although they are interdependent, of course.

Notes for this section begin on page 91.

On one level theory is "meta-theory:" it reflects *on* historical studies and by doing so it becomes a different discourse in itself. On the other level theory is "object theory:" it is a part of the work done *in* historical studies. From a metatheoretical perspective, one looks at historical study itself, at its distinguishing characteristics, its scientific nature, the principles of historical knowledge, the rules of historical research, historiography, etc.[3]

An object theory of historical studies is concerned with 'real' history, with what happened in the past. Here the issues are theoretical statements of the temporal changes people and their world undergo in history, the interrelations of history, the present and the future in general, the description of historical phenomena in general, comprehensive hypotheses explaining historical change and related themes.[4]

One may find discussed certain questions within a metahistory of historical studies: for example, can history be a science? Does historical research use theories? Does this research lead to historical laws which can be used to explain history in a scientific manner? The object of metatheory is what actually happens in historical studies; its aim is to explicate the construction of historical studies as far as this construction characterizes history as its subject. Furthermore, it aims to show that this construction, as well as the principles underlying it, can be made visible and explicit and can be analyzed, interpreted, and proved.

To think "theoretically" is thus to be distinguished from the "practice" of gaining knowledge through historical studies. Theoretical thinking is, therefore, acquiring knowledge in a reflective way; this is the aim toward which historians (together with philosophers) should work—that is, to make the principles on which their practical work rests so transparent and conscious that they can carry out that work more efficiently. It will enable them to prove, defend, develop, and better their argument in a way which will decisively place their practical work on a higher level than would be the case without this knowledge.[5]

The following three questions play an essential role in this reflection. First, is the scientific nature of historical studies dependent on the ability of the relevant historical knowledge to theorize or not? Second, whether and how should historical research use theoretical knowledge of the human past as history and if so how does it proceed? Finally, can historical study itself develop such theoretical knowledge, and if so, how? These questions deal with the actual acquiring of scientific historical knowledge, of which metatheory is an essential ingredient. When these questions are being discussed on a meta-theoretical level, the discussion has the practical aim of being of use toward acquiring knowledge within historical studies, to develop that knowledge, to reconstruct and to expand it.

Theory as metatheoretical reflection on basic principles: the task and functions of metahistory (*historik*)

Since antiquity the development of historiography has been accompanied by a theory of its principles. This theorizing belongs to the field of rhetorics, and primarily concerns historical studies' rules of art (*historica*). From the second half of the eighteenth century, however, historical thinking started to become a science, changing the nature of metahistory (*Historik*). The historian came to know his subject and the science of historical thinking on the meta-level as part of knowing his own task as a historian. This was, of course, done in anticipation of practising historiography; it did not only expressed what historians were doing. Metahistory explicated and justified new principles constituting science, thereby serving the professionalism of historiography as an academic subject. It laid down standards for historical knowledge, controlling these rules distinguished the historian from the laity as an expert; by fulfilling them his historiography became part of science's claim to truth and cultural status.

Metahistory fulfilled the function of reflecting the justification and professionalism of historiographical principles in different ways. There are five argumentative strategies.

1. Metahistory honored the (humanist) tradition of rhetoric and poetics within historiography.
2. Metahistory has formulated historical knowledge as encyclopedic entities which, as the result of previous research, were not to be discarded, but needed to be expanded and deepened.
3. Metahistory, as the methodology of historical research, has formulated the rules which must be followed by historical thinking in dealing with history (and its sources) in order to arrive at lasting progress in knowledge.
4. Metahistory, as history's theory of knowledge, has formulated history's scientific status and characteristics which differentiated it from other sciences.
5. Metahistory, as philosophy of history, has formulated the criteria and leading insights followed by historical thinking when it makes the human past present as history, thereby placing it in a close relationship with the present as well as with the future.

These strategies are seldom used alone; they usually appear as a mixture of different aspects of historical studies, and are made explicit in principles and points of view. It is J.G. Droysens's metahistory[6] that has gained classical status because of its comprehensive systematization which integrated all the above-mentioned strategies, as well as all the aspects which have developed from them. His metahistory was, however, exceptional only because of the wide range covered by its systematization and because of its high level of argument. It is not a basis for discussing the basic principles of historical studies today.

Metahistory describes the status of historical studies as a discipline. It does so by relating two points of view to each other, which are both characteristic of historical studies: on the one hand, it puts down the principles for methodological rationality in historical studies by which it is defined as science, with other sciences. On the other hand, it defends the characteristics of historical studies that differentiate it from other sciences, especially from the natural sciences, if one considers this to be an ideal and an example for being scientific.

In the academic tradition of nineteenth-century historicism *(Historismus)* the second point of view was decisive. Because of the scientific ideal of the exact (natural) sciences, an ideal which was positivistic, the individuality of historical studies was based on the necessity of research in a methodologically correct way, with "history" as a specific object of knowledge. Historical studies coming to know their object by way of "understanding" *(Verstehen)* were distinguished from the natural sciences in particular, which defined their object by "explaining" it *(Erklären)*. In the theory of knowledge the same distinction was made with the following opposites: the ideographical versus the nomothetical method, or the individualizing versus the generalizing method.

This distinction had and still has important consequences as to whether or not historical studies can be theoretical. "Explaining" and "generalizing" have a bearing on sciences which acquire and utilize knowledge in the form of theories, which manipulate the objects of their research. In "understanding" and "individualizing," on the other hand, theoretical knowledge plays no role (or its theoretical status is completely different from the character of explaining regularities). It is often thought that historical studies cannot and need not theorize. This thesis defends the methodological autonomy and the special status of historical study as a discipline.

An attempt, however, to show that the same methodological rationality prevails in historical studies and in the natural sciences, has been made within this thesis. As a result, the development and expansion of theories about history are looked upon as a legitimate method to acquire historical knowledge.

The discussion[7] on the scientific nature of historical studies, and on its specific features as a discipline, is still being characterized by the contrasting strategies below. First, there is the analytical theory of science works with paradigms of rational explanation *(Erklären)* valid for all sciences. This type of theory indicates by complex argument how and why these models also apply to historical studies. The Hempel-Oppenheim model of rational explanation takes an important role in this respect.[8] In this model nomological knowledge (that is, knowledge acquired from facts which are related according to laws) is indisputable, since it is possible to explain facts "rationally" (that is, specifically within a science) only with nomological knowledge. Against this subjection of historical studies to an ideal scientific method—a method which has as its example the natural sciences—the objection has been raised that historical knowledge, because of its specific nature, obviously has a narrative structure.[9]

This is the second strategy. Accordingly, historical knowledge must be explained in a specifically historical way—that is, as narrative explanation, as explanation through narration. This explanation follows its own logic, and it is to be distinguished from explanation which uses the help of knowledge acquired through laws.

The peculiarity and individuality of a historical way of thinking are thus expressed. In the attempt to prove explanations in historical studies with the help of a theoretical form of knowledge, characteristics like peculiarity and individuality are not discussed and are usually referred to only as negative deviations from the example of the other sciences, which explain phenomena strictly according to laws.

The narrative nature of historical knowledge is, however, regarded as an embarrassment to its scientific potential. It is argued that "narration" as the fundamental mode of historical knowledge is a poetical or rhetorical act of speech, which, ultimately, cannot be scientific. It places historiography within the field of the arts, moving it further away from becoming scientific.[10]

This is, however, not necessarily a result of historiography as narration. The scientific nature of historical studies becomes problematic only when one regards this model of explanation in a positivistic way in which the laws of the natural sciences play an essential role, as the only model which is scientific. It is quite impossible to identify such scientific laws by the narrative structure of historical knowledge and to predict the future, from a historical insight into the past, by means of these laws. When one uses more general and flexible criteria for science—principles of argumentation, of conceptual thinking, as well as of method—then one can establish how and whether argumentation within the narrative forms of historical knowledge can be scientifically proved and developed.

Of course, the status of historical study as a discipline does not only raise the above mentioned fundamental questions on a specifically historical type of rationality and the scientific and methodological nature of this rationality. It also raises the full range of questions specifically concerning the complex structure of historical study as a discipline. These specific questions can be thus systematized if historical studies can be structured into a disciplinary matrix, held together by the cognitive principles of historical thinking. Such principles, each singular principle as well as all principles as a whole, constitute history as a discipline.

These basic principles, the inner coherency of which constitutes historical study as a discipline and as an academic subject, can be listed as follows:[11]

1. Interests generating historical knowledge, based on people's needs to orientate themselves toward practical life—needs which are decisive for historical thinking.
2. Dominant perspectives on the human past, placing "history" in meaningful coherence with the present and the future.

3. Principles constituting historical method as a set of rules for empirical research.
4. Principles concerning the forms of historiography in which historical knowledge, which has been gained through research, is addressed to potential recipients.
5. Principles providing historiography with a function within the present culture (which is the raison d' être of historiography)—the function of orienting people in the course of time.

While reflecting the principles which constitute historical studies in the form of metahistory, it is now our task to describe, based on these factors and their inner systematic coherence, the central theme of history as an academic subject: at how the development of knowledge within this subject is possible and how this knowledge can be implemented practically into the present culture.

To summarize one can list the most important ways of questioning and arguing the disciplinary matrix and its individual functions.

1. The dominant theme in the discussion on *the type of knowledge which is of decisive interest to history as a science,* focuses the fact that this knowledge is dependent on the point of view from which historical thinking ensues.
2. The second part of this theme treats the perspectivity and relativity of historical knowledge which result from this dependency.
3. The third point of discussion is the claim for objectivity in historical thinking. How can objectivity be possible vis-à-vis the dependence of historical knowledge on viewpoint and perspectivity.[12] In this argument the ground for points of view are seen in norms reflecting standpoints in social life. These norms were discussed in respect to the question of whether they can be generalized, so that a critical comparison of different perspectives and a broadening of historical perspectives are possible.

The question is raised whether the dominant perspectives from which historical studies address the needs of people in the present, orientate them towards experiences of the human past.[13] This question is important for the status of historical studies as an academic subject. It concerns the form in which these perspectives, through which the events of the past are made a history for the present as well as its hope for the future, can and should be incorporated into the process of arriving at scientific knowledge. It is an undisputed fact that such perspectives exist. They indicate what in the human past is (as history) worth remembering in the present and within its hope for the future.

The human past is not automatically history. The present must give the latent historical character of the past the status of history. Such elevated status is structured by the historical perspectives already mentioned. It must be asked, however, in which form the perspectives can be conceived within history as an academic subject, and how they can be used validly in acquiring historical knowledge. Herein lies the problem of theorizing within historical studies.

The problem thus stated brings to the fore the question of whether historical thinking is scientific, especially whether it is possible to theorize on central historical perspectives on the human past. From a scientific point of view these perspectives can occur as theories only when the subject matter of historical studies is continually defined and structured as "history." When the perspectives cannot be theorized they may only serve as elements of a rhetorical and poetical presentation. The scientific status of historical studies may thus become an embarrassment.

It is still an open question, that is controversial and not often discussed, as to what form theorizing on these perspectives should take. Do these theories not have a completely different structure from other sciences which arrive at knowledge through laws and use these theories for explanation and prognosis? When historical thinking has a fundamentally narrative structure, it should be made clear that the theories on its dominant perspectives have a narrative form. Up till now this has not been fully realized.

The question of theory inevitably leads us to the third element of the disciplinary matrix—that is, to the rules of historical research. Traditionally, historicism has canonized three basic ways of doing systematic research, which constitute the multi-facetted unity of "the historical method." They are heuristics, source critique and interpretation, following one another in succession. The three operations activate the processes of historical research, thus enabling progress in the acquisition of knowledge. The above-mentioned problem of theorizing within historical studies should necessarily indicate how and what role theories play in correlating heuristics to criticism and interpretation—that is, historical interpretation.[14]

Since historical study has become the object of scientific research, the question of the rules of historical method also becomes the question of the forms of historiography. In relation to the basic question of theorizing and its ability to provide historical knowledge with criteria and perspectives, an important theoretical problem has been introduced into historical study, namely, the remarkable revaluation of the forms of historiography.[15]

The principles according to which historical knowledge is given form become relevant in giving meaning to history and in transforming the events of the past into histories for the present and its future.[16] The historiographical moulding is regarded as constituting and giving meaning to historical knowledge acquired through research. The writing of history is seen not only as a function of research, but as an independent act of the historian that is not derived from research alone.

The question of the cognitive structure of this operation is still open, as is especially the question of its relationship to explanatory theories on dominant perspectives and the methodological rules of empirical research.

By writing history the functional aspect becomes a theme in laying the foundations of metahistory. When science is understood solely as the technology of historical research, then questions on the practical function of historical knowledge are seen as problems outside the subject of history, although practical insight into the work of the historian is not to be disregarded. The functional aspect of historical knowledge becomes more and more important as the interest in historical knowledge and the audience to whom the historian addresses herself or himself become indispensable actors in structuring historiography, and are discussed on the metahistorical level.

The following question has become an important issue within another academic component, the *didactics* of history. The question is if and how history, as an academic subject, can manipulate knowledge that it has produced itself, intending to develop criteria by which the correct and incorrect usage of its knowledge can be judged? For a long time the didactics of history have simply been seen as a technique to be applied to the production of scientific knowledge; its usage was seen as lying definitely outside science.

Because of the process of reflection within historical studies, the didactics of history in the meantime has developed its own basic principles as a discipline.[17] At last, when historical knowledge has built up an identity of its own in the social context of historical studies, and when the process of building up its own identity is seen as a process of learning, then the functional aspect of historiography, as a reflection on the didactics of history, has become an integral component of metahistory.

Levels of theorizing

In the process of acquiring historical knowledge theorizing is done on more than one level. Simplifying the issue, one can distinguish three levels: level one, the level of broad basic principles; level two, the level of specific paradigms of historical interpretation; and level three, a mediating level of a general periodization.

Level One

On the deepest level categories of basic principles are developed. On this level a field of knowledge is opened up for concepts, a field popularly called "history." It is a field in which historians also treat the human experiences of the past as objects which must be researched and written about as meaningful history.

J.G. Droysen considers the following as the most important question regarding this most basic level of historical theorizing: "How is history construed from events?" With this question he correctly formulates the insight that temporal events in the human world do not acquire the specific quality of being historic simply because they are part of the past—past events do not automatically become the objects of historical studies. Rather, a set of qualifications typical of this past is needed before they can be described as history. They bring about a qualification which concerns their meaningful coherence to the present experience and future orientation of historians and their audience.

These qualifications can be divided into three perspectives—the contents, the forms, and the functions of historical knowledge.[18]

As far as the contents are concerned, categorization of an inner coherence between the past, the present, and the future is of primary concern. This coherence is used as a general criterion to give a historical qualification to the course of time and to give meaning to the experience of the past. Well-known examples of coherence are "progress," "development," "evolution," "process," and "according to laws." Such coherence of periods of time has been addressed in the discussion on historical theory within the category of "continuity."[19] When history is thus qualified in terms of content, a differentiation is made between specifically historical experiences and other experiences. The qualification also defines the area of historical knowledge, thereby formulating the way in which his area should be researched and studied. Thus different strategies of thinking can lead to a concept of "history" as a model for what can be historically known. The experiences of the temporal changes of people and their world in the past can thus be organized: the philosophy of history generally formulates the meaningful coherence of the temporal changes of people and their world (the most famous example is Hegel's philosophy of history); historical anthropology describes the characteristic elements of people's actions and sufferings and deduces from them general characteristics of historical time (well-known examples are Jacob Burckhardt's theory of the three potencies and their six relationships,[20] as well as the *Feuerbach* chapter in the *German Ideology* of Marx and Engels); historical materialism develops a system of the general laws of historical time, which intentionally encompasses the past, the present, and the future.

A different way of categorizing historical knowledge is needed for formal qualifications to define thinking and knowledge as specifically historical. "History" is not only the contents of the subject matter of historical statements, it is also a qualification of the forms of the statements. "Continuity," that is, coherence of experience, is the categorical qualification for historical contents; analogous to this type of "narration" is the categorical qualification of historical forms. In the most recent discussion, "narration" characterizes the form aimed at in thinking and knowledge which can be defined specifically as "historical." This categorical criterion for form indicates that thinking is historical when it constitutes a history which is based on narrative acts of speech.

This criterion is also very general and abstract, and can be developed in different ways into a theory of historical formation. Famous expressions of such theories are rhetorics for the prescientific phase of development in historical thinking, poetics of historiography; for example, as stressed by

Gervinus,[21] a typology of historiographical forms of presentation or possibilities of presenting historical interpretation (Droysen, Nietzsche,[22] White,[23] and Rüsen[24]). By means of conceptual argument, theories of this kind open up the space in which historical knowledge can be historiographically presented; they address themes such as how the historian's audience should be treated; they deal with quality as the art of writing, with the communicative structure of historical thinking, its character as a work of art, the richness of historiographical forms, their relationship to historically researched experience, as well as all the factors which have to do with the linguistic productivity of historians.

Finally, theorizing on historical knowledge includes categorizing its functions. The cultural function of historiography is indeed not only external, but so very much part of the historian's work (either as an unconscious presupposition based on the expectations of their audience, or as conscious, pedagogical or political intentions). Historical knowledge is (partly) constituted by the need to orientate toward the present. It determines the disciplinary discussion of historians in the form of interests in knowledge; the type of needs decide what will be regarded as meaningful history on the cultural level. Here the functional criterion, which is valid in acquiring historical knowledge, is derived from "historical identity:" from stories which present the experience of the past under categories acceptably coherent with the present and the future, people form conceptions of themselves regarding the status of their lives in the process of the temporal changes of their world and themselves. These conceptions of the diachronical extent of their subjectivity are components of their individual and societal identity. By means of these conceptions they come to an agreement with themselves about who the other people are with whom they have to live.

Theoretical explanations of this category of functions within historical thinking are especially given to create usable forms of self-understanding about the changes in generations. National identity as a dynamic, integrating, factor thus permanently becomes part of modern societies through historical education which is organized by the state—this identity is thus reflected both pedagogically and politically. In such cases points of view are stated and proved according to which historical consciousness is intentionally formed in the process of socializing and individualizing. Thus they secure, from within, the assurance that a society's cultural form of life will continue. The relevant theories come to the fore as concepts of historical education in different (political, aesthetic, didactic) forms of expression.

Level Two

Historical categories determine the spheres of the possible contents, forms and functions of historical thinking, and organize them conceptually. The mental procedures of historical consciousness are based on categories, but they follow, more or less their own theoretical guidelines. The guidelines do not develop and organize the overall field of possible history, but only single fields of real history. They distinguish these fields from others and characterize periods of time and their determinants which are decisive or "typical" to them. This concerns explicit frames of historical interpretation by which results obtained from the sources, the (so-called) facts of the past can be put together as meaningful stories. These frames have the character of conceptual construction by means of which the experience of the past can be made present as historical time. They are the real core of theorizing on historical knowledge; they determine whether and how the research findings from the sources can be developed in a concrete and specific way, by means of the knowledge of abstract and general coherence of times. (Therefore they are also the basis for further reflection.) They prove the intellectual power and austerity of historical categorizing; they translate the categorical possibilities of stories—stories which are true to experience, which are meaningful and which can be communicated—into intellectual forms, so that they correspond to the actual temporal processes. They extract concrete historical experiences from the sources, and they translate their facts into broader fields of temporal events which do not appear in the sources as such, but which give the sources their value, their historical quality, and their status by means of what specifically happened in history.

The character, status, and function of knowledge in general, which historians possess to develop the specifically historical contents of the sources, is a controversial matter in historical studies (as well as in philosophy). It is, however, undisputed that there are conceptual elements by means of which the informational or factual contents of the sources can be historically explained and interpreted. These elements are the decisive factor in evaluating and organizing source information into a specific historical timespan.

Level Three

On a third level ideas mediate between the fundamental level of theorizing and the level where frames for the historical interpretation of sources function. The broad lines of historical development which were drawn by these ideas no longer treat potential history or historical possibilities, but real history. They concern general periodization, which thus mediate between different time concepts—the time which has been theorized upon within frames of interpretation, and other times outside this frame, to indicate clearly the status of time which has been given prominence within general historical experience. These criteria for periodization categorize dominating present expectations and future expectations (the "not anymore" and the "not yet") into presentations of the courses of time ("continuity") and thereby acquire points of view to distinguish qualitatively between periods of time. The best known periodization is that of antiquity, middle ages, and modern times—a periodization questionable in respect to its empirical and theoretical evidence obtained through historical research.

Periodization plays an important role in the theoretical work of historical studies, where theoretical concepts of comprehensive temporal processes or broad historical developments are related to a strong present expectation that a qualitatively new future can be brought about through the experience of the past.

This is especially the case in Marxism and Leninism. Here, even the most highly differentiated periodizations have been, and still are, worked upon and discussed in the form of a general theory of historical development (with the claim to prognostic power). Five major epochs in the history of humanity are distinguished here: primitive society, slave-owning society, feudalism, capitalism, and socialism. Each epoch is characterized as the formation of a specific type of society. The individual epochs are then combined—under the category of predictable progress—into a collective presentation of historical time as an unambiguous future perspective for directing action.

The problem with such a periodization is that a specific time (e.g., within European history) is generalized into history itself, and that one interpretation of the present (e.g., a position in the present) and one future expectation have categorical (absolute) meaning. Other experiences, points of view, explanations, and expectations are thereby discriminated against and robbed of their potential to develop through experience and to direct people in time. On the other hand, the renunciation of periodization clearly leads to the horizons of historical experience becoming blurred and historical knowledge losing its power to orientate itself toward the actual practice of life.

The compulsion to theorize

The extent and nature of theorizing in historical studies are controversial. To what extent historical thinking is able to theorize, and to what extent historical research can be theoretical, are by no means simple issues within the work of historians, neither are they indisputably part of the self-understanding of people working in this field. Yet tendencies and thrusts toward theorizing have been established in the development of historical studies, by means of which the present situation may be explained and the most pressing problems may be more precisely stated.

Even before the scientification of historical thinking and historiography theorizing was done on the work of historians: rhetorics discussed the form of historiography under the dominant perspectives of their literary status and their function to orientate people toward practical life. The thrust to develop toward the scientification of historical thinking during the late eighteenth and early nineteenth centuries did not weaken this rhetorical theorizing, but brought about new categorical possibilities concerning the contents of historical thinking. Now "history" could be thought of as a complete whole and as a coherent object of historical knowledge. Before, there had been only a multiplicity of histories that depicted different periods of time. This multiplicity was embraced by a presentation of time meaningful only within religion, but which did not really treat or understand these histories as "the history."[25]

The categorical constitution of such an object of knowledge is accompanied by a qualitative change of criteria that are authoritative and meaningful for historical thinking. The interpretation of the experience of the past is no longer concerned with giving full historical examples of general rules for behaviour and with demonstrating the possibilities of how to apply them in practice. Giving meaning to temporal experience by means of examples was replaced by giving meaning to history from a genetic perspective: the experience of the past was treated and interpreted from the perspective of a general historical development of humanity; the past, the present, and the future were linked together as a dynamic development that can most effectively be described by the fundamental historical category of "progress."

This type of theorizing in which "history" became the object of a specific type of scientific knowledge, belongs to the presuppositions of historical studies and remains active only in the form of implicit hypotheses. Real work on theory was actually done in the initial phases of scientification within the discussion on the "plan" of historiography during the latter part of the Enlightenment (Gatterer),[26] when the possibility of moving deliberately beyond an "aggregate" of different histories toward a "system" of a comprehensive universal history (Schlözer) was considered.[27] However, these theoretical concepts were not really developed and used as research instruments; they were discussed only as forms of presentation, although with (still unconscious) consequences for the decision as to what could and should be considered as the contents of history.

As long as historians primarily directed their attention toward the course of human interaction, and in an one-sided perspective looked at time, namely that of action and how it was influenced by intentions of the actors, no explicit need was articulated for a theory on the analysis of sources, nor has it been until now. It was considered to be sufficient to understand and explain what happened in the past; this asked for no more than an everyday knowledge of the relationship between the intentions and the execution of actions.

Nevertheless, during the era of historicism there was implicit serious theorizing on the inner linking of temporal sequences of events in the past to a meaningful whole. Historicism presupposed that the course of human interaction was regulated by ideas, in which culture was formed through human actions. It was through this regulation that time acquired its specific historical character. Since the operation of these ideas constituted "history" as the contents of historical knowledge on the level of the intentional regulation of actions, it became necessary to explicate these historical presuppositions theoretically. Thus an appeal was made to understand actions and their course by means of the intentions which regulate action. Moreover, theorizing on historistic concepts of ideas became more difficult because historical studies were critical of an idealistic philosophy of history which regarded only the ideal substance of temporal development as history and which could not be reconciled with historical studies as a discipline. To guarantee source research historical–philosophical theorizing was dismissed as something opposed to empirical source analysis (although it presupposes source research).

Using theory implicitly in historical research became problematic when the presuppositions of historicism—presuppositions which as theories regulated historical studies—lost their force as leading criteria in historical interpretation. It became even more problematic when social sciences established themselves among historical studies, claiming theoretical status for the knowledge produced by them. The meaning of this knowledge for historical knowledge could not simply be dismissed.

As the disciplinary need for an explicit model for historical interpretation grew, the problem of theory in historical studies was again on the agenda. It was inevitable that it would emerge again as historical thinking had to cope with a profound change in the experience of time: temporal change was experienced as a change in life conditions which could no longer be adequately explained by means of the conscious intentions of individual actors. Anonymous motives beyond or below such intentions forced historical studies to take a look at itself; new concepts for the interpretation of historical studies became necessary.

The problem of theory which was thereby opened up presented itself from the perspective of form and contents. Formally, the aim was to develop theoretical frames of reference for historical interpretation as working concepts in empirical research. As far as contents are concerned, the aim was to make the factors of temporal change within humanity and its world understandable by means of such frames of reference in order to view these changes not only in the light of the intentions which accompanied actions. Since historical studies complied with both these requirements in the long term (although in different and, until today, in disputed ways), it transcends the borders set by historicism for the disciplinary use of theory.

Formally, different strategies were developed to introduce theoretical elements into researching historical interpretation. The two best known forms of the use of theory for interpreting sources are the process of generating and using ideal-types, as developed, methodologically reflected upon, and used practically by Max Weber, Otto Hinze and others; and second, historical materialism, which developed a theory about the working of history according to laws, which placed a Marxist-Leninist orientation at the disposal of historical studies as an instrument of research.

As far as contents are concerned, the compulsion to theorize—which led historical studies away from historicism's concept of science—guides the historical perspective toward a deep structure of temporal processes in which structural conditions for action prescribe temporal changes in people and their world. The economic and social factors of human life, which within an idealistic concept of history were treated as peripheral historical events or even as natural factors, were now viewed as essential areas of historical knowledge. Historical change was no longer seen as short-term events and their sudden changes, but as long term processes of structural change.

This development led to the features of historical studies which are typical of the twentieth century and are the starting point of historical thinking today.

Notes

This chapter was first published as "Theorie der Geschichte," in Richard van Dülmen, ed., *Fischer Lexikon Geschichte*, vol. 2, Frankfurt am Main, 1994, 32–52.

1. Lunyu 1.2, cited in Heiner Roetz, *Konfuzius,* Munich, 1995, 22 (German quotation translated into English).
2. Aristotle, *Poetics*, 9, 1451 b.
3. In German the term *Historik* has become common for this type of theory, whereas in English the established term is "metahistory." Cf. Frank R. Ankersmit, *Denken over Geschiedenis. Een Overzicht van Moderne Geschiedfilosofische Opvattingen,* 2nd edn., Groningen, 1986; Chris Lorenz, *De Constructie van het Verleden. Ee Inleiding in de Theorie van de Geschiedenis*, Amsterdam, 1987; Chris Lorenz, *Konstruktion der Vergangenheit. Eine Einführung in die Geschichtstheorie,* Beiträge zur Geschichtskultur, vol. 13, Köln, 1997; Josef Meran, *Theorien in der Geschichtswissenschaft. Die Diskussion über die Wissenschaftlichkeit der Geschichte*, Göttingen, 1985. Bibliographical information can be found in special issues of the journal *History and Theory*; Helmut Berding, *Bibliographie zur Geschichtstheorie*, Göttingen, 1977.
4. See Jörn Rüsen and Hans Süssmuth, eds., *Theorien in der Geschichtswissenschaft,* Düsseldorf, 1980; Jürgen Kocka, "Theorien in der Sozial- und Gesellschaftsgeschichte. Vorschläge zur historischen Schichtungsanalyse," *Geschichte und Gesellschaft* 1 (1975), 9–42; idem, "Theorieorientierung und Theorieskepsis in der Geschichtswissenschaft," *Historical Social Research* 23 (1982), 4–19.
5. See Rüsen, *Historische Vernunft*; Rüsen, *Rekonstruktion der Vergangenheit*; Rüsen, *Lebendige Geschichte.*
6. Droysen, *Historik*; this contains lectures, posthumously published, which Droysen wrote from 1857. The "outline" of these lectures, which were given by Droysen to his students, was also translated into English: Johann Gustav Droysen, *Outline of the Principles of History,* Boston, 1893, reprinted New York, 1967.
7. William H. Dray, ed., *Philosophical Analysis and History*, New York, 1966; Frank Ankersmit and Hans Kellner, eds., *A New Philosophy of History,* Chicago, 1995.
8. Carl G. Hempel, "The Function of General laws in History," *The Journal of Philosophy* 39 (1942), 35–48.
9. Arthur C. Danto, *Analytical Philosophy of History*, Cambridge, 1968; Paul Ricoeur, *Time and Narrative,* 3 vols., Chicago, 1984–1988; White, *Content of the Form*; Henry S. Hughes, *History as Art and as Science. Twin Vistas on the Past*, New York, 1965.
10. The most important book in this respect is White, *Metahistory.*

11. This matrix is explained further in chap. 18.
12. See also Reinhart Koselleck, Wolfgang Mommsen, Jörn Rüsen, eds., *Objektivität und Parteilichkeit,* Beiträge zur Historik. vol. 1, Munich, 1977.
13. Cf. Jürgen Kocka and Thomas Nipperdey, eds., *Theorie und Erzählung in der Geschichte,* Beiträge zur Historik, vol. 3, Munich, 1979.
14. Cf. Christian Meier and Jörn Rüsen, eds., *Historische Methode,* Beiträge zur Historik, vol. 5, Munich, 1988.
15. An overview is given by Pietro Rossi, ed., *Theorie der modernen Geschichtsschreibung,* Frankfurt am Main, 1987. Cf. also, Stephen Bann, "Analysing the Discourse of History," in idem, *The Inventions of History. Essays on the Representation of the Past,* Manchester, 1990, 33–63; Peter Burke, ed., *New perspectives on historical writing,* Cambridge, 1989. A contribution to the theory of historiography which has been widely discussed is Lawrence Stone, "The Revival of Narrative: Reflections on a new old History," *Past and Present* 85 (1979), 3–24.
16. Cf. White, *Metahistory*; idem *Tropics of Discourse: Essays in Cultural Criticism,* Baltimore, 1978; idem *Content of the Form.*
17. Cf. Jörn Rüsen, "The Didactics of History in West Germany: Towards a New Self-Awareness of Historical Studies," *History and Theory* 26 (1987), 275–86.
18. See Jörn Rüsen, "Der Teil des Ganzen. Über historische Kategorien," in Rüsen, *Historische Orientierung,* 150–67.
19. Hans Michael Baumgartner, *Kontinuität und Geschichte. Zur Kritik und Metakritik der historischen Vernunft,* Frankfurt am Main, 1972.
20. Burckhardt, *Force and Freedom,* ("The Three Powers," and "The Reciprocal Action of the three Powers").
21. Georg Gottfried Gervinus, "Grundzüge der Historik (1837)," in idem, *Schriften zur Literatur,* ed. G. Erler, Berlin, 1962, 48–103.
22. Friedrich Nietzsche, "Vom Nutzen und Nachteil der Historie für das Leben (Unzeitgemäße Betrachtungen, zweites Stück)," in idem, *Sämtliche Werke,* Kritische Studienausgabe in 15 Einzelbänden, vol. 1, Munich, 1988, 243–334. (Friedrich Nietzsche, *On the Advantage and Disadvantage of History for Life,* trans. Peter Preuss, Indianapolis, 1980.)
23. White, *Metahistory.*
24. Ibid., chapters 1 and 2; Rüsen, "Die vier Typen des historischen Erzählens," 153–230.
25. See Koselleck, "Historia magistra vitae," 38–66 (as to the term "the history" cf. notes 8 and 9 in chap. 4).
26. Johann Christoph Gatterer, "Vom historischen Plan und der darauf sich gründenden Zusammenfügung der Erzählung," in *Allgemeine historische Bibliothek,* 1 (1767), 15–89, Reprinted in Horst Walter Blanke and Dirk Fleischer, eds., *Theoretiker der deutschen Aufklärungshistorie,* 2 vols, Stuttgart and Bad Cannstatt, 1990, vol. 2, 621–62. On Gatterer, see Peter H. Reill, "History and Hermeneutics in the Aufklärung: The Thought of Johann Christoph Gatterer," *Journal of Modern History* 45 (1973), 24–51.
27. August Ludwig Schlözer, *Vorstellung einer Universalhistorie,* Göttingen, 1772, reprinted, ed., Horst Walter Blanke, Hagen, 1990. For theorizing on the basic principles of historical studies in the later part of the German Enlightenment see Blanke and Fleischer, eds., *Theoretiker der deutschen Aufklärungshistorie;* Peter H Reill, "Science and the Science of History in the Spätaufklärung," in Hans Erich Bödeker, ed., *Aufklärung und Geschichte. Studien zur deutschen Geschichtswissenschaft im 18. Jahrhundert,* Göttingen, 1986, 430–51.

Chapter 6

New History: Paradigms of Interpretation

> Es existiert kein menschliches Verhältnis zur
> Geschichte, wenn daran nicht gearbeitet wird;
> ein sachliches Verhältnis ist aber überhaupt keines.
> Das Problem liegt daran, daß nicht einmal die
> Sensibilität unterstellt werden kann, daß dies als
> ein Problem empfunden wird.
>
> Oskar Negt, Alexander Kluge[1]

We cannot say that the development of historical studies in the twentieth century has provided a canonically established use of theory in dealing with sources. There have been different procedures in the developing and use of theory in the methodical procedure of interpretation for historical research. "If" and "how" and "what type" of theories should be developed and used were open questions. Different paradigms for historical interpretation were developed according to different concepts of historical studies. In the following pages I want to characterize some of the more important of these disciplinary structures within historical studies of the twentieth century[2], on the grounds of the procedures used when applying theory to interpretation. They developed their specific feature of "new" history[3] by their attempt to overcome the hitherto developed disciplinary structure of historical studies in the nineteenth century, which can be called "traditional" or "historicist."

My method of characterizing some of the paradigmatic structures of the "new," (i.e., post-historistic historical thinking) is an idealtypological one. Marxism, Annales School, and societal history are realized in a broad variety of different manifestations and developments, due to different political circumstances and scholarly traditions. It is not my intention to present this variety but rather to characterize a mode of historical thought, its basic assumptions, concepts, and approaches. I inquire, so to speak, more into its logic than into its history. Neither can be divided, but one can be emphasize at

---

Notes for this section begin on page 106.

the cost of the other. Concentrating on basic and constitutive patterns of historical interpretation, I prefer abstract features to concrete examples. This way of presenting "logics" of history is somewhat arbitrary yet acceptable as long as the features are used as conceptual means to understand what shapes the work of the historians in the core of cognitive practice; they can even disclose the scope of flexibility and change—within a clear limit set by fundamental assumptions on the nature of history, and the way of gaining meaning out of the experience of the past.

Marxism

Marxism has taken hold of modern presentations of the dynamics of historical change, in which the future overbids the past. It conceptualizes these dynamics in a comprehensive theory of progress. It places this progress into the field of material life relationships. In this concept the specifically historical character of the temporal changes in people and their world are constituted. Marxism takes a definite ideological-critical stance against the hermeneutic tradition of historicism: the powers working within history cannot be seen as ideas regulating human actions. On the contrary, they themselves are regulated by the external factors of material needs. Marxism, therefore, has developed a theory of history in the form of a historical materialism, according to which the real historical dimension of practical human life is constituted by production relationships, the social forms and technical means by which nature makes physical life possible.

Historical materialism offers historical studies the possibility of doing research based on the internal laws of this historical life, which have been constituted materialistically. These historical laws are related to the synchronic and diachronic dimensions of historical experience. From a synchronic perspective the "basis superstructure-statement" formulates a criterion according to which the different factors of practical human life (scientific, social, political, legal, cultural, etc.) can be evaluated and brought into relationship with one another. It gives priority to social economic factors and uses them to explain phenomena and development in other fields of human advancement. From a diachronic perspective, historical experience is reconstructed and arranged by means of a theory which regards the progressive development of productive forces and their contrasting relationship to the whole system of production as the decisive grounds for changes in human life relationships.

Historical materialism explains the factors of human life that decisively shape its particular temporal form, as the basic structure of an epoch (that is, the formation of a society). Likewise, it points at the contradictions in this basic structure, which are essential for the structure of changing from one epoch to another. Together, both these aspects are defined by a complex system of laws in the construction and changing of forms of human life; time and again these laws theoretically explain the distinguishing characteristics of a specific time found in the sources.

Today this claim for laws in historical studies is controversial, if not generally negated. What a historical law really is and how it can be distinguished from the laws of other sciences (especially natural sciences), and whether historical studies are really capable of making forecasts in order to produce technically useful knowledge, are questions that have not been answered by historical materialism. Historical materialism cannot prove that its claim to provide a theoretical basis for scientific historical knowledge can be regarded as a sure ingredient of the selfunderstanding of historical studies.

The Annales School

The historians, who have grouped around the journal *Annales* (since 1929),[4] offer a concept of science for historical studies that is characterized by means of a new method of analyzing the deep structures of historical experience. These historians also advocate the integration of historical studies into other human and social sciences.

History is disclosed as a discipline dependent on other disciplines for gaining and developing knowledge: that is, disciplines that are concerned with man and his world. These disciplines become especially important when they do not primarily focus on historical developments but on the systematic coherence between human life relations. They include linguistics (in its systematic-synchronistic form), anthropology, ethnography, geography, and, of course, economics, with their mathematical approach to laws and regularities. With the help of the existing knowledge of these disciplines, historical studies are able to enlarge the horizon of historical thinking considerably. In the form of an integrating *histoire totale,* historical studies represents the unity of human nature within the wide space of historical experience. It no longer fills this space with the knowledge of occurrences which change with time, since in them it sees only the surface of a much more important dimension of experiencing the powers which regulate human life. Events and occurrences are replaced by structure, as Fernand Braudel put it, they are a game played together, a texture, actually a reality, which is not dependent on time and which can move forward for a long time.

The historical perspective is fixed on the regular, on what repeats itself in time, on frames within human life which last for longer periods and which—in relation to the processes of change within modern societies—have a low capacity for change. These are seen as a solid basis, a comprehensive determinant for significant changes in the past. As far as their contents are concerned these structures are characterized as the social climate, as the comprehensive form of society, as the profound mentality, as economic laws of change of direction, as frames for the inclinations of human nature, as trends of population development, as attempts towards alphabetization, as cycles of agricultural production, as long term changes in complex ownership relations, as attitudes towards sexuality and death, as life forms of childhood, etc. Historical time has got a new quality: it is "no longer the periodical and mysterious compulsion which makes things happen; it should rather be compared with the rhythm of a revolution, which is now measurable."[5] With the corresponding methods of comparative research, of quantification and the in-depth hermeneutical reconstruction of mental life forms historical research obtained a new standard of methodical rationality and interdisciplinary activity.

Along with Marxism, the Annales School shares a thorough-going insight into structural conditions of human life, which lie below of level of intentionally guided activity. It differs fundamentally differs from Marxism's theory of development according to laws, in that it turns away from the present dynamics of modernizing processes. It uses historical experience as an alternative to modern society: that is, the alternative experience of the deep structures of premodern societies. The question of historical processes that developed into present life relationships is ignored.

There is another essential difference between the Annales School and Marxism. The Annales School does not support their new methods of interpreting historical experience by explicitly theoretical presuppositions of the new deep structure of historical experience. Its scholars do not offer any proof for their work by means of explicit theorizing or the explicit use of theory in the construction and interpretation of information about historical structures, obtained from the sources. Their insight into the interpretation of historical structures in the human past remains implicit. They have, so to speak, disappeared in reconstructed and interpreted material: that is, in the historical description of life relationships.

Societal history, historical social science

In the late 1960s and early 1970s historical studies in West Germany developed a crisis as far as its basic principles were concerned.[6] The boundaries of the traditional concept of historical studies were critically rejected by young historians who wished to constitute historical studies not in line with, or even in opposition to, historicism.[7] Instead they preferred working with theoretical elements of knowledge as instruments of research, thereby opening up a new potential for gaining knowledge within historical studies. Max Weber's idea of constructing and using ideal types was thus pragmatically tested.[8] The names of Societal History (*Gesellschaftsgeschichte*) and Historical Social Science (*Historische Sozialwissenschaft*)[9] indicate how the insights, as they are formulated by these concepts, are directed toward the field of historical experience. History, as found in the Annales School and in Marxism, is no longer primarily established on the level of intentional interaction, but on the deeper level of structural conditions and circumstances for action. Actions and actors are analyzed against the background of systemic life circumstances which determine their actions: that is, their determination goes essentially beyond the intentions and self-understanding of the actors. Society is seen as the entirety of all things according to which history can be sought after theoretically and empirically.

This concept of history also brings historical studies into the realm of the social sciences; indeed, it can be understood as a social science itself, with a specific perspective on the historical dimension of human social life. This concept of history was developed theoretically and established in opposition to the tradition of historicism and the practice of the Annales School, but in formal accordance to Marxism. In the form of a bundle of theories it was used as an instrument in empirical historical research. Societal history works with explicit theoretical frames for doing historical research: that is, with "explicit and consistent systems of concepts and categories which serve to explain specific historical phenomena, but which cannot be adequately deduced from the sources" (Kocka).[10] As to their contents, these theoretical concepts tend to move within the sphere of a general modernizing theory. Consequently, societal history refers to historical subdisciplines, which have the same theoretical approach in research, such as historical demography or economic history. The same is true for overlapping fields of historical research for instance sociological research on the family and social stratification. The work usually done there is picked up for the acquisition of historical knowledge; by doing so sociological theory can be criticized according its a-historical character and be transformed into a historical shape. But in general the practical use of theories to disclose and interpret empirical findings, as in the social sciences, has become a paradigm for historical studies.

The extent to which this working with conceptual constructions determines the work of historians can be observed as a high level of argument in historiography to which societal history is committed. This type of historiography explicitly presents its perspectives not in the form of interpreted facts, but for itself as a framework of historical interpretation. Thus the interpreting perspectives themselves become a matter for argument, and the process of obtaining knowledge for historical presentation becomes transparent.

Criticism of theory and new approaches

The concept of doing history by the means of theory has been urgently challenged by concepts of historical studies. Everyday history, historical anthropology, and some directions in women's history have tested new approaches to historical experience.[11] They start from a new experience of the present which provokes a radical criticism of modernity, and also looks very critically at the future of modernization. A new, consistent, and homogeneous scientific paradigm has not yet crystallized from all of this; yet some tendencies within the new developments in historical studies can, however, be summarized and described as new approaches to the experience of history.

These new approaches criticize all those theoretical frameworks of historical interpretation, which I have described above: here the real people of the past, their actions and sufferings have no audible voice. Theories are "cold," they don't pay sufficient attention to the subjectivity of the people involved: by this theoretical grip on historical experience the authoritarian attitude of modern rationality has been extended to historical work. And since the problems caused by this rationality in relation to nature, and in political power structures, have been exposed the theoretical approach, it cannot be left uncriticized in historical thinking—and it must be replaced by other forms of thinking.

As an alternative to the concept of historical studies which are dominated by modernity and its idea of progress, a new concept of history is now proposed, that is not concerned with the comprising process of development from the present to the future; objective thinking on the manifold and varied changes in the past is no longer dominant. Instead, particular occurrences, events, and individual developments are studied. Their historical meaning is no longer brought about by placing them in a macro historical development, but by understanding them as representations of options of human self-manifestation and the dangers of human self-neglect. Development as transformation in time, which is directed toward future human activities, is no longer of primary importance. Now it is important to relativize the idea of historical development along the line of one comprehensive development in favor of different possibilities of human life in different times.

Macro history, which has dealt with a comprehensive history up to modern times, is now being replaced by numerous micro histories, each of which is meaningful in its own right. Historical experience is no longer considered as the potential for a process of rationalizing human life pointing into the future; instead, there prevails a deep distrust of the idea that human life can be mastered by means of rationality. The historical perspective is not primarily directed toward the history of comprehensive systems like the economy, society, and politics, but toward concrete people and social life relationships in the light of their subjective experience and interpretation. "Everyday life" is the common characteristic of this historical insight, which until now has not been adequately developed as a coherent concept. While societal history addresses the interactions and relations among people in the past with sociological terms such as "classes" or "strata," the concept of "the people" is again used critically to indicate the subjective inner dimension of a comprehensive social whole.

It is no accident that these new insights into historical experience have not been developed in the form of theoretical constructs. This is so because theoretical constructs are replaced by "thick description" is—to quote a term formulated by cultural anthropology.[12] The use of analytical concepts is substituted by participatory observation. With this research strategy historical studies enter the field of ethnology and cultural anthropology and go back to hermeneutical models to reconstruct the human past.[13]

Women's and gender history is carried out across this alternative between the constructive or descriptive character of historical knowledge. On the one hand, it uses the common instruments of modern historical research to give profile to the female as subject matter of history. With its new approach, theoretical constructs, which take a narrow and closed view towards this "object," are criticized. New insights into historical experience are thereby presented to make "the other half of humanity" visible. On the other hand, radical feminist criticism is launched against a scientific and methodical rationality, which is seen as an effective cultural means of male domination. Only in new discourses, which follow a logic different from these rational and theoretical constructs, can the cognitive power of female self-experience be developed and historically described.[14]

This strong criticism against theoretical and methodical rationality in historical studies converges with the intellectual trend of postmodernism. Postmodernism critically questions the presuppositions of historical studies as an academic ("scientific" in a broader sense of the word) discipline, namely the idea that history is a definable, pregiven ("objective") field of experience with its own concept of time and a corresponding scientific nature of historical thinking. In a postmodern understanding "history" is only a product of the narrative representation of the experience of time, characterized by a poetic or rhetorical nature that is not in need of methodical rationality. The theoretical efforts—which have been undertaken since the end of the eighteenth century to open up historical thinking for science and to establish historical studies as an academic discipline in order to rationalize work of the historical memory—are now exposed as falsely pretending to be scientific, and are therefore rejected in favor of the historian's poetic act of writing.

Historical studies can meet this challenge only by the continuing reflection of the (meta-)theoretical foundation of its own principles, as it has done when developing into modern historical studies. Despite the objections against the development and use of theories, the work done on the standard of the construction of theories is not simply discarded; but its application is investigated as to whether this work can be applied to the new tendencies of opening up new fields of experience for historical knowledge. This is possible when the concept of societal history, or historical social science does not exclude the alternatives which were developed against it, but incorporates them as complementary, looking at them critically from a meta-theoretical point of view. So, it is possible to bring these perspectives into balance with one another.

A "thick description" without theory is a concept of doing history with a limited potential of insights, since there are theories related to horizons of subjective understandings and sense generation of the people in every day life (like the sociology of the human life world).[15] Even his adversaries should give credit to Max Weber who, in his sociology of religion, paradigmatically stands for theorizing the humanities (at least in the eyes of historical social science), for emphasizing the fundamental importance of "culture" as a subjective factor in the interpretation of human structures.[16]

"Experience" and "meaning" or "sense" as principles opposing the construction and use of theories, can be theoretically conceptualized. In this form they can be used as theoretical means for historical interpretation. In a theorized form these principles provide an opportunity for giving profile to the subjectivity of the people in the past, in an argumentative and not an emotional way.

An outright negation of a comprehensive, macro-historical presentation of the past is not a convincing research strategy at all. It may succeed in pointing out the limitations of perspectives which were provided by formulating theories. It does not, however, present any way in which the course of time can be given historical meaning, and the coherence of temporal change can be addressed. Historical phenomena which have been identified micro-historically still have to be interpreted with concepts which put them into a perspective of temporal change and development.

The feminist critique of a dominating male perspective on historical experience should not be too eager to eliminate the formulation of theories within historical interpretation. If the plea for a new direction in historical studies is not to end in a fatal confirmation of the stereotype of feminine irrationality, then new categories of historical experience should be developed, in accordance with radical feminist criticism, and be used as an outline for new ways of doing historical research. The criticism that theories of historical studies are predominantly formulated from a male perspective should not lead to the female perspective being presented simply, without theory. On the contrary, to the extent to which theories are criticized by a theoretical argument, and to which theories with a broader perspective are developed and used in empirical research, feminist partiality can be made plausible. It can raise the potential for argument within historical studies in general and lead to a generally accepted new historical orientation toward gender. Similar work on explaining gender as a historical category, and a similar restructuring of the empirical perspective, have already been successfully.[17]

The challenges for historical thinking by postmodernism and its radical criticism of rationality and science, can be adequately met by historical thinking only through further fundamental reflection on basic criteria and agendas for making sense of history and representing it. The claim of historical studies to be scientific (in the broader sense of the word) depends on the proof that criteria for historical meaning can be theoretical and that the historical discourse can be methodical. When historical studies asks for its status, it deliberately enters the tradition of historicism, which at the emergence of history as an academic discipline reflected upon its claim to be scientific and justified it. Postmodern critique of historical studies understanding its own scientific nature, indicates that important deficiencies exist in the traditional self-understanding of historical studies. These deficiencies in self awareness are based on tendencies in the development of science, which can be described as the process of turning research into technology, of taking didactics out of historiography, and of making historical-sense criteria irrational.

In summary, a narrowing of the professional perspective on the basic principles of historical studies has been effective. The potential of theories in research, the role of the addressees in historiography and the possibility of describing historical knowledge's fundamental criteria of sense and meaning by reflecting on the basic principles of historical studies, should be recovered.

The practice and methodology of theoretical work

How should the procedures, the tasks, and the functions of the research work done with theory be described? One has to look at the conceptual means of research and take into account the discussion about the use and disadvantage of historical theories. Doing so, one can distinguish three types of problems: the relationship of historical studies to the theoretical knowledge of other sciences; the categorical criteria of the sense and meaning of historical cognition; and the practical work with theoretical frameworks of historical interpretation.

The theoretical knowledge of other sciences plays an important role in historical studies at all levels of research. It is applied without problems when the facts of the past are established by means of source criticism. To create information from sources historical studies use a multitude of methods of the auxiliaries, in which the theoretical knowledge of other sciences has been incorporated. Early history, for instance, uses physics (a highly theoretical science) as an auxiliary in order to date archaeological findings by means of the C-14 method. Problems of formulating specific historical theories only appear when theoretical knowledge of nonhistorical sciences are used for a specific historical interpretation of the information gained from the source material. If historical studies are not to be reduced to a production of facts to be interpreted with the methods of other disciplines, it must develop specific methods of interpretation on its own. Historical studies must develop its own concept of temporal change in the human world. Doing so it can use the theoretical knowledge of other sciences but must give it a specifically historical shape and logic. It is, however, historical studies which decide what knowledge is to be used for which historical goal and in what form it should be used.

It cannot be denied that there is a practical use of theoretical knowledge of other academic disciplines in historical research. Decisive for this use is its transformation in a historical perspective of the human world. This is decided by the historical categories which, admittedly, are not always reflected and explicated in the usage of theoretical knowledge in research and are not formulated as criteria for converting this knowledge into the parameters of historical studies. When the relation of historical studies to other disciplines is being questioned, normally no explicit formulation of categories of criteria is presented. But an eclecticism in the practical use of the theoretical knowledge of other disciplines by historical studies cannot replace an explanation and foundation of authoritative points of view.

How can historical categories be explicated? A common way of doing this in historical studies is historical semantics, or the history of basic concepts (*Begriffsgeschichte*).[18] It is obvious to state that basic historical terms have their own historical dimension, an internal temporal dynamic. Historical studies confirms this internal historicity against forms of knowledge which claim for a general validity, based on an unhistorical fixation of elements and factors of the human world. But historical semantics itself presupposes basic categories of historicity, that make clear what is specifically historical in the human world, that is, what characterizes the internal temporal dynamics of the basic concepts which express human life relationships and their temporal change in language. A systematic reflection on this presupposition does not belong to the daily task of the professional historian's understanding of his or her discipline. Only in Marxism and Leninism are these presuppositions systematically explained. The nature of this explanation, however, and the related problems of dogmatization, of narrowing the historical perspective through political conditions, and the instrumentalization of historical knowledge have not been effective in encouraging non-Marxists to systematically reflect categories or basic principles.

Finally, such a reflection is only possible at the intersection of philosophy and historical studies. Recently, the narrative structure of historical knowledge and the narrative linguistic procedures of historical consciousness have been analyzed in this area. By doing so some essential points of view have been explicated which illuminate what is specifically historical in dealing with people and their world; this is of higher plausibility than the traditional distinction between explanation and understanding, and between generalization and individualization. It may be a promising possibility to reformulate and give new attention to the old theme of the "sense of history" in analyzing the narrative coherence of historical knowledge.

The narrative coherence of historical knowledge depends upon the degree of plausibility with which stories about the meaningful changes of people's life world are told. As an academic discipline, historical studies is committed to certain standards of plausibility by doing research. Research is a very important way in which the claim for validity in historical thinking is substantiated. This claim is related not only to statements about the past, but on its meaningful relationship to presence and future as well, as history is not simply the past, but its meaningful and sense-bearing relationship to the present and its future perspective. Now historical theories stand for nothing more than conceptual constructions, that serve the purpose of making plausible the claimed coherence of past facts and their meaningful relationship to present and future.

Seen only from the perspective of logic, patterns of historical significance are at stake when the facts established by source criticism are placed in a coherent and meaningful relationship. Historical theories provide general features of narratives. They shape narratives in a way that they may provide the facts of the past, brought about by source critique, a temporal connexion. This furnishes them with meaning and significance for the presence and its future perspective. Max Weber described ideal types as conceptual elements of such narrative constructs. (He, however, used a neo-Kantian terminology and strategy of argument, that left undefined the specifically historical character of the ideal types, by which they are distinguished from the concepts common to other sciences.)

The same is true of the Marxist presentation of historical laws. The specifically historical character by which such laws are distinguished from those of other sciences (especially those of the natural sciences) untill now has not been adequately taken into account by Marxist historical theory. Consequently, the misconceptions about how historical knowledge can make predictions and be used politically as a technical tool of shaping the human world have not been resolved.

A series of criteria can be constructed for the development and use of historical theories in practical research. They bring the highly abstract view closer to the work of the historians so that the plausibility of stories is increased by the theoretical explanation of constitutive narrative constructs.

1. In the research process points of view and perspectives serve to distinguish between important and unimportant source findings. In relation to these findings they have a theoretical character. They are grounded upon categorical principles which determine what, in the course of time, should be considered historical and should be researched.
2. Historical research starts by asking questions. Questions are more fruitful when they are put to the sources in the form of explicit hypotheses. Indeed, the more constructively they are formulated, the more fruitful these questions are. In this respect constructive elements become elements of practical research. They serve the aim of extracting facts from sources to a much higher degree of analytical differentiation than was possible "from the sources alone." This applies, of course, especially to the extraction of facts which do not appear in the sources at all, but must be deduced from different source information by means of complicated processes of aggregation. Such facts are theory-laden and do, indeed, only come into being through the application of theoretical constructs at source information.
3 With the help of theoretical constructs concrete historical phenomena can be more precisely described than the references in common sense language

or the language of the sources only are. For instance, concrete manifestations of political domination can be made more understandable with the help of a typology of legitimation, the systematic coherence of legitimating principles.[19] A historiographical text can be interpreted with the help of a typology of historical sense criteria, so its constitutive pattern of significance becomes visible.

4. Periodization is not possible without a general and explicit (theoretical) characterization of periods of time, their differences and similarities. As indicated above, the constitutive criteria for periodization mediate between the level of fundamental historical categories and the level of frames of historical interpretation, which are determined by practical research.

5. In all historical explanations theoretical moments occur. The clearer the explanatory theories are the more understandable and fruitful the explanation. Yet, not every explanatory answer is necessarily specifically historical, although it may be the answer to a question with a historical reference, since ways of explanation (including theoretical knowledge which is used specifically for explanation) which are of divergent natures exist within historical studies. An explanation is specifically historical when a why-question can be answered by narrative statements in the form of a story. The explanatory theoretical form is a narrative construct. It explicates the generality of a temporal course and it historically explains an event by putting it into the concept of this course. Such concepts are constructed by historians as "tendencies," as "the processes of development," or whatever the usual terms for them (including historical laws) are. The reason for explanatory laws can be misunderstood when the fundamental difference between a historical and a nomological explanation becomes blurred. Historical studies differ from the nomological sciences in that they do not deduce the result of a historical development from its starting point in connexion with a general law of development. Historical theories explain changes by indicating that they contain the essential elements and events of their course. Historical theories do not deduce changes (something that is different at a later point in time than at an earlier point in time) and also not their course (something which has happened or which has ended) from comprehensive (covering) laws. Historical theories also do not present historical predictions along these lines, not because of the complexity of the relation between historical facts, but because of the (narrative) logic of historical explanation.

6. Every historical comparison needs a paradigm according to which things can be compared: for instance, a criterion which would establish what is common and what is specific. Such a criterion has theoretical status over and against the facts. Every historical typology presents such a theoretical basis for historical comparison. Such comparisons are specifically historical insofar as they are not exclusively concerned with establishing generalities. Historical comparison does not intent to establish generalizations as

an aim in itself, so that the value of knowledge depends upon its generality and abstractness (as the nomological sciences do which consider theoretical knowledge the more valuable the more general it is). Historical comparison is as much concerned with the establishment of generality as with the precise extent of differentiation (which is known in the historical tradition as "individuality"). In historical comparison, generalizing and individualizing are two sides of the same cognitive operation. For example, if we want to formulate a theory about nationalism for the specific aim of doing historical research, we have to typologically establish every nationality's identity in according to its differences in region and time. A theory about nationalism which deals only with generalities is of little use for practical research in historical studies because of its abstract generalization. A theory, however, which clearly formulates the synchronic and diachronic typological differences between national identities and correlates them with the social and political factors of historical developments in the relevant period, is of high heuristic and explanatory value.
7. Even the opposite of a comparison—that is, an internal differentiation of historical phenomena in synchronic and diachronic components—can be constructively executed by means of theoretical knowledge. Individual components of interrelating historical facts are analyzed, whereby the complexity of their interrelations become evident.
8. By means of theoretical knowledge, which covers the whole field of empirical findings because of its relative generality, missing segments of empirical knowledge can be established. It is by means of an overview that lacunae in knowledge become evident. It is a theoretical presentation of the relevant historical interrelations which reveals the size of empirical confirmations and the corresponding lacunae in knowledge.
9. Finally, without theoretical generalizations and summaries of historical knowledge it would be impossible for historians to establish what should in practice be directed toward building a historical identity. If the unavoidable question about the relevance of historical knowledge is to be taken seriously, such knowledge should provide answers to this question within its own theoretical structure.

Prospect

Historical theories are not per se an aim of research; they do not stand for themselves simply by being constructed and by being proved empirically. Their task is to obtain historical knowledge of which they themselves become structuring elements. However, this knowledge is more than and different from a theoretical construct—since a story is something different from the constructive ideas it follows.

Whether and to what extent the theorization of historical knowledge—besides encouraging research—can lead to the increase of the narrative coherence of historical knowledge gained through research, ultimately depends on the manner in which such knowledge is presented historiographically. Theory can contribute a mode of argument to historiographical presentation so that the story which is told can be understood and accepted only if the addressees mobilize their own ability in discursive argument. In this case the writing of this history may augment the competence of its addressees of making sense of the past through an increase in historical experience, as well as in the possibilities of its interpretation. In all these cases theorization in historical studies may become an essential element in giving meaning to history.

For history as an academic discipline the question of central importance is whether and to what extent its methodical rationality reaches into the core of the sense-generating mental processes of historical consciousness. For historical studies theorizing is not a cognitive operation that may be carried out or ignored. If theorizing does not work toward historical knowledge as a factor of narrative coherence, it would separate the historical consciousness that gives meaning to history from the methodical rationality of historical research. Then it would become merely the poetics of presenting time; research only brings about facts without making clear what the specifically historical character of facts is. In such circumstances theory will become the whore of the intellect which serves the beauty of mystical sense generation. The discipline of methodical rationality would change into a strategic means of rhetoric. The truth of knowledge would disappear in the beauty of form, and historical knowledge could no longer be used in practice as the criterion for rational proof but is applied in the field of uncontrollable aesthetic immediacy.

Against this postmodern irrationalization of historical consciousness, historical studies could find its place within the medium of discursive argument. With this medium historical studies could, through theorizing, make its contribution to the forming of a historical identity and historical orientation in practical human life.

Notes

1. (There is no human relationship to history, except one works on it; a factual one is none at all. The problem is that we can´t even assume the sensibility that this is understood as a problem.) Oskar Negt and Alexander Kluge, *Geschichte und Eigensinn*, Frankfurt am Main, 1981, 597.
2. An informative overview is given by Georg Iggers, *New Directions in European historiography*, Revised edn., Connecticut, 1984.

3. A good descripton of the "new" history is given by Ignacio Olabarri, "'New' history: a longue durée structure," *History and Theory* 34 (1995), 1–29.
4. A collection of representative texts on fundamental issues of this school can be found in Jacques Le Goff and Pierre Nora, eds., *Faire de l'histoire: Nouveaux problemes*, Paris, 1974.
5. Francois Furet, "Quantitative History," *Daedalus* 100 (1971), 151–67.
6. I use the Westgerman case for characterizing a general trend, effective in other countries as well. Cf. Jürgen Osterhammel, "Sozialgeschichte im Zivilisationsvergleich. Zu künftigen Möglichkeiten komparativer Geschichtswissenschaft," *Geschichte und Gesellschaft* 22 (1996), 143–64.
7. Hans-Ulrich Wehler, "Historiography in Germany Today," in Jürgen Habermas, ed., *Observations on The Spiritual Situation of the Age*, Cambridge, 1984, 221–59. Georg Iggers, "Introduction," in idem, ed., *The Social History of Politics: Critical Perspectives in West German Historical Writing since 1945*, Leamington Spa, 1985, 148; Hans-Ulrich Wehler, "Sozialgeschichte und Gesellschaftsgeschichte," in Wolfgang Schieder and Volker Sellin, eds., *Sozialgeschichte in Deutschland*, vol. 1, Göttingen, 1986, 33–52; Hans-Ulrich Wehler, *Historisches Denken am Ende des 20. Jahrhunderts. 1945–2000*, Essener kulturwissenschaftliche Vorträge, vol. 11, Göttingen, 2001.
8. See Jürgen Kocka, ed., *Max Weber, der Historiker*, Göttingen, 1986.
9. Jürgen Kocka, "Sozialgeschichte—Strukturgeschichte—Gesellschaftsgeschichte," *Archiv für Sozialgeschichte* 25 (1975), 1–42; Idem, *Sozialgeschichte, Begriff—Entwicklung—Probleme*, 2nd edn., Göttingen, 1986; Hans-Ulrich Wehler, *Geschichte als historische Sozialwissenschaft*, Frankfurt am Main, 1973; Jürgen Kocka, "Historische Sozialwissenschaft heute," in Paul Nolte, Manfred Hettling, Frank-Michael Kuhlemann, Hans-Walter Schmuhl, eds., *Perspektiven der Gesellschaftsgeschichte*, Munich, 2000, 5–24.
10. Jürgen Kocka, "Theorien in der Sozial- und Gesellschaftsgeschichte. Vorschläge zur historischen Schichtungsanalyse," *Geschichte und Gesellschaft* 1 (1975), 9–42, quotation p. 9.
11. An overview is given by Roger Fletcher, "Recent Developments in West German historiography: The Bielefeld School and its Critics," *German Studies Review* 7 (1984), 451–80.
12. Clifford Geertz, "Thick Description: Toward an Interpretative Theory of Culture," in idem, *The Interpretation of Culture: Selected Essays*, New York, 1973, 3–30.
13. Programmatically formulated by Hans Medick, "Missionare im Ruderboot? Ethnologische Erkenntnisweisen als Herausforderungen an die Sozialgeschichte," *Geschichte und Gesellschaft* 10 (1984), 295–319.
14. See Jörn Rüsen, "'Schöne Parteilichkeit', Feminismus und Objektivität in der Geschichtswissenschaft," in Rüsen, *Historische Orientierung*, 130–67.
15. I only mention the work of Alfred Schütz, Peter L. Berger, Thomas Luckmann, *The Social Construction of Reality*, Garden City, 1966.
16. Cf. Friedrich Jaeger, "Der Kulturbegriff im Werk Max Webers und seine Bedeutung für eine moderne Kulturgeschichte," *Geschichte und Gesellschaft* 18 (1992), 371–93.
17. Cf. Dorothee Wierling, "Keine Frauengeschichte nach dem Jahr 2000!," in Konrad Jarausch, Jörn Rüsen, Hans Schleier, eds., *Geschichtswissenschaft vor 2000. Perspektiven der Geschichtstheorie, Historiographiegeschichte und Sozialgeschichte. Festschrift für Georg Iggers zum 65. Geburtstag.* (Beiträge zur Geschichtskultur, Bd. 5), Hagen, 1991, 440–56.
18. See Reinhart Koselleck, ed., *Historische Semantik und Begriffsgeschichte*, Stuttgart, 1978.
19. The best example is Max Weber's Typology, Max Weber, "Die drei Typen der legitimen Herrschaft," in idem, *Gesammelte Aufsätze zur Wissenschaftslehre*, ed. Johannes Winckelmann, Tübingen, 1968, 475–88.

Chapter 7

Theoretical Approaches to an Intercultural Comparison of Historiography

> Es scheint an der Zeit, eine in größerem Stile vergleichende Betrachtung der verschiedenen Formen anzustellen, in denen in den verschiedenen Kulturen und Gesellschaften historische Fragen, Betrachtungsweisen, Interessen mit den Problemen, Perspektiven und Bedürfnissen, mit bestimmten Weisen des Handelns, der Veränderung, der Erwartungen und mit bestimmten Struktureigentümlichkeiten der Gesellschaft korrelieren.
>
> Christian Meier[1]

Why theory?

Most works on historiography have been done within the framework of a national history.[2] A broader perspective is related to European or Western historiography[3], or to the historiography of non-Western cultures. The latter mainly deals with a single country or a single culture such as China[4] or India.[5] Comparative studies have been rare so far.[6] There are a lot of reasons for this but I will only mention two: the difficulty of combining the competences of research in different historical cultures, and the dominance of Western historical thinking in historical studies even in non-Western countries. This dominance draws the academic interest on the origins and development of the specific modern way of historical thinking. On the other hand, there is a growing demand for intercultural comparison simply and unavoidably because of the increasing growth of international and intercultural communication, not only in economics and politics, but also in various fields of cultural life.

But how should such an intercultural comparison be done?[7] It is not sufficient simply to put different histories of historiography side by side. Thereby

---

Notes for this section begin on page 125.

we may get a useful and even necessary overview of the available knowledge, but it is no comparison whatsoever as the different stocks of knowledge lack a common framework for its cognitive organization. Every comparison needs an organizing parameter. Before looking at the materials (texts, oral traditions, images, rituals, monuments, memorials etc.), one should to know what realm of things should be taken into consideration and in what respect the findings in this realm should be compared. To put it as a simpler question: what are the conformities and where are the differences in historiography?

This simple question asks for a very complex answer. Intercultural comparison of cultural issues is a very sensitive matter—it touches the field of cultural identity, and it is therefore involved in the struggle for power and domination between different countries, especially in respect to Western dominance and non-Western resistance in nearly all fields of intercultural relationship. But it is not only a political struggle for power that in the field of historical thinking raises problems for an intercultural comparison. Beyond politics there is an epistemological difficulty with enormous conceptual and methodological consequences for the humanities: each comparison is done in the context of a pregiven culture, so it is involved in the subject matter of the comparison itself. Looking at historical thinking in other cultures with a historical interest is normally undertaken by an aspect of historiography, which is pregiven in the cultural context of the scholar. As historian he or she has a concept of what historiography is, and therefore has no urgent reason to reflect or explicate it theoretically. This pregiven knowledge of what historiography is functions as a hidden parameter, as a norm, or at least as a unit for structuring the outlook on the variety of historical thinking in different places and times.

So nonawareness is the problem: the use of a single case for historical thinking has an unreflected meta-status. Therefore, this approach is more than only a matter of comparison, it prescribes its results: of course the "real" or the essentially "historical" mode of historiography can only be found in one's own pregiven paradigm, and the other modes get their meaning, significance and importance only in relation to it.[8] Comparison here simply means measuring the proximity or distance from the presupposed norm. Usually this norm is the mode of one's own historical thinking. Only in rare cases does the scholar use projections of alternatives into other cultures in order to criticize his or her own culture's point of view; but even in this case he or she never gets a substantial insight into the peculiarities and the similarities of different modes of historical thinking and historiography.

To give an example of underlying concepts I would like to question how we should deal with elements of fiction and poetical imagination in representing the past. We can either evaluate these elements as a-historical, or nonhistorical, or even antihistorical or as necessary factors of making sense of the past in its historical representation. This depends on our presupposed concept of historical thinking and historiography. Another example may be the question of the importance of writing. Because of a presupposed conviction about the constitutive role of writing for historical thinking for a long time, we have become used to qualifying cultures with only oral tradition as a-historical, even as not belonging to history at all.[9] Introducing the medium of writing into these cultures was propagated, legitimated or confirmed as means of bringing them history, which they did not have before. Such a view prevents an insight into the culture-specific kind of historical thinking beyond or before writing.

There is no chance of avoiding the clashes between involvement and interest concerning the historical identity of the people whose historiography must and should be compared. Such involvement and interest has to be systematically taken into consideration, they must be reflected, explicated and discussed. There is at least one way of doing so. It opens not only a chance for comprehensive insights and cognition but also for a potential agreement and consensus among those who feel committed to, or at least related to, the different cultures in question. I am thinking of theory, that is, a certain way of reflecting and explicating the concepts and strategies of comparison. Only by a theoretically explicit reflection can the standards of comparison be treated in a way that prevents or at least corrects any hidden cultural imperialism or misleading perspective.[10]

Which theory?

How can we avoid a simple generalization of our own traditional way of historical thinking? The answer to this question is to look for anthropological universals of historical consciousness. To do so we have to go beyond the limits of professional and academic historiography and its rational procedures of historical cognition. Historical studies as an academic discipline cannot serve as a model or paradigm for historiography. Instead, we have to ask for basic mental procedures which can be found in every human culture. Is there something like an anthropological universal called "historical consciousness?" We know that thinking historically in the usual meaning of the word "history" is a result of a long process of cultural development and cannot be presupposed in all types of human society. But if one looks at some basic mental procedures constituting historical consciousness it is possible to identify them as universal. To explicate these procedures leads to a general theory of cultural memory.

There is no human culture without a constitutive element of common memory. By remembering, interpreting and representing the past, the people understand their present-day life and develop a future perspective of themselves and their world. History in this fundamental and anthropologically universal sense is a recollecting interpretation of the past serving as a cultural means of orienting present-daylife. A theory which explicates this fundamental and elementary procedure of making sense of the past in respect to the cultural orientation of present-day life is a starting point for a theoretical perspective of intercultural comparison. Such a theory thematizes the cultural memory or the "historical consciousness" that defines the subject matter of comparison in general.[11] It serves as a categorical definition of the cultural field in which historiography is placed in its various forms. In the framework of such a theory there is no presupposed specification of what historiography is like. On the contrary, historiography appears in the framework of such a general theory of historical consciousness or cultural memory as a specification of a universal and basic cultural practice of human life.

The theoretical framework of an intercultural comparison has several tasks: it must define the realm of what should be compared; it has to open up a perspective within which historiography or historical thinking as a matter of comparison come into view; and at the same time it should offer a set of points of view which render the variety of differences visible. In order to do so it must be clear how this variety of differences is constituted. First of all, it depends on the circumstances in which historical consciousness works. What are the challenges which bring it about? What functions does it have to fulfill? Furthermore, one has to look for the cultural practice by which historical consciousness is pursued as a process of communication, as an element of social life. In a third respect one has to look for the mental processes themselves by which the past obtains the specific quality which we call "history."

Here, our special interest should be directed to the principles of sense which govern this reconstruction of history. They decide about the logic of historical interpretation, about the poetics and rhetorics of forming a representation, and about the possibilities of understanding the past as something relevant and important for the cultural orientation of present-day human activities. An excellent description of what is meant can be found in Hao Chang's book on Chinese thinking at the turn of the twentieth century.[12] He speaks of an "orientational symbolism," a "general interpretation of life and world" which enables the people "to maintain coherence and order in the universe of meaning." This symbolism is related to three main subjects: self, society, and cosmos. It shapes also the modes of historical thinking. As to history, it is expressed in concepts of time and temporal change that define the relationship between past, present and future. These time concepts put the human world into an order which enables people to handle the experience of contingency by which their lives are permanently threatened. They also define their social life forms by structuring basic views of identity, of togetherness, and of otherness. In Chinese one could speak of the "Tao" of history, which can be compared with the "logos" of history or its "sense" in the West. The related principles and modes of thought draw a line between sense and senselessness in respect to the temporal dimension of human life. (So one should not forget to ask not only for sense, meaning, and significance, but for its contrary as well. What is defined as being senseless, chaotic, threatening etc.?)

Finally one has to look for modes, processes and factors of change and development concerning the work of historical consciousness. Can the variety of different manifestations of making historical sense of the past be put into a temporal sequence? Is there anything comparable in the structural change of historical thinking across the lines of different cultures? In respect to this question one has to be especially careful not to generalize European history or historical thinking into an entire of change direction comprehending all different cultures.

On the following pages I would like to deal with some particulars of these points. This should be done in a systematic order of arguments; however, this would demand a comprehensive and differentiated theory of "making sense of history," which hasn't yet been offered.[13]

A methodical problem of comparison

An intercultural comparison presupposes cultures as the subject matter of its work. It is an open question how these units of comparison should be looked at. Are there pregiven entities well distinguished in time and space? If an intercultural comparison uses a theoretical framework it has to be very careful not to start from presuppositions, which are problematic. This can be easily shown in respect to the sense criteria that constitute historical thinking in general. These sense criteria are an essential part of a cultural code which defines the units of comparison. Consequently, cultures can be compared along the line of their fundamental concepts which define the forms and realms of reality and human self-understanding. So a typology of such a conceptualization is a very useful theoretical means for a comparative approach.

Johan Galtung has proposed a well-structured typology of this kind.[14] He characterizes six different cultures (occident 1, occident 2, indic, buddhic, sinic, nipponic) in respect to seven basic concepts (nature, self, society, world, time self, time society, transperson, episteme). In the framework of such a typology the specificy of cultural codes becomes visible. But what is the status of such a code constituted by the systemic interrelationship of basic concepts and sense criteria? It makes culture become something very static, immovable and clearly discriminated in space and time. The relationship between cultures is one of monads, interrelated as if there were isolated configurations of sense and meaning, separated from each other and only following the regulative force of their deeply rooted cultural codes.

The danger of such a theory of cultural differences is its tendency to substantiate or even reify the single cultures concerned. Their internal historicity, their manifold interferences and mutual conditioning are lost from sight. Comparison is only a statement of dichotomy or clear alternatives: historical thinking either follows this code or another one. The related forms of cultural identities look like special realms with clear borderlines. Nothing seems to exist beyond or across the single codes. But the typology itself transgresses this borderline in a decisive step, and indicates a mode of thinking which does not necessarily follow one cultural code differently from the others. A typology of cultural differences is methodically necessary as a hypothetical construct, but it has to avoid the constraints and misleading views of a concept of cultures as pregiven units and entities.

The idea of cultures as being pregiven units and entities is committed to a cultural logic which constitutes identity on a fundamental difference between inside and outside. Such a logic conceptualizes identity as a mental territory with clear borderlines and a corresponding relationship between self and otherness as being strictly divided and only externally interrelated. This logic is essentially ethnocentric, and ethnocentrism is inscribed into a typology of cultural differences which treats cultures as coherent units which can clearly be separated from each other.

I would like to propose a method of using theoretical conceptualization which avoids this ethnocentrism. Ethnocentrism is theoretically dissolved if the specifics of a culture are understood as a combination of elements which are shared by all other cultures. Thus the specifics of cultures are brought about by different constellations of the same elements. The theoretical approach to cultural differences which is guided by this idea of cultural specifics does not fall into the trap of ethnocentrism. On the contrary, it presents the otherness of different cultures as a mirror which enables a better self-understanding. It does not exclude otherness constituting the peculiarity of the cultural features of oneself, but includes it. Cultural specifics bring about an interrelationship of cultures that enables the people, who have to deal with their differences, by providing the cultural power of recognition and acknowledgement.

What should be compared?

Historiography as the subject matter of comparison is a manifestation of historical consciousness; it cannot be understood without going back to a complex set of prepositions, circumstances, challenges, and functions, which altogether shape its peculiarity. How is it possible to compare peculiarities? It is necessary to decompose them into their constituent parts and reconstruct them as a specific relationship and synthesis of various elements. If it can be shown that these elements, or at least some of them, are the same in different manifestations of historiography, a comparative analysis can be done in a systematic way. So the first step to creating a theoretical parameter for comparing historiography is a theory of the main components of these specific cultural manifestations called historiography.

In order to do this one has to identify anthropological universals in the works and results of historical consciousness. This universality consists of a specific experience of time and a specific mode of dealing with this experience. It is an experience of time which can be called "contingency." Contingency means that human life is embedded in a course of time which always irritates human life. It is the irritation of rupture, of unexpected occurrence in one's own world, like death, catastrophes, accidents, disappointed expectations—in short, it is the experience which can be described by Hamlet's words: "The world is out of joint; - O cursed spite/that ever I was born to set it right."[15] "To set it right" means to develop a concept of the course of time, of temporal change and development, which makes the contingent occurrences senseful and meaningful in respect to the orientation of human activities vis-à-vis the permanent changes of the world and of the people in question.

Another example can be found in a Chinese expression in the Kung-yang-commentary to the *Spring and Autumn Annals*: "To set to right things which have been thrown into chaos and to restore the world to order, there is none better than the '*Spring and Autumn Annal*'."[16]

The experience of temporal change which structurally threatens human life and disturbs the concept of an unproblematic, ongoing, familiar process in one's own life and world[17] has to be interpreted in order to adjust human activities to it, and mentally to give it an order enabling the people who are threatened to continue with their daily lives. In order to do so they have to put it into a type of temporal order that gives an answer to the challenge of contingency. The work of historical consciousness can be described as a procedure by which such an idea of the temporal order of human life is brought about. It deals with the experience of the temporal change of life and world, which is stored in the halls of memory. It provides a sense of change by interpretation, which can be applied to the understanding of the world of today. Thus it enables people to expect the future and to guide their own activities by this future perspective according to the experiences of the past.

So the work of historical consciousness consists of recalling the past and understanding it as an accumulated experience of temporal change. Thus, the world of today becomes understandable and the future appears in a realistic perspective of expectation. This work is done in specific activities of cultural life. I would like to call them "the practices of historical narration." By these practices historiography becomes a part of human life, a part of culture as a necessary element of the human life form. Any intercultural comparison has to take into account systematically these practices, and has to interpret their specific forms of the universal cultural activity of making sense of the past by narration. I would not deny that there are non-narrative elements effective in the work of historical consciousness and that the narrative representation of the past has its limits, but the peculiarity of the cultural phenomenon called history cannot be described without the cultural practice of narration.

This activity of narration has its mental counterpart, history as a mental construct, in which the past is present as a determination or orientation of present-day life, including its future perspective. What are the substantial elements of this mental construct called history? In order to distinguish it from every other content of human memory one should first explicate its specifics as a memory of a past, which goes beyond the limits of one's own personal recollection, or (more objectively) beyond one's own life span. This temporal extension of memory is a necessary condition for giving the past the quality of being historical. Accordingly the future perspective, opened up by historical consciousness, transcends the limit of one's own life span as well. Historical consciousness enlarges the mental concept of the temporal dimension of human life into a temporal whole which goes far beyond the lifetime of the people who do the historical work of recollection.

The simple enlargement of the temporal horizon of memory is a necessary, though not sufficient condition for the specific historical quality of going back to the past. The human mind has to fill this dimension with a specific sense, that makes the past, as experience, significant for the present and future. This "historical sense" is an image, a vision, a concept, or an idea of time that mediates the expectations, desires, hopes, threats, and anxieties moving the minds of people in their present-day activities with the experiences of the past. Recalled real time becomes synthesized with the projected time of the future; past and future merge into an entire image, vision or concept of temporal change and development that functions as an integral part of the cultural orientation in the life of the present. Examples for this idea of time as a meaningful order of human activities are the ideas of the regular and incessant change of order and disorder,[18] the category of progress, the belief that God governs the world, or that there is an entire, moral, world order (such as *Tao*).

All these concepts are based on the idea of the order of time. Thus time concepts are the basis or the foundation of the sense of history; time related to the human world and its precarious balance between the experience of the past and the expectation of the future preforms any sense and meaning of the past as history. For comparative purposes a basic dichotomy has often been used: the difference between cyclic and linear time. This distinction as a simple alternative is not very useful for characterizing fundamental modes of historical thinking, as there is no concept of history that does not make use of both of them. So the emphasis of disclosing characteristic time concepts should be directed to the modes of synthesis of cyclicity and linearity of time.

The comparative outlook on historiography has to identify these criteria of historical sense and meaning. Normally they do not occur in an elaborated form. Very often they are implicit principles or highly effective presuppositions. All the more reason why it is necessary to identify and explicate them. So a system of basic concepts can be explicated, governing the entire historiography, structuring its way of transforming the experience of the past into a sense and meaningful history for the present. By such a system the semantics of history will be disclosed and prepared for comparison.

These basic categories may appear as ideas of a divine order of time, as a twofold world in which the occurrences of the human world are less important than the imaginative world of a higher temporal order, devoted to divine beings or higher principles of civilization or progress beyond the triviality of everyday human life. Examples of these basic concepts in the Chinese and in the European tradition of historiography may be the following: first of all, the concepts of record keeping (*chi*) and of "warming up the old [precedents] to know the new" (*wen ku erh chih hsin*), of memory, sense, and history, to be completed by basic notions like tradition, continuity, discontinuity, development, process, revolution, restoration, evolution, transformation through virtue, progress, decay etc. Then we should take into account different "philosophies of history," embedded in a moral world order, sacred history, divine providence; the philosophy of history since the enlightenment; and the concept of modernization. For comparative purposes it is necessary to find corresponding basic concepts in all other historiographies.

Today these sense criteria are mainly considered to be fictional, as inventions which have nothing to do with the reality. In this view the cultural creativity of historical consciousness is recognized, unfortunately, in a one-sided way, as one cannot deny the element of experience which moulds the mental construct called history as well as the images, symbols and concepts used to interpret it. Very often these interpreting elements are a part of the experience itself, so it is misleading to identify, explicate, and interpret them as being substantially fictional.

In the whole realm of the various cultural practices of historical narration, and of different manifestations of the mental construct called history, historiography can be distinguished as one species of cultural practice and of mental structure. It is an elaborated presentation of the past bound into the medium of writing, and its possibilities and limits. It presupposes the social life form of a historiographer characterized by a certain degree of specialization and even professionalization, and his or her function in a social and political order. For the purpose of comparison the following questions are important:

- What social rank do the historiographers have?
- Who do they depend on?
- What is their functional position in the system of political domination?
- What role does their work play in legitimating or delegitimating political domination?
- What role does gender play in constituting the specific competence which defines historiographers as a social group?
- What other groups or persons are concerned with recalling the past?
- Who do the historiographers have to defend against?
- Who legitimates their profession?

Historiography is a specific form of manifesting historical consciousness. Generally it is characterized by its presentation of the past in the form of a chronological order of events which are presented as "factual," that is, with a special quality of experience. For a comparative purpose it is important to know how this relationship to the so called facts of the past is organized and presented.

Another characteristic of historiography is its linguistic form. Is it presented in verse or in prose? What do these two main modes of writing indicate? Is this indication the same across the lines of cultural differences? In Western culture prose indicates a certain rationality, a discursive character of moulding the experience of the past with an idea of integrating sense, and a foundation of the report of the past on empirical evidence.

The whole comparative approach to historiography depends on the line of difference which defines the units to be compared. What does it mean to compare Chinese historiography with Western historiography? Before going into detail it is necessary to clear the plausibility of this presupposition of units of historiography and the modes of their conceptualization. Are they simply drawn from present-day distinctions or is there any correspondence to the presupposed unit in the conceptual framework of the historiographical work itself? For China this question might find a simple answer since, at least paradigmatic works of Chinese, historiography is related to China as a cultural unit in the minds of the historiographers and their audience. But what about Europe? Is the horizon of self-understanding or the elaboration of historical identity always "European" in the historiographical works of the West? Without explicating the internal horizon of the historical space which gives the past its specific perspective, comparative interpretation might simply be a misrepresentation or a naive reflex of an assumption of the interpreter.

Synchronic comparison

Synchronic comparison should be done in respect to types of cultural practices of historical narration; types of historical sense or meaning; conditions of the activities of historical consciousness; strategies and operations of the mental procedure of making historical sense; topoi of historical sense; forms of representation, media, and species of historiography; and functions of historical orientation.

Concerning the types of cultural practices of historically recalling the past, historiography has to be placed on a scale of different modes in order to find out its context and relationship to nonhistoriographical modes of dealing with the past. What is its relationship to rituals, ceremonies, festivities, public holidays, religious performances such as pilgrimages and other performances of collective memory? What is its relationship to popular culture? Can it be an integral part of popular culture? Another question puts historiography into a social perspective concerning its presentation of the past: how is history writing placed in social hierarchy? Does it reflect its social position by looking at human affairs,—a view from the top of the hierarchy or from below?

A very important perspective of the social history of historiography is related to gender. It is necessary and highly useful to distinguish between male and female voices in the representation of the past, systematically taking into account the realm of experience presented by historiography in respect to males and females. The same is to be done in respect to the orientation function of historiography: what kind of identity is presented by it, or more precisely, how is gender identity related to history?

In respect to the types of historical sense one should use a comprehensive typology which furnishes the interpretation of historiography with a clear and distinct conceptual framework. In respect to historiography in its elaborated scriptural form, there are at least four typologies of historiography worked out in the Western metahistorical discourse of the last centuries:

1. Droysen distinguishes in his "Topik" the investigative, narrative (in a more narrow meaning), didactic, and disputative presentation of the past.[19]
2. Nietzsche has described three types of dealing with the past: monumental, antiquarian, and critical representation.[20]
3. Hayden White has presented the most elaborated typology of historiography. He bases historical sense on four tropes of combining single facts into a meaningful history by narration: metaphor, metonymy, synecdoche, and irony. He adds three further dimensions of historical sense in the form of a typology; four modes of emplotment (romantic, tragic, comic, satirical); four modes of explanation by formal argument (formist, mechanistic, organicistic, contextualist); and four modes of explanation by ideological implication (anarchist, radical, conservative, liberal).[21]
4. My own typology combines functional and structural elements of historical narration, and distinguishes between four different modes of making sense of history: traditional, exemplary, critical, and genetical modes of historical narrative.[22]

In respect to the cultural context of historiography one should look at the presupposition of religious criteria for sense and meaning, as in most societies—at least, of the premodern type—religion is the main source for sense of the kind that historiography refers to for its relationship between past and present. It is trivial to say that the distinctive nature of historical thinking in the West is deeply influenced by Christianity, even at the time of historicism, when historical studies achieved its academic form as a discipline with its own methodical strategy of research. Relationship to religion can function as a key to decipher the language of sense, meaning, and significance in historiography.[23]

In order to understand why specific sense criteria of history have come into use, one should first consider the challenges that constitute the activity of historical consciousness and which demand a historiographical answer. I have already characterized those challenges as a rupture and irritation in the course of time, concerning the temporal coherence of human life. Examples for this challenging experience of discontinuity are the French Revolution for historicism, the fall of Rome for Augustine's concept of sacred history, the new political structure and role of Athens in the late fifth century for Herodotus;[24] and the founding of the empire of the Ch´in and Han dynasties for Ssu-ma Ch´ien. As not all incoherence in respect to time can be mastered by historical narration one should look for those specific time experiences which find their answer in historiography. What kind of problem will be solved by historization?

In respect to the internal operations and strategies of historical consciousness one should first of all look at the specific narrative structure of historiography. Is it structured as a narrative at all? If not, like the classical annals in China, what does it mean for the underlying criteria of historical sense? If there is no real historical representation of the past without narrative elements, where will we find these elements if important texts are structured differently? Additionally, one should look for the existence and role of non-narrative elements such as images and symbols, which do not represent narratives but may initiate them, or at least give a framework of significance for them.

A list of historical topoi is very useful. These topoi organize the narrative presentation of the past by ascribing it a specific significance for the attitude toward the problems of present-day life. Historical topoi can be defined as forms of perception and representation within the texture of the historical sense of the past, which occur as repetitive patterns related to diverse contents.[25] The most famous topos of historical significance is, of course, expressed by the Ciceronian slogan *historia vitae magistra* (history is the teacher of life) and in China by the metaphor "mirror"(*chien*).[26] Historiography that represents the past according to this topos teaches general rules of human conduct by examples; it is governed by the logic of judgment, that is, the generation of rules from cases and the application of rules to cases. Mostly these rules are related to politics and addressed to the rulers in order to commit them to ethical principles of legitimacy of power and domination.[27] There are, of course, a lot of other topoi. For the purpose of comparison they should be listed and brought into the systematic order of a rhetoric of historiography. Such a rhetoric doesn't yet exist. So I can only mention some topoi, drawn in a systematic form from empirical findings in a recent investigation of the historical consciousness of young people:[28] the past as a place of evasion; the past as a utopian counterimage of the present; the past should be altered; the past presents obligatory traditions; the important things of the past are still lasting; the important things of the past are changing; the past has to be explicitly mediated with the life conditions of the present; the past can teach us something, so history is a matter of learning.

There are a lot of other points of view which may function as a parameter of comparison. I cannot explicate all of them in a systematic order; so I will simply enumerate them:

- How are events of the past related to each other? What kind of rationality governs this relationship?
- What level of synthesizing different elements of experience and signification prevails?
- How much does historiography reflect itself in respect to its structure and principles?
- How deep do the analysis and the explanatory strategies of historical representation go?
- What role do values and norms play in structuring the past as history?
- To what degree is the past historicized?
- A very important question is related to the way, historiography deals with the experience of other cultures, different from the historian's. Are they marginalized, used as a focus for projecting one's own desire, or is there an ability to recognize them?
- I have already mentioned the problem of the foundation of historiography in experience on the one hand, and elements of fictionality in its interpretation of the past on the other. According to this relationship there should be an effort to find typical constellations between factuality and fictionality in dealing with the past. This relationship may even indicate a stage of development, since, I think, a clear distinction between factuality and fictionality demands a highly developed historical culture, which has specific procedures of making sense of history emphasizing the factuality of the reported past.
- A very important element of comparison is the form of historiography. What different forms[29] can be observed and what systematization has been given them in their time? Does this order correspond to our strategies of systematization?
- Even more important than the form is the medium of presentation. Whether historical narratives are realized in an oral, a scriptural or in one of the new media makes substantial differences in understanding and interpreting the past.[30]

Finally the practical function of historiography should be systematically taken into account. This function lies in the cultural orientation of human life. Its most remarkable manifestation is the articulation of the historical identity of the people to whom historiography is addressed. For comparative purposes there is a need for different points of view concerning identity. The most important view is related to the spatial extent of historical identity and to the norms and values which determine this extension. Who is included, who is excluded in the historical narratives? How is the relationship between both presented? Where is the borderline between self and other, between togetherness and strangeness?

Diachronic comparison

Diachronic comparison is related to change in historiography. Theoretically undertaken, it has to identify comprehensive factors, modes of processes, and directions of change. But before explicating corresponding perspectives of change in historiography, a general periodization should be reflected within which historiography gets its historical significance related to the entire process of change in the human world. Such a periodization realizes the dependence of historiography on its context, by which it gets its constitutive challenges, its basic sense criteria, and within which it fulfills (or misses) its orientationfunction. It is an intensively debated question, whether the main epochs of European history could be applied to other cultures. If not, the different periodizations should at least be compared in respect to the criteria which determine the division of epochs. For the purposes of historiography a general periodization which relates to the dominant media of human communication is useful. Nobody will deny that a distinction between three epochs, defined by the three media orality, scribality, and "electronality"[31] can serve as a first approach indicating a comprehensive perspective of cultural change.

Coming closer to the specific development of historiography one has to look at those factors and elements that cause change in the procedure of making sense and representing the past. To give at least one example for such a moving force of changing historiography, I would like to consider the increase of knowledge about the past. It can challenge new categorizations, and these new categorizations reshape and restructure historiography in general. Without the exploding increase of knowledge the rise of historicist thought in the late eighteenth century could not be sufficiently explained. There was a similar accumulation of historical knowledge in China, but it doesn't seem to have brought about a shift in the underlying categories of historical perception and interpretation.

Another question is related to the presentation of change in historiography. Is there anything like the experience of progress, based upon self-esteem of a successful group that historiographers can associate with?

The most important parameter of diachronic comparison is the direction of change. Is it possible to develop tendencies of change which cover different cultures? Today even this question is highly disregarded. It seems too much loaded with the ideological burden of Western supremacy. But a rejection of Western ideology should not lead to a prohibition of asking questions. I think that such a question is unavoidable, since today all countries of the world today are directly or indirectly involved in the process of modernization, and this modernization is a challenge of historical identity for them all. It is of high importance to know whether there are tendencies in one's own cultural history which point into the same direction as Western development. And for Westerners it is useful to know whether there are tendencies in non-Western cultures which have a similar direction of development of their own. If there is a cultural development or evolution potentially involving all countries, then the modernization process will be more than only a threat of alienation, it may even be conceptualized as a chance of gaining or regaining one's own identity in a broader perspective of humankind.

So Max Weber's concept of the universal rationalization and disenchantment should be reformulated as a question for a comparative analysis of historiography. There is no historiography without rationality, that is, a set of rules which bind the sense-making process of historical consciousness into strategies of conceptualization, of bringing empirical evidence into the representation of the past, and of coherent argument. This rationality should be reconstructed and investigated in respect to its development toward a growing universality of its validity. The same should be done in respect to the norms and values that constitute historical identity. Do they show a directed development, which can be described as a process of universalization, and does the spatial extension of historical identity develop accordingly? I think we can observe such a process of universalization in many cultures:[32] It starts from a small social group in archaic times and leads to mankind in modern history. Alongside this universalization a corresponding regionalization very often takes place. Additionally, one should look for a process of particularization and individualization; it may be a reaction to universalization or a consequence of it.

Another direction of development can be conceptualized in respect to the treatment of "facts" in relationship to the presupposed order of time. Is there a comprehensive process of "positivation" of historiography by increasingly integrating positive facts and principles of temporal order? In archaic societies the "facts" occurring in human life are not important for the narrative presentation of the divine order of the world in space and time. Myths as narratives that present world order, are not very much related to chronologically fixed dates given and proved by empirical evidence. As a result of a long development the mythical order has vanished or has been mixed up with the temporal chain of positive, that is, "factual" events and structures.

Following this line of argument, I dare to outline a periodization that is basically related to the media of cultural communication and their transformation and may at least function as a heuristical and hypothetical means of giving historical thinking a comprehensive temporal order. It even indicates a possible development (post-historic period), which presents an ideal type, composed of the most challenging elements of postmodern historical thinking.[33]

Modernization is, of course, one of the most important perspectives of diachronic comparison. It should be concretized as an internal process of rationalization in dealing with the past. Historical studies as an academic discipline

TABLE 7.1 SCHEMA FOR A UNIVERSAL PERIODIZATION OF HISTORICAL THINKING

Pre-Historic
Sharp distinction between paradigmatic time of world order ("archaic" time of myth) and the time of every-day human life; the latter is meaningless for the order of world and self. Contingency is radically sorted out. Dominance of the traditional type of historical narration. Medium of oral tradition

Historic
Intermediation of both "times." Contingent facts (events) are loaded with meaning concerning the temporal world order. Contingency is recognized as relevant for this order and bound into a concept of time which orientates practical activity and forms human identity. Medium of writing.

Modern	Traditional
Minimalization of the transcendent dimension of timeorder. The entire sense of history tends to become innerworldly. Human rationality is able to recognize it by the means of methodical research of the empirical evidence of the past. Dominance of the genetic type of historical narration	The entire order of time has a divine character. Religion is the main source for sense of temporal change. Dominance of the exemplary type of historical narration.

Post-Historic
No comprehensive order of time including past, present, and future. The past is separated into a time for itself. Facts of the past become elements of arbitrary constellations which have no substantial relationship to present and future. The human past becomes detemporalized. Contingency loses its conceptualization by ideas of temporal order valid for present-day life and its future. Medium of electronics.

SOURCE: Jörn Rüsen, 2004

indicate forms and stages of this rationalization. But rationalization is only one side of the coin of modernization. There is always a reaction against it, a re-enchantment in the relationship to the past which, at least compensates the loss of sense and meaning brought about by the rationality of methodical strategies of research. So the comparative approach to historiography should always be a double one: the view at disenchantment as well as at its compensation by an irrational re-enchantment or at its complementation by new or reformulated ("reformatted") sources and potentials of sense, meaning, and significance of the temporal dimension of human life.

Another strong indicator of modernity is the emergence of the concept of "the history" as an entire field of human experience, as a temporal totality of development comprising all cultures in the past, present, and future.[34]

New questions

The twentieth century has brought about fundamental challenges of historiography in respect to its basic criteria of sense and meaning. I think of the traumatic experience of the Holocaust and similar occurrences of mass murder and other radical irritations of sense in the course of time in the human world. (A Chinese example is at hand, too: the Taiping Rebellion, for example, cost 20 million victims.) Such experiences cause traumatic reactions and very often suppress important elements of collective memory into the unconscious. Looking at historiography this unconscious level has to be disclosed as a silent factor in the past which, nevertheless, influences the present. In order to make this plausible one has to identify indications of this suppression in the articulated representations of the past. In order to meet these challenges our interpretation of historiography systematically has to take into account intended or unintended procedures of a negative mode of making sense of history. This negative sense or the sense of senselessness can be demonstrated as "limits of representation," which have already been paradigmatically discussed in respect to the Holocaust.[35] It seems to be a fruitful quest to look for such limits, even in ordinary historiography, thus bringing to our awareness a dimension of historical consciousness in which historiography speaks the language of silence.[36]

In the introductory remarks to this chapter I pointed to the fact that every work in historiography, including comparison, is involved in the process of identity forming and is guided by practical interests. This is true for the proposed strategy of pursuing comparative interpretation of historiography as well. The practical objective of this strategy is a negative and a positive one. Negatively, it should prevent ideological generalizations of cultural peculiarity from becoming presuppositions and guidelines for the study of historiography, thus avoiding the widespread dichotomy between self and other and the related strategy of exclusion in identity-forming habits. Positively, it should enable the scholars to present the historiographical traditions of different cultures, peoples and societies in a mental movement between sameness and difference. Those whose identity is at stake, should be put into the position of becoming aware that otherness is a mirror for their self-awareness. Then their communication can become an effort of mutual recognition and acknowledgement.

Notes

1. Christian Meier, "Die Entstehung der Historie," in Reinhart Koselleck and Wolf-Dieter Stempel, eds., *Geschichte—Ereignis und Erzählung,* Poetik und Hermeneutik V, Munich,

1973, 251–306, cit. 256. (Time seems to have come, to install an elaborated comparative view of the different forms, within which the different cultures and societies correlate historical questions, world views and interests with certain ways of activity, of change, of expectation, and with certain structural peculiarities of society.)
2. A recent example: Horst Walter Blanke, *Historiographiegeschichte als Historik*, Fundamenta Historica, vol. 3, Stuttgart/Bad Cannstatt, 1991.
3. Ernst Breisach, *Historiography—Ancient, Medieval, and Modern*, Chicago, 1983; Georg G. Iggers, *Geschichtswissenschaft im 20. Jahrhundert. Ein Überblick im internationalen Zusammenhang*, Göttingen, 1993. Iggers' "international relationship" is exclusively European–American—the older *International Handbook of Historical Studies: Contemporary Research and Theory*, ed. Georg Iggers and Harold T. Parker, Westpoint, CT, 1979 includes most of the non-Western countries.
4. E.g., William G. Beasley and Edward G. Pulleyblank, eds., *Historians of China and Japan*, London, 1961; Yu-sha Han, *Elements of Chinese Historiograph*, Hollywood, 1955; Charles S. Gardner, *Chinese Traditional Historiography*, Cambridge, 1961; George Kao, ed., *The Translation of Things Past: Chinese History and Historiography*, Hong Kong, 1982; Rolf Trauzettel, "Die chinesische Geschichtsschreibung," in Günther Debon, ed., *Ostasiatische Literaturen*, Wiesbaden, 1984, 77–90; "Extrême-Orient/Extrême-Occident," IX; *La référence à l'histoire*, Paris, 1986.
5. E.g., D. Devahuti, ed., *Problems of India Historiography*, Delhi, 1979; B. Kölver, *Ritual und historischer Raum. Zum indischen Geschichtsverständnis*, Munich, 1993; Pratima Asthana, *The Indian View of History*, Agra, 1992; Michael Gottlob, "Writing the History of Modern India historiography," *Storia della Storiografia* 27 (1995), 123–44.
6. E.g., Donald E. Brown, *Hierarchy, History and Human Nature: The Social Origins of Historical Consciousness*, Tuscon, 1988. A recent approach to bring non-Western cultures into view in dealing with the history of Western historiography is the series *Geschichtsdiskurs*, ed., Wolfgang Küttler, Jörn Rüsen, Ernst Schulin, vol. 1, *Grundlagen und Methoden der Historiographiegeschichte*, Frankfurt am Main, 1993; vol. 2, *Anfänge modernen historischen Denkens*, Frankfurt am Main, 1994; vol. 3, *Die Epoche der Historisierung*, Frankfurt am Main, 1996; vol. 4, *Krisenbewußtsein, Katastrophenerfahrungen und Innovationen 1880–1945*, Frankfurt am Main, 1997; vol. 5, *Globale Konflikte, Erinnerungsarbeit und Neuorientierungen seit 1945*, Frankfurt am Main, 1999; cf. Horst Walter Blanke, "Zum Verhältnis von Historiographiegeschichte und Historik—Eine Analyse der Tagungsbände Theorie der Geschichte und Geschichtsdiskurs," *Tel Aviver Jahrbuch für deutsche Geschichte* 29 (2000), 55–84.
7. Cf. Jürgen Osterhammel, "Sozialgeschichte im Zivilisationsvergleich. Zu künftigen Möglichkeiten komparativer Geschichtswissenschaft," *Geschichte und Gesellschaft* 22 (1996), 143–64; Heinz-Gerhard Haupt and Jürgen Kocka, eds., *Geschichte und Vergleich. Ansätze und Ergebnisse international vergleichender Geschichtsschreibung*, Frankfurt am Main, 1996.
8. A typical example is Donald E. Brown, *Hierarchy, History and Human Nature: The Social Origins of Historical Consciousness*, Tuscon, 1988. Franz Rosenthal reflected the problem when dealing with the subject matter of "Muslim historiography." He identifies it as "those works which Muslims, at a given moment of their literary history, considered historical works and which, at the same time, contain a reasonable amount of material which can be classified as historical according to our definition of history ...," Franz Rosenthal, *A History of Muslim Historiography*, 2nd revised edn., Leiden 1968, 17.
9. E.g., Leopold von Ranke, *Weltgeschichte*, vol. I,1. 4th edn., Leipzig, 1896, VIII. Cf. Andreas Pigulla, *China in der deutschen Weltgeschichtsschreibung vom 18. bis zum 20. Jahrhundert*, Wiesbaden, 1996.
10. I have tried a first approach to such a theoretization for the sake of an intercultural comparison (concerning the history of human rights) in: Jörn Rüsen, "Die Individualisierung des Allgemeinen—Theorieprobleme einer vergleichenden Universalgeschichte der Menschenrechte," in Rüsen, *Historische Orientierung*, 168–87.

11. For the following cf. Jörn Rüsen, "Was ist Geschichtsbewußtsein? Theoretische Überlegungen und heuristische Hinweise," in Rüsen, *Historische Orientierung*, 3–24.
12. Chang Hao, *Chinese Search for Order and Meaning 1890–1911*, Berkeley, 1987, 7.
13. In doing so I will refer to a lot arguments, hints, and ideas I got during the work of a research group of the Center for Interdisciplinary Study at the University of Bielefeld, which has treated the issue "Making sense of History—Interdisciplinary Studies in the Structure, Logic, Function, and Intercultural Comparison of Historical Consciousness." I feel especially indebted to Klaus E. Müller, Burkard Gladigow, and (concerning China) Helwig Schmidt-Glintzer and Joachim Mittag. Joachim Mittag has substantially enriched my comparative approach to historiography. I owe to him most of the Chinese examples in this text. Further argument on "making sense of history" can be found in Rüsen, *Zerbrechende Zeit*.
14. Johan Galtung, "Six Cosmologies: an Impressionistic Presentation," in idem, *Peace by Peaceful Means*, London, 1996, 211–22; idem, "Die 'Sinne' der Geschichte," in Klaus E. Müller and Jörn Rüsen, eds., *Historische Sinnbildung. Problemstellungen, Zeitkonzepte, Wahrnehmungshorizonte, Darstellungsstrategien*, Reinbek, 1997, 118–41.
15. William Shakespeare, *Hamlet*, Act I, Scene V, 189 sqq.
16. Kung-yang chuan, *Ai-kung 14th year*.
17. In Chinese it is expressed by the *term pien* (change with meaning of turmoil).
18. Cf. Mencius, III B, 8.
19. Droysen, Untersuchende, erzählende, didaktische und diskussive Darstellung, *Historik*, 217–83 and 445–50. Cf. Jörn Rüsen, "Bemerkungen zu Droysens Typologie der Geschichtsschreibung," in Rüsen, *Konfigurationen des Historismus*, 267–75.
20. Friedrich Nietzsche, "Vom Nutzen und Nachteil der Historie für das Leben (Unzeitgemäße Betrachtungen, zweites Stück)," in idem, *Sämtliche Werke. Kritische Studienausgabe in 15 Einzelbänden*, vol. 1, Munich, 1988, 243–334, esp. 258–70. Friedrich Nietzsche, "On the Uses and Disadvantages of History for Life," in *Untimely Meditations*, trans. R.J. Hollingdale, Cambridge, 1983, 83–100.
21. White, *Metahistory*, 1–42.
22. Ibid., chapters 1 and 2.
23. Cf. Jörn Rüsen, "Historische Methode und religiöser Sinn—Vorüberlegungen zu einer Dialektik der Rationalisierung des historischen Denkens in der Moderne" in Wolfgang Küttler, Jörn Rüsen, Ernst Schulin, eds., *Geschichtsdiskurs, Anfänge modernen historischen Denkens*, vol. 2, Frankfurt am Main, 1994, 344–77.
24. Christian Meier, "Die Entstehung der Historie," in Reinhart Koselleck and Wolf-Dieter Stempel, eds., *Geschichte—Ereignis und Erzählung,* Poetik und Hermeneutik V, Munich, 1973, 251–306. Meier speaks of a "politically determined process of an entire rapture, a deep shift of measures," 254.
25. Jörn Rüsen et al., "Untersuchungen zum Geschichtsbewußtsein von Abiturienten im Ruhrgebiet," in *Geschichtsbewußtsein empirisch*, eds. B. von Borries, H.-J. Pandel, J. Rüsen, Pfaffenweiler, 1991, cit. 286.
26. Cf. Chun-chieh Huang, "Historical Thinking in Classical Confucianism—Historical Argument from the Three Dynasties," in Chun-chieh Huang and Erich Zürcher, eds., *Time and Space in Chinese Culture*, Leiden, 1995, 72–85, cit. 76, "Chien originally meant 'mirror', and mirror is that by which we examine ourselves, how we look at people, the representative of our 'conscience'. The character, chien, then turned later to meaning 'lesson, norm, pattern', without totally shedding the original meaning of normative mirroring."
27. This topos seems to be universal in all advanced civilizations. It is, e.g., the basis for Ibn Khaldun's (1332–1406) *Book of Examples and Collection of Origins* as well as for Ssu-ma Kuang's (1019–1086) *Comprehensive Mirror for Aid of Government*.
28. Jörn Rüsen, Klaus Fröhlich, Hubert Horstkötter, Hans Günther Schmidt, "Untersuchungen zum Geschichtsbewußtsein von Abiturienten im Ruhrgebiet;" Jörn Rüsen, "Geschichtsbewußtsein von Schülern und Studenten im internationalen und interkulturellen Vergleich," in

Bodo von Borries and Jörn Rüsen, eds., *Geschichtsbewußtsein im interkulturellen Vergleich. Zwei empirische Pilotstudien*, Pfaffenweiler, 1994, 79–206.
29. E.g., "grand" or "master" narrative, essay, presentation of research results, article in a journal, monograph, documentation of sources, comment on canonic scripture, etc.
30. I refer to this aspect of media in my rough sketch of a comprehensive development of historical thinking at the end of this chapter.
31. Albert D'Haenens (Louvain la Neuve) once in a debate used the slogan "oralité, scribalité, electronalité," which I pick up here.
32. I have tried to conceptualize such a process in respect to the question for their universality of human rights and the general issues of humankind, selfness, and otherness in Jörn Rüsen, "Die Individualisierung des Allgemeinen—Theorieprobleme einer vergleichenden Universalgeschichte der Menschenrechte," in Rüsen, *Historische Orientierung*, 168–87; and Jörn Rüsen, "Human Rights from the Perspective of a Universal History," in Wolfgang Schmale, ed., *Human Rights and Cultural Diversity*, 28–46; Jörn Rüsen, "Vom Umgang mit den Anderen—Zum Stand der Menschenrechte heute," *Internationale Schulbuchforschung* 15 (1993), 167–78.
33. I have put three of the four types of historical sensemaking into a clear periodic order. This is misleading, since they play a much more complex role in all periods. But, nevertheless, they can be used to characterize an epoch-related type of historical thinking.
34. As to the term "the history" cf. note 7 in chap. 4.
35. Saul Friedländer, ed., *Probing the limits of representation. Nazism and the 'Final Solution'*, Cambridge, 1992.
36. Concerning the fall of Nanking in 1867 an already established literary pattern of suppressive memory was applied, which articulated a weariness of looking back: "And I fear to look back, to read too carefully Yü Hsin's fu," Stephen Owen, "Place: Mediation on the Past at Chin-ling," *Harvard Journal of Asiatic Studies* 56 (1990), 417–57.

Chapter 8

Loosening the Order of History: Modernity, Postmodernity, Memory

Bei der Erörterung der übergreifenden Zusammenhänge und bei der Hervorhebung der großen Linien jedoch sind die Ausführungen der Gelehrten selten von umfassendem Verständnis gekennzeichnet und ihre Prinzipien treffen die entscheidenden Punkte nicht.

Liu Zhiji: Chun Qiu[1]

Topical challenges

Historical studies as an academic discipline is under discussion, which treats its roots, functions and principles in a way that render them at the same time satisfactory and uncomfortable. The satisfaction may result from the new attention history has got in the realm of the humanities. One of the most dominating issues here is memory and its role in human culture. "Memory" covers the entire field of dealing with the past, thus including the realm of history as a subject matter and as a mode of recalling the past into life of its representation in the cultural framework of human activities. On the other hand this awareness of historical representation may generate a feeling of discomfort among professional historians, as it very easily transcends and even neglects those strategies of dealing with the past which constitute historical studies as a discipline or as a "science," and the professionality of historians.

The discourse on memory lacks the cognitive procedures which furnish historical knowledge with the element of rationality, and which give the view of the past the validity of objectivity and legitimate professionalism with claims of truth. But it also seems to put aside historical studies as a culturally inhabitated place for dealing with the past: vis-a-vis the lively forces of moving memories in the life of individuals, groups, nations, and whole cultures,

---

Notes for this section begin on page 142.

the academic relationship to the past seems to be a realm of shadows. The light of practical importance does not seem to enlighten its work of research. Disclosed in the places of memory (*lieux de memoire*) history seems to have emigrated from the fields of academic research and professional historiography into the open field of symbolizing representation where it is not bound by the constraints of reifying and alienating methodical procedures.

The uncomfortable situation of historical studies has been considered for a long time by the discourse on postmodernism. This brought about a radical doubt in the cognitive principles of historical thinking and historiography in its specific "modern" form of historical studies. The discussion about postmodernism as a challenge to the humanities has become weaker, but the challenge for historical studies is still very strong. Its "disciplinary" structure and form, still effective in the study of history and the professionalization of historians, including teachers of history, has lost its voice. Instead of the professional academic practices of producing historical knowledge, the cultural practices of recalling the past as history and representing it in the symbolic order and orienting forces of cultural life, have gained an enormous interest not only in the humanities but even more so in public life, where memorials, monuments, anniversaries, and other institutions and ceremonies of collective remembrance play an important role.

Historical studies as a discipline and the professionality of the historians finds itself in a context within which the clear features of its cognitive achievements are fading away. Put onto the ground of living memory, historical studies seem to lose its fundamental principles of cognition. Can the role historical memory plays in shaping human identity and orienting human activities simply be applied to historical studies as an academic discipline or as a "science" in the broader sense of the word? If it is recognized at all in the discourse of memory it simply appears as an agent of ideology, presenting history according to the interests and needs of elites, as a weapon in the struggle of power to be used by those who have the power to define the semantic terms of trade in the field of constructing, deconstructing and reconstructing collective identity. Related to the poetic and rhetoric strategies of furnishing the past as history with the life of topical human activities, it appears as a hermaphrodite of scientific rationality and literary shape, as an ambiguous figure synthesizing scientific rationality and literary textuality: to put it bluntly, as a failure (an outage) with a very doubtful cultural function.

Metahistory

Most of the arguments which threaten historical studies by ignoring its specific cognitive procedures, or criticizing its ideological function, are delivered and worked out on a level of discourse which can be described as "metahistorical."

It reflects history and its various modes of dealing with the past; it is not a mode of this dealing but a theory about it—even if this reflection is not directly or explicitly related to historical studies. Nevertheless, it cannot be neglected as at least some of its issues aim at the heart of historical studies: mainly the sense criteria which were used to give the past its specific historical meaning and significance for the present, the constitutive role of needs and interests in dealing with the past, and the function of remembering in orienting human activity and forming all kinds of identity are of constitutive importance for historical studies.

So historical studies have to pick up this reflection and have to relate it to its cognitive strategies in bringing about solid knowledge of the past and in professionally writing historiography. Doing so it continues a tradition of reflecting itself, of doing metatheory in pursuing its work of remembering, recalling and representing the past, which is even older than its status as an academic discipline.[2] Such a reflection has already been done in the tradition of rhetoric in historiography. It has played an important role in bringing about and legitimating historical studies as an academic discipline with special claims for scientific rationality and corresponding validity of its interpretation. In Germany, for example the process of professionalization and "scientification" of historiography got its first push on a metatheoretical level rather than on the level of concretely dealing with the past.[3] Metahistory as self-reflection of historical studies is a tradition in the development of the discipline.[4] It accompanies historical research and history-writing in its development, in all its changes, crises, stagnations, revolutions, and debates concerning its status as an academic discipline, its relationship to other disciplines, its epistemological preconditions, its cultural functions, and the principles of its cognitive work.[5] In Germany there even exists a term which designates this specific self-reflection of historical studies: "Historik." Here we find a tradition of arguing about the principles of historical studies, an innerdisciplinary preestablished discourse, that enables historical studies to bring its specificy into the discourse about the general and fundamental issues of dealing with the past.

To the same extent to which historical studies are challenged by the postmodern criticism of the modern way of doing history, which puts their "scientific" image into radical doubt, and by the discourse on memory, which lets their disciplinary structures dissolve, historical studies have to mobilize and to revise their tradition of self-reflection. They have to reflect themselves again, to explicate, legitimate and also criticize their cognitive status and their claims for a certain validity brought about by the methodical procedures of research. They can do this work in keeping up the already established modes and results of metahistory as a discourse within their disciplinary constitution.

In order to do so, at first they have to explicate and elaborate their cognitive structure, from which they get their specific shape in the vast field of culture where history is done in different modes of remembering, recalling, and representing (and at the same time forgetting and suppressing) the past.

A model of historical studies

This cognitive structure of historical thinking cannot be explicated without systematically taking into account its constitution and function in practical human life, as its specific logic is constituted by its relationship to the cultural needs of human activities. It is one of the most important merits of the topical discussion on historical memory to illuminate this point: that historical thinking takes place in the realm of memory and is committed to its mental procedures, by which the recalling and representation of the past is dedicated to the cultural orientation of human life in the present. Recalling of the past is a necessary condition of furnishing human life with a cultural frame of orientation, that opens up a future perspective, grounded on the experience of the past. On the other hand, it would be misleading, if historical thinking, and with it the whole work of historical studies, is stressed only by following the cultural needs of practical human life; it has its own logic as well—logic that is mainly characterized by the methodical rationality in treating the empirical evidence of the past. Both sides, the relationship to practical needs and functions and the rationality of methodical cognition, have to be seen together.

This can be done in the form of a schema, which explicates five principles of historical thinking and its systematic relationship, (see figure 8.1). One can pick up the term of Thomas S. Kuhn and speak of the "disciplinary matrix" of historical studies (without following his argument concerning the development of sciences and the impossibility of applying his ideas of science to the humanities).[6] The five principles are:

1. Interests in cognition generated out of needs for orientation in the temporal change of the present world.
2. Concepts of significance and perspectives of temporal change, within which the past gets its specific feature as "history."
3. Methodical rules of empirical research.
4. Forms of representation, in which the evidence of the past, brought about by interpretation into the concepts of significance, is presented in the form of a narrative.
5. Functions of cultural orientation in the form of a temporal direction of human activities and concepts of historical identity.

Each of these five factors is necessary, and all of them together are sufficient in constituting historical thinking as a rationally elaborated form of historical memory. (It may be useful to underline that not every memory itself is already a historical one. Only if memory goes beyond the limits of the lifespan of the person or group concerned should one speak of a specific "historical" memory. "Historical" indicates a certain element of temporal distance between past and present, which renders necessary a complex mediation of both. The

```
                    Methods
                  of treating the
                    experience
                    of the past

    Concepts
   of significance
(theories, perspectives,                         Forms
     categories)                             of representation

                    Principles
                 of historical sense

                                        Functions
                                     of cultural orientation
                                        (temporal-direction
         Interests                     of human activities,
   (needs for orientation                  concepts of
   in the temporal change                historical identity)
        of the world)
```

Level of theoretical reflection

Level of pragmatic reflection

Level of practical life

1: **semantic** strategy of symbolization
2: **cognitive** strategy of producing historical knowledge
3: **aesthetic** strategy of historical representation
4: **rhetorical** strategy of offering historical orientation
5: **political** strategy of collective memory

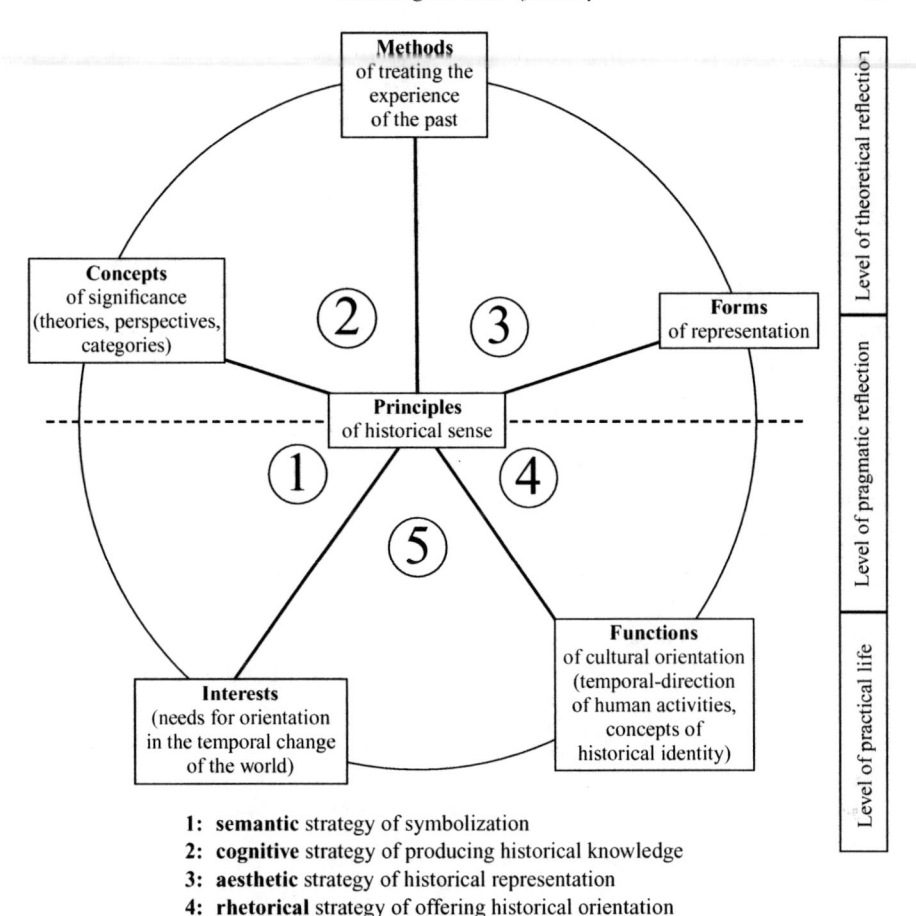

FIGURE 8.1 SCHEMA OF HISTORICAL THINKING

five factors may change in the course of time: that is, in the development of historical thinking in general and historical studies in specific, but their relationship, the systematic order, in which they are dependent on each other will remain the same. In this systematic relationship all of them depend upon one main and fundamental principle: the principle that gives their relationship its coherence and characteristics, which historical studies have in the variety of historical change and development. This main and fundamental principle is the sense criterium, which governs the relationship between past and present, within which the past gets its significance as "history."

During most of the periods of its development historical studies has mainly reflected the cognitive dimension of itself on the level of metahistory. It was eager to legitimate its "scientific" status and its claims for truth and objectivity, thus participating in the cultural prestige of "science" as the most convincing form, in which knowledge and cognition can serve human life. This has been done in a broad variety of different conceptualizations of this "scientific character." In most of these manifestations historical studies claimed for a certain epistemological and methodological autonomy in the field of the academic disciplines. Doing so, it remained aware of some noncognitive elements still valid and influential in the work of historical studies, mainly in history writing. But only after the linguistic turn these elements and factors have been seen as being as important as the cognitive ones.

This can be made plausible in the proposed structure of the five factors in the schema of historical studies (figure 8.1), if one looks at specific relationships between them.[7]

1. In the relationship between interest and concepts historical thinking is originated as a fundamental semantic strategy of symbolizing time by relating it to human activity and suffering in a meaningful and sense bearing way. In this realm of the human mind principle criteria of meaning and sense of history are decided upon.
2. In the relationship between concepts and methods historical thinking is mainly committed to a cognitive strategy of producing historical knowledge. (This strategy constitutes under certain conditions of modernity the "scientific" character of historical studies. It subjugates the discourse of history under the rules of methodical argumentation, conceptual language, control by experience, and gaining consent and agreement by rational means.)
3. In the relationship between methods and forms an aesthetic strategy of historical representation takes place. Historical knowledge, based on experience, gets its form in which it becomes an element of cultural communication on the temporal dimension of human life. Knowledge of the past gets the features of present-day life and becomes furnished with its forces to move the human mind.
4. This communication is initiated within the relationship between the forms of representation and the functions of cultural orientation. Here historical thinking is ruled by a rhetorical strategy of offering cultural orientation.
5. Finally, in the relationship between interests and functions historical studies is committed to a political strategy of collective memory. It places the work of the historians into the struggle of power and recognition and makes it a necessary means of legitimizing or delegitimizing all forms of domination and government. Taking all the strategies together, historical thinking can be made visible as a complex synthesis of dealing with the past in five different dimensions: semantics, cognition, aesthetics, rhetoric, and politics. This synthesis stand for an order of history as an integral part of culture.

The proposed scheme of the constitutive factors of historical studies shows how the work of historians is influenced by and related to practical life on the one hand, and how it has its own realm for gaining knowledge beyond the practical purposes of life orientation on the other. It makes plausible the reason for history being rewritten—according to the changes in interests and functions of historical knowledge in human life—and why, at the same time, there is a development, even a progress, in the cognitive strategy for getting knowledge about the past. With this schema it is possible to pick up the tension between modernity and postmodernity and the challenge of the discussion on memory and to bring into interdisciplinary self-reflection of historical studies, thus moving it toward a deeper and more up-to-date awareness of itself.

It is my intention to correct misleading confrontations. Most of the postmodernist attitudes to history and historical studies have brought about the impression that there is a strong contradiction between modern and postmodern elements of historical thinking. Following the guidelines of the proposed schema this contradiction can at least be relativized, and even changed into a strategy for argumentation, which opens up a perspective of development of historical studies, in which modern and postmodern features can be synthesized.[8] The same is true in respect to the distinction between memory and history: the liveliness and relevance of memory very often have been seen as contradictory to the strength and rationality of historical knowledge gained by methodical research. There seems to be a contradiction between serving human life, even being an element of it, on the one hand, and putting memory into the cages of accumulated knowledge without a direct function in practical life, on the other. This contradiction makes us forget the fundamental interrelationship between memory and history. It produces a wrong awareness of historical studies as a cognitive procedure. It is the intention of the following arguments to overcome this opposition of arguments in favour of a discourse which shows how historical studies can develop and gain a new self-awareness according to its new perspectives and strategies of its work.

As every scheme illuminates complex phenomena and at the same time takes parts of it outside our awareness, it should be briefly indicated that there are elements in dealing historically with the past, that are not addressed by the proposed system of principles: in the realm of constitutive interests there is already an "experience" of the past. It is substantially different from the experience treated methodically in the realm of empirical research. The past has already been present when historical thinking starts with questions, initiated by needs for and interests in historical memory. It plays an important role in shaping these interests and needs. This is the case in very different forms: as an effective tradition, as a fascination of alterity, as a traumatic pressure and even as forgetfulness, which, nevertheless, keeps the past alive by suppressing it.

Modernity—the strong order of history

Modernization in respect of the principle of historical sense means at the same time a new concept of history and a new approach to the empirical evidence of the past. The new concept consists of a category that discloses the temporal relation between past, present, and future by an idea of a comprehensive internal connection called "the history."[9] History as a totality of the temporal change of man and world is categorized by the idea of "progress" or "development." The new approach is categorized by rational means of cognition. They enable the historian to disclose the moving forces of temporal change of the human world and constitute the entire entity and totality of "the history."

Modernity in historical thinking has brought about the idea of "the" history. Before the middle of the eighteenth century one couldn't speak of anything like "the" history. Instead of this totality or temporal whole, comprising past, present and future, there were only histories, stories, and historiographies, but not the idea that there is a phenomenon called "the history." "The" history means a factual entity of temporal change, which internally combines past, present, and future into one comprising totality of time. The late enlightenment has conceptualized this entity with the historical category of progress. Historicism has stuck to it and has changed its categorical form into the concept of "development," and modern historical studies has explicated it with different concepts of structural change. The development of historical studies can be described as a development in conceptualizing this entity called *the history*. Historicism thought that "the history" is constituted by the mental and spiritual forces of human activity. In the German language this force has been called "*Geist*," and it has given the humanities the name of "*Geisteswissenschaften*." The Annales School, Marxism, and the various concepts of modern historical studies as societal or structural history have brought about different and much more complex concepts of the entity, which we call "the" history. In a critical turn against the historicist idealistic idea of history they understand history as constituted by a very complex relationship between material and mental forces.

The second essential of historical sense, which is common to all its manifestations of historical thinking in the process of modernization, is method. The academically professionalized historians are more or less convinced that there is a rational method that enables them to find out by research, (in Ranke's famous words) "what really has happened."[10] Using the methods of research will bring about insight into that very entity called "the" history. The first step of conceptualizing historical method was taken in the Enlightenment when the procedures of source critique were systematized. The next step was done by historicism which, for the first time, brought about the idea of historical interpretation as the essential operation of research. (Many historians today still think that the essential methodical operation of historical studies is source critique – which means that they haven't yet learnt the methodological lesson of historicism.) Interpretation changes the mere facts, the findings of source critique, into historical facts by putting them together along the line of the idea of history as a meaningful temporal relationship of past, present, and future. Interpretation transforms empirical evidence into history.

The last step of developing historical method was the already-mentioned step of theoretization. In the Annales School theoretization was done mainly implicitly, whereas in Marxism and in social or societal history it was done explicitly, as it was proposed and paradigmatically realized by Max Weber.

Postmodernism—the broken order of history

Postmodernism is first of all a critique of the principles of modern historical thinking. On the level of the constitutive principles of historical sense this criticism says that the modern idea of the history is nothing but an eurocentric ideology without any factual evidence. Since it destroys all other forms of cultural identity it is not at all a historical thought mainly guided by rational argument (reason, method, and theory), but by the will of the European nations to have power over the rest of the world. Therefore it is ideological, it is destructive, and it doesn't open up a future perspective at all. The only future perspective of this concept of history, based on the idea of progress and development, is that of a catastrophy.

The postmodernist concept of history radically and totally negates the idea that there is anything like one single and comprising historical process of the development of humankind. History is not a factual entity at all: it is nothing but a fictional image. According to this, postmodern metahistory describes the principles of historical thinking a completely different manner: it does not emphasize method in the form of rational argumentation and rules of empirical research, but it stresses the poetics and the rhetoric of narration. So the concept of postmodern historical thought is the opposite of modern historical studies.

In its modern form historical thinking furnishes human activity with an orienting idea of temporal change, which can be used as a guideline for changing the world and bringing about a collective identity at the same time. Postmodernism destroys the plausibility of this orientation function and replaces orientation by imagination. Since there is no real entity called "the" history, this historical imagination is constituted by elements of fiction. So in principle it cannot orientate practical activity, (a practical activity, oriented by fictions, will end in complete disaster). But, nevertheless, according to my five principles of historical cognition, there must be an orientation function. Postmodernity in history indeed offers an orientation function, but a very specific one: it is a way of orientating human life comparable to dreams. Psychoanalysis has taught us that we need dreams in order to come to terms with reality. And to me, this seems to be the orientation function of postmodernist historiography and theory of history. In a way, it is a compensation of negative results of modernization; it is an aesthetic consolation brought about by historical memory in respect to the crisis of progress and to the threat of a catastrophy into which a simple continuation of the process of modernization will lead the world.

What are the new elements of historical thought brought about by postmodernism in historical studies? There is a very essential point, which defines the difference between a postmodern form of historical thought and a modern one. A modern form of historical thought realizes a genetic connection between past and present by its concept of temporal change. Historical thinking gives the impression that the past moves toward the present-day situation. This genetical connection between past and present is completely destroyed and negated by postmodern historiography. By doing so postmodernism claims to give back to the past its own dignity.

There is a German word, that expresses this dignity to be won by cutting the genetic ties between past and present: "Eigensinn."[11] Its meaning combines significance of its own with elements of obstinacy and stubbornness. It is an obstinacy against the integration of past forms of human life into a process, leading to our own life form. *Eigensinn* means a significance against this integration. Little children who don't like to obey their parents are *eigensinnig*, they react against their parents' will by a stubborn activity of their own. This is the way the past is presented by postmodern historiography. We should not forget that already Leopold von Ranke, the leading German representative of historicism, has formulated a principle of *Eigensinn* by saying: "Jede Epoche ist unmittelbar zu Gott."[12] But Ranke, at the same time, always accepted the idea of a comprising temporal development bringing past, present and future together in the totality of "the" history.[13] This idea is completely refuted in the postmodern concept of history and historiography. So postmodern historiography is strongly fighting against the concept of development. The most radical conceptualization of this negation of development can be found in Walter Benjamin's theory of history.[14] Here he speaks about the commitment of historical memory to a time concept, which he characterizes by the metaphorical expression of "the tiger's leap of the moment."[15] In this image every temporal chain between the different phenomena in the past is cut off in favor of a unique occurrence, thus gaining a substantial historical significance. In this temporally condensed significance it becomes apparent in present life through historical memory, like a tiger who jumps into our minds and brings about an irritation of our common consciousness in respect to the awareness of the temporal change of our lives. This is postmodernism *avant la lettre*. Here we can find the most interesting concept of antidevelopmental or antigenetic ideas of history.[16]

Postmodern historiography thus produces counterimages to the present-day situation. These counterimages are presented in new forms of historiography. We call them narrative, but this is a misleading term because every historiographical form of text is narrative. Besides this logical or epistemological meaning, narration means a specific form of historiographical presentation, which can be distinguished from others. "Narrative" means a historiographical presentation, that prefers events and interactions. If we compare Natalie Davis' story of the return of Martin Guerre[17] to the productions in the usual academic form of social and economic history, loaded with footnotes, statistics, and graphics, we can understand the quality of a "narrative" historiography. Narration stands against explanation,[18] lively description against abstract analysis, or—to use a revitalized metaphorical dichotomy—warm empathy against cold theory.

Another specific trait of postmodern historiography is microhistory. As the very postmodern form of presenting history it is opposed to macrohistory. A single person like Menocchio[19] or Martin Guèrre, and not a society or a class are shown; a life span or even only a few days, instead of an epoch or a long-run development; one day[20] and not a century; a small village and not a state or an empire are dealt with. This is the subject matter of postmodern historiography.

Postmodern historiography claims to have developed a new and different research strategy. It is opposed to developing and using theoretical concepts. In order to characterize its new methical approach to the past, postmodern historians like to quote the cultural anthropologist Clifford Geertz who proposed "thick description" instead of theory construction.[21] "Thick description" is the methical means by which the past will gain its own significance, its *Eigensinn*. The past will no longer be submitted to genetic structures, by which it is combined by modern historical thinking with the present-day situation in one line of historical development.

This turn against genetic theories is essentially bound to a new hermeneutical approach to inquiring into the lives of people in the past. Historians have become less interested in reconstructing the structural conditions of human life in the past and by doing so explaining the real lives of the people. But instead, they stress the way the people experienced and interpreted their own world. They inquire into the awareness of life conditions by the people in question, thus trying to give them back a cultural autonomy for dealing with their own world in their own specific way, which is different from ours. The paradigmatic methical strategy of this new approach to the people's own awareness and understanding is oral history.

In respect to the content of historical commemoration one can say that postmodern historiography is in favor of the victims of modernization, mainly of the lower classes, minorities, and not to be forgotten, is in favor of women. Women's and gender history is not in all parts, but in many parts closely related to the postmodern concept of historical studies. In the leading conceptualizations of historical experience postmodern historiography gets its inspirations from cultural anthropology and ethnology. In respect to the orientationfunction of historical commemoration postmodern historical studies present a growing interest in the aesthetic quality of historical experience. History has to produce a picture, an image of the past with an aesthetic quality.

Order through memory?

The thematization of historical memory came alongside with the postmodern attitudes in history. It could be understood as an attempt to open up a new source for historical sense generation. It has disclosed new plausibilities, which are grounded in the fundamental and universal cultural function of memory as a means of identity building and orienting practical life. Metahistory, indeed, should start its work of reflecting, criticizing, and legitimating the principles of historical studies with an analysis of memory as the root of historical thinking. Doing so it supports the postmodern attitude toward the sense-creating creativity of the human mind, set into work by those who recall and represent the past in order to live their present-day lives. It affirms imagination and other noncognitive forces of the human mind, such as politics, as essential for recalling the past and placing it through memory into the moving mental forces of present-day life.

In the traditional forms of metahistory the rootedness of historical cognition in practical life and its dependence upon it has been discussed mainly as a problem of standpoints and perspectives to be solved in accordance to claims of truth and objectivity with which historical studies transmit the use of history for practical purposes into the realm of solid and valid knowledge of the past.[22] By thematizing memory historical studies get a much broader and deeper insight into their relationship to contemporary practical life. They disclose the mental force of their guiding sense principle that they could not become aware of simply by asking for truth and objectivity as a matter of the method of empirical research. They have to realize that the cognitive procedures of gaining solid and valid knowledge out of the empirical evidence of the past is always substantially related to aesthetic principles of representing and to political principles of using the past in the cultural framework of present-day life human activities. Thus, realizing memory as a source for a powerful constitution of sense criteria, historical studies can accept the postmodern emphasis on aesthetics and rhetorics as a necessary contribution to its metatheoretical self-understanding.

On the other hand, metahistory is still committed to cognition as an element of making sense of history, which cannot be neglected at all (as long as cognition is a necessary element of orienting human life). Doing so, it reaffirms the methodical rationality of historical thinking by placing it into the depths of memory itself. There is no memory whatsoever without a claim for plausibility, and this claim is grounded on two elements: the transsubjective element of experience and the intersubjective element of consent. Memory is essentially related to experience; only the one-sidedness of postmodern criticism has neglected this essential. So in the metahistorical discourse of the last decades memory could be handled as a strong argument in favor of an unlimited subjectivism categorically conceptualized by the term "fiction." This term characterizes the ontological status of history as a matter of memory and representation. Stressing the essential relationship of memory and experience metahistory thus can resubstantiate the methodical rules of historical research as a specific way of treating experience. Doing so the rationality of the historical method can no longer be seen as alienating and reifying history, or as depriving it of its use for human life. The order of history brought about by the creative forces of the human mind in recalling and representing the past brings back the solidity of being grounded in experience.

Intersubjectivity is the other element of historical sense, which cannot be neglected in recalling and representing the past through the mental forces of human memory. History cannot play its cultural role without the consent of those to whom it is addressed. If it was realized as mere fiction, immediately it would lose its cultural power. But its plausibility not only depends upon its relationship to experience. It depends also upon its relationship to norms and values as elements of historical sense, that are shared by the community to which it is addressed. In this respect metahistory has to reflect the rules of discourse, which bring about intersubjective consent as methodical elements of historical cognition. This will tie it back to modernity, as modernity can be explicated as a certain mode of dealing with norms and values. The formal structure of universal validity itself is a sense-building principle in historical cognition. This principle is rooted in the fundamental and constitutive intent to consent and agreement of historical memory. Thus, history gains a normative order with which it can fulfill its cultural function.

Regaining the order of history

There have been only a few attempts by metahistory to bring about this new self-awareness of mediating and synthesizing modern and postmodern features of historical by memory. Concerning the constitutive principle of historical sense the main question remains: How can the universalist approach of modernity towards history become mediated with the ideology critique and the particularist approach of postmodernity?

The postmodernist critique of the concept of "the history" has to be taken very seriously. I think we have to accept this criticism insofar as it pointed at an ideological generalization of one history to "the" history. And this has really been the case in the process of modernization from the Enlightenment until now. So I think we have to concede that there is only a multitude of histories and not "the" history as a factual entity. But, nevertheless,—and this is my modernist point of this argument—we need an idea of the unity of historical experience. Otherwise historical thinking will lead into complete relativism. And the price for relativism is too high. We still need historical categories of logical reasons; without them we can't think historically. Additionally, we need a concept of history, that meets the topical experience of the growing one-world. (To emphasize micro-history while living in a macro-historical process sounds like pushing away a challenging experience instead of meeting it by historical interpretation.)

But how can we bring about a concept of the universality of historical development and, at the same time, accept that there is only a multitude of different histories or a multiperspectivity in historical thinking? Within the diversity of historical perspectives a unity of history can only be brought about by universal values in the methodical operation of historical interpretation. The point is that we need a leading value-system, a universal valuesystem, that affirms the differences of cultures. I think that there is a fundamental value, that can be brought into a strategy of historical interpretation; a value that is both universal and at the same time legitimates multiperspectivity and difference. I think of a normative principle of mutual acknowledgement and recognition of differences in culture. This principle can be elaborated into a cognitive structure, that will strengthen the hermeneutical element of historical method, and this structure, which bring about a new approach to historical experience, that synthesizes the unity of mankind and temporal development on the one hand, and the variety and multitude of cultures on the other.

Based on such a principle of historical sense, historical studies can develop a metatheoretical self-understanding, by which it does not only meet the challenges of its time at the beginning of the third millennium, but also contribute to the auspices of the third, in which humanness remains an issue of the order of history

Notes

1. Michael Quirin, *Liu Zhiji und das Chun Qiu*, Frankfurt am Main, 1987, 75f. (When they discuss the entire connexions and mark the important lines the presentations of the scholars are only rarely characterized by comprehensive understanding, and their principles don't meet the decisive points).
2. Cf. Horst Walter Blanke, Dirk Fleischer, Jörn Rüsen, "Theory of History in Historical Lectures: The German Tradition of Historik 1750–1900," in *History and Theory* 23 (1984), 331–56.
3. This is one of the main points of Blanke and Fleischer, eds., *Theoretiker der deutschen Aufklärungshistorie*, 2 vols, Stuttgart/Bad Cannstatt, 1990; cf. idem, *Aufklärung und His-*

torik. Aufsätze zur Entwicklung der Geschichtswissenschaft, Kirchengeschichte und Geschichtstheorie in der deutschen Aufklärung, Waltrop, 1991.
4. The classical text in the German tradition is Droysen, *Historik*. English translation of the "Grundriß" (the part given to the students as a scheme of the main argument): *Outline of the Principles of History*, Boston, 1893, reprint New York, 1967.
5. Cf. Blanke, Fleischer, Rüsen, "Theory of History in Historical Lectures," 331–56; also in Rüsen, *Studies in Metahistory*, 97–128.
6. Thomas S. Kuhn, *The Structure of Scientific Revolution*, Chicago, 1962.
7. I am deeply grateful to Achim Mittag for his stimulating suggestion to complete my concept of this interrelationship.
8. Cf. Jörn Rüsen, "Historical enlightenment in the age of postmodernism: history in the age of the 'new unintelligibility'," in idem, *Studies in Metahistory*, 221–39; Jörn Rüsen, "Historical studies between modernity and postmodernity," *South African Journal of Philosophy* 13 (1994), 183–89; I use some parts of this text in the later parts of my chapter.
9. I prefer the term "the history" according to the German "die Geschichte," although it is not used in English. The word "History" (with capital H) might be misunderstood.
10. "… wie es eigentlich gewesen," Ranke, *Geschichten*, p. VII.
11. Cf. the reflection about this word in Alf Lüdtke, *Eigen-Sinn. Fabrikalltag, Arbeitserfahrungen und Politik vom Kaiserreich bis in den Faschismus*, Hamburg, 1993, especially 9 sqq.
12. (Every epoch is immediately related to God.) Leopold von Ranke, *Über die Epochen der neueren Geschichte*, ed. T. Schieder and H. Berding, Aus Werk und Nachlaß, vol. 2, Munich, 1971, 59.
13. In the same text where the just quoted word is said, we find the following passage: "In der Herbeiziehung der verschiedenen Nationen und der Individuen zur Idee der Menschheit und der Kultur ist der Fortschritt ein unbedingter;" (Ibid., 80). (In attracting the different nations and individuals to the idea of humankind and culture there is an unconditional progress.)
14. Walter Benjamin, "Über den Begriff der Geschichte," in *Gesammelte Schriften*, vol. I, 2, Frankfurt am Main, 1991, 691–704.
15. Ibid., 694, 701.
16. Cf., Lutz Niethammers very enlightening interpretation of Benjamin's theory of history; *Posthistoire. Ist die Geschichte zu Ende?*, Reinbek, 1989, 116 sqq. [Lutz Niethammer, *Posthistoire: Has History come to an End?*, London, 1992].
17. Natalie Z. Davis, *The return of Martin Guerre*, Cambridge, MA, 1983.
18. Cf., Lawrence Stone, "The Revival of Narrative: Reflections on a New Old History," *Past and Present* 85 (1979), 3–24.
19. Carlo Ginzburg, *The Cheese and the Worms*, Baltimore, 1980.
20. George Duby, *Der Sonntag von Bouvines*, Berlin, 1988.
21. Clifford Geertz, "Thick Description: Toward an Interpretative Theory of Culture," in idem, *The Interpretation of Cults Selected Essays*, New York, 1973, 3–30.
22. Cf., Reinhart Koselleck, Wolfgang Mommsen, Jörn Rüsen, eds., *Objektivität und Parteilichkeit,* Beiträge zur Historik, vol. 1, Munich, 1977.

III: ORIENTATION

Chapter 9

Historical Thinking as *Trauerarbeit*: Burckhardt's Answer to a Question of our Time

> Hörst du den ewigen Jammer, der nie sich stillt?
> Verschmachtet ist in Plagen der Erdenball—
> Doch ausgelitten ist sein Elend—
> Aber wer endet die Ewigkeiten?
>
> Jacob Burckhardt[1]

At the end of the millennium—the challenge of historical experience

Some years ago the Getty Research Institute for the History of Art and the Humanities organized a conference at the Warburg Institute on "Memory, History, Narrative: A comparative inquiry into the representation of crisis." At the end of this conference Saul Friedländer tried to summarize the main issues and the decisive points of view concerning the Western concept of history and the idea of its practical function today. He said that looking back at the catastrophes of the twentieth century one has to raise the question again: "What is the nature of human nature?"

It is this question on which modern intellectual life has focussed its endeavor to understand and to interpret the human world, and even to answer the decisive philosophical questions. Kant, for example, has distilled the three key questions of philosophy, "What can I know?," "What shall I do?," and "What can I hope for?," ("Was kann ich wissen?," "Was soll ich tun?," "Was darf ich hoffen?'") into one question: "What is the human being?" (Was ist der Mensch?).[2] The work of historical studies in the humanities has been anthropologically founded and framed. Apparently, Friedländer was not convinced that this modern foundation of the humanities was sufficient to meet the chal-

---

Notes for this section begin on page 158.

lenges of twentieth-century history of which we are aware at the start of the third millennium.

Indeed, there is a strong indication that the experience of contemporary history challenges our ability to conceptualize an anthropological pattern of historical significance, into which our own past would fit in such a way that we can come to terms with it and can develop a reliable future perspective. It is not by chance that "Trauma" has become one of the central issues of metahistorical discussion.[3] This category has opened our eyes to a fundamental breakdown and lack of sense and meaning in dealing with the past and shaping acceptable features of human identity.

A similar symptom of an unsolved problem in the categorical foundations of historical thinking is Michel Foucault's declaration of the end of man in history.[4] It expresses the shortcomings of the hitherto developed anthropological patterns of historical thinking, in which basic principles of sense and meaning enabled the human mind to come to terms with the experience of the past in the form of a sense-bearing and meaningful history. Here past and present were combined into a unity of temporal development into which the present-day activities could be placed in such a way that they provided a guiding future perspective. Today the traditional criteria of historical sense in modern Western societies have lost their credibility: i.e. civilization, progress, and development combined with ideas of humanity and freedom have guided the historians' work for 200 years. They are still effective in everyday-life orientations and are implicit in many works of historiography as well, but on the level of deliberate and reflective historical thought they have been put more and more into radical doubt.

The limits of these sense criteria of the anthropological paradigm of history become evident when the horrific experiences of contemporary history, the most challenging of which is the Holocaust, are concerned. Our present-day awareness of them initiates an attempt to fundamentally reconceptualize our relationship to the past which we call "history."[5]

History is a narrative bridge that follows the natural stream of time, starting from the past and leading into the future. This mental bridge of historical narration serves to orient our activity in the sphere of practical life, as well as in the internal life of the human self.[6] But bridges of this kind that have been built and used in our historical culture are now broken. On the cultural level of sense and meaning time cannot flow any longer. Dan Diner has expressed this rupture of time vis-à-vis the Holocaust with the metaphor of a "bottled up time." He argues that we cannot think of a convincing relationship of the Holocaust to a previous and to a later time in a way in which a comprehensive idea of temporal change and development could provide any historical meaning of it.[7] The limits of such an idea become evident when the horrific experiences of contemporary history are in concern. It would be completely misleading if one picked up this disturbing quality of the Holocaust and similar catastrophes in a way that would put it outside usual historical thinking into a metahistorical or transhistorical field close to myth and religion.[8] In this case history and historical thinking would remain untouched by one of the central experiences and events in the twentieth century. The opposite should be the case. The Holocaust should be regarded as a historical experience of metahistorical importance in order to reshape our framework of reference within which we pursue the discourse of history. By doing this, our historical perspective will change and we will become aware of a fundamentally catastrophic dimension of history which has not yet been conceptualized in the established discourse of professional historians.[9]

How can we treat this experience of a loss and lack of historical meaning in relation to the "bottled up time" of the catastrophes of our century? By the very act of acknowledging it we effectively rule out all notions of a historical sense and meaning. Meeting it prevents a concept of a comprehensive continuity of those elements of human activity that constitute collective and personal identity. In modern historical culture these identity-constituting principles of historical experience and significance are centred around an idea of humanness. To be a human being is in itself a value of universal validity shaping the experience of the past into a feature of oneself, providing sameness and coherence of one's own self in the temporal changes of the world. Humanness has been an elementary principle of recognition and acknowledgement, an effective presupposition of understanding and communication in the cultural life of modern societies.[10] Droysen, for example, explicated history as a mirror of experience which furnishes everybody who looks into it with an awareness of the centre of his or her self: "History is the gnôthi sautón of humankind, its conscience."[11]

This presupposition has become uncertain now, and even seems to vanish. The mirror of history destroys our self-awareness based on this principle of humanness. This is a challenge to the humanities as it prevents the coherence of selfness without which social life is impossible. How can we overcome its loss? Vis-à-vis the metahistorical consequences of the experiences of contemporary history we cannot simply restitute humanism as a basis for identity building and leave it to the good will of the humanists.

I would like to contribute to the general effort currently being made to deal with this uncertainty through a specific argument about the role of history. History provides the possibility of treating the loss of certainty concerning our self-understanding as human beings, for it has always represented the potential of the human mind to come to terms with ruptures of continuity and with uncertainties in presumed concepts of cultural identity. To meet the challenge, history does not simply have to integrate new realms of experience into its interpretative work; its modes of recognition and representation should reflect this interpretative work. I would like to propose a specific mode of historical thinking as an answer to the challenge of the loss of humanness in contemporary history: mourning as a mental operation of historical consciousness.

Mourning is a general and fundamental cultural practice of dealing with a loss in the realm of self-esteem, of subjectivity. So it seems obvious to commit historical thinking to mourn the loss of basic principles of historical identity, cognition and representation in order to regain them in a new form. It is all the more astonishing that we do not know what mourning could mean in the realm of the established strategies and functions of historical consciousness. Mourning can be found in modern societies, of course, but it is not an established procedure of a genuine historical culture. There is an established theory of mourning in psychoanalysis, but only very few attempts have been made to translate it into the specific modes of historical thinking, and even less to use it as a cognitive strategy in historical studies.[12] The reason for this may be that mourning has not been considered as more than only an emotional operation, so it has still to be reflected and pursued as a mode of thinking and cognition as well.[13] On the level of cultural tradition the practice of mourning is influenced by religious ideas of reconciliation, but it is quite obvious that they fail to meet the specific qualities of catastrophes like the Holocaust, which do not bear any concept of healing and reconciliation.[14] Therefore we find an intellectual reluctance to pick up mourning as a major subject or a way of meeting the challenges of contemporary history through historical thinking.[15]

This lack of tried and proven intellectual practices of mourning in the discourse of history leads us to inquire into the history of historical thinking and historiography. Is there any chance of finding this problem already treated here, so that we can pick up an already established strategy of historical thinking as an act of mourning? If we can, we will not be leaving the discourse of historical studies in dealing with mourning as a fundamental principle of historical thinking, but will be continuing it, thus confirming its function as a means of cultural orientation and identity building. Then we can develop it further into a mode of thinking that may meet the challenge of our historical awareness at the end of the millennium.

I think that Jacob Burckhardt's work in historiography, as well as in metahistory, provides us with such a chance. Burckhardt has taught us to look into well-known texts over and over again with great alertness so that we may find a first-rate fact hidden in it.[16] I would like to apply Burckhardt's advice concerning Thukydides to study his own work. Doing so I will rely mainly on his lectures "On the Study of History," but I think that his historiographical work, above all the "Culture of the Renaissance in Italy" and his "Cultural History of Greece," can serve as a "practical" complement and proof of the "theoretical" argument concerning basic sense criteria of historical thinking.

A pathological view of history

Burckhardt did not speak of mourning as a historical category at all. But, nevertheless, he had already picked up the matter. He uses keywords which form a network of significance by which historical thinking comes close to mourning:

misery (*Elend*), despair (*Verzweiflung*), lamentation (*Jammer*), suffering (*Dulden, Leiden*), consolation (*Trost*). One can easily find the constitutive elements of mourning in Burckhardt's way of doing history: from loss as a rupture of subjectivity to working the rupture through and regaining coherence in subjectivity.

Burckhardt's historical thinking is moulded by the following three constitutive mental elements:

1. The experience of a fundamental loss of humanness in the temporal changes of the human world, that is inspired by his awareness of modernity as a crisis of culture.
2. The method of working through this experience by means of conceptual thinking, thus shaping the experience of the past into an idea of history as "of culture"[17] into a totality of time. It represents "the history of the life and suffering of mankind as a whole;"[18]
3. The presentation of history as a bridge across the gap of the loss, which provides present-day life with an orientating idea of historical continuity. It allows a "compensation" of the lost humanness and offers a valid ground for self-esteem and a principle for cultural identity.

The loss of humanness

First of all, one has to realize that Burckhardt's relationship to modernity is that of a fundamental crisis.[19] He interprets the revolutionary age of his time as a loss of the only reliable principles of cultural life that were achieved in the long course of European history from Ancient Greek times through a continuation of permanent renewals and realizations of cultural creativity along the line of individualism and personal freedom. Burckhardt thinks of European history as a continuity of culture originating in antiquity and reaching up to his own time. "The continuum is magnificent ... Exclusively here the postulates of the spirit become realized; only here development takes place and no absolute fall but only transformations."[20] But the revolutionary era is seen by Burckhardt as a definite end of this continuum, a radical break of cultural continuity constituting Europe as a place for individualism and spiritual freedom in different realms of human life: in education, society, politics, and culture. It is the idea of individualistic "*Bildung*" brought about by a creative will of freedom and self-determination which is realized in a wide variety of cultural forms, the rise and fall of which represent the creative force of the human mind. Modernization—as it is seen by Burckhardt—brings this continuity to a definite end.

We can use Max Weber's interpretation of modernity[21] and characterize Burckhardt's awareness of the crisis of modernity as a loss of value rationality which has founded cultural creativity in the course of time; now it is dissolving into a value-free instrumental rationality, driven by a blind will to power and a blind need for material goods. So the accelerating process of modernization that Burckhardt could witness as a destiny of his own world was seen by him under the dominant category of "loss"—a loss of the specific qualities of cultural life that constitute the essence of history, and accordingly the essence of historical identity made up by the totality of the cultural creations of Europe.

It is important and even decisive for the purpose of my argument that Burckhardt does not look at this loss of culture and cultural continuity in his time as if there was something in the past which stands for its opposite, as if a human way of life of the past could serve as a paradigm to regain the lost cultural qualities of human life in the future. This kind of critique of modernity is well known: it is simply antimodern and reactionary. In this case modern culture is completely condemned, and the whole effort of historical thinking is to go back to the lost past in order to evoke it or to restitute it in a more or less fundamentalist way. Burckhardt's historical thinking is beyond this simple dichotomy of gain and loss, distinguished by temporal differences. Burckhardt does not simply play off the intact past against the rotten present, but—and this is my point—for him the past itself is determined by the same destructive elements of human nature, even in its prime times of cultural flourishing. Those tendencies of human activity which have brought about the radical breakdown of cultural continuity in his time have always been effective in human history. Therefore there is no valid and lasting historical paradigm for realizing humanness in a comprehensive and coherent formation of culture.

This can easily be proved by Burckhardt's presentation of the origin of modern culture,[22] the Renaissance. Here humanness had reached its most advanced realization in all branches of cultural life: here for the first time the humans and humankind had been completely recognized in their deepest essence.[23] The Renaissance stands for the "recognition of the individual on all levels," for the "development of personality." "The immortal art" of the Renaissance could "present the perfect human being in his very essence as well as in his characteristic appearance."[24] Here the highest forms of human subjectivity and—as the other side of the same cultural advancement—the approach of objectivity toward nature and the human world were worked; Europe has been committed to this ever since.

At the same time, Burckhardt recognized the Renaissance as an "incredible amount of immorality:"[25] Crime in a new "specific personal consistency,"[26] an "excess of unlimited egoism"[27] and other unbound destructive forces of the will to power were integral parts of the "modern Italian mind," which was "to become a paradigmatic model for the Occident."[28] The spirit of freedom to be admired in great works of art originated in a context of political violence; they belong to "lawless political conditions which look like a glorious and permanent victory of the evil."[29]

So Burckhardt's way of treating the crisis of his time is not a simple reaction, but an analysis and a critique of modernity that can be characterized by the Freudian concept of "working through." Burckhardt has worked through the threatening experience of cultural discontinuity as a loss of humanness in his time by conceptualising a general theory of history, which he characterized as "pathological." He inscribed the loss of coherent humanness in his time into the general signature of history itself. He developed an anthropological theory of human historicity, explicating the temporal character of human life in such a way that it constitutes the permanent change of human forms of life, and principally prevents the possibility of realizing the highest value of humanness in any form of human life in a full and unbroken way. Burckhardt commits historical thinking to "the one point accessible to us, the one internal centre of all things—man, suffering, striving, doing as he is and was and ever shall be. Hence our study will, in a certain sense, be pathological in kind." [30] Burckhardt transformed the experience of loss into the historical category of suffering.

Working through the loss

This transformation is the first step of working through the loss of continuity and coherence in the identity-building features of modern history. For Burckhardt, human historicity is principally determined by misery, despair, suffering, and lamentation.[31] As a leitmotif he permanently points to the human costs of establishing empires or of any political activity whatever, of economic competition and the pursuit social inequality. Thus he writes of "a picture of horror when we imagine the sum of despair and misery which went to establish the old world Empires, for instance."[32] The resistance of the small subjugated peoples is mentioned as "ghastly last struggles of which all knowledge has been lost. Did they fight in vain?"[33] One could borrow one of Burckhardt's own metaphors and characterize his idea of human creativity as building culture in the "smoking ruins of the world."[34] In respect to fourteenth-century Italy—the paradigmatic origin of European culture to which Burckhardt himself feels committed—he writes that the "misdeeds" of political violence in the Italian states—one of the conditions, in his view, of the cultural creativity of the Renaissance—"cried forth loudly."[35]

Burckhardt relates this suffering to human nature which is present and effective in all historical changes of the human world. History is anthropologically rooted in a force of evil, which originates from human nature itself. In his explication of these constitutive evil forces of human historicity Burckhardt comes very close to Darwin.

Excursus: Burckhardt and Darwin

At first glance there is a lot of Darwinism in Burckhardt's historical thought. He uses the concept of "race" in a naturalistic meaning,[36] and in his historiography as well as in his metahistorical considerations we can find references to natural forces guiding human activities explained by the drives of the struggle for existence ("Kampf ums Dasein"). Burckhardt never mentions Darwin, but uses at least one of his key concepts which underlines the role of nature in history: "The history of nature shows a terrifying struggle for existence; this struggle deeply reaches into human life and history."[37] The whole realm of history is determined by this natural force:

> It is violence, the right of the stronger on the weaker, already performed in the struggle for life, which covers the whole nature, the world of the animals as well as the world of the plants, continued in humankind by murder and robbery in earlier times, by driving out, respectively, by destruction or enslavery of weaker races, weaker peoples within the same race, of weaker state formations, of weaker social classes within the same state and nation.[38]

But Burckhardt is no Darwinist. On the contrary, for him the essence of history lies beyond the realm of nature and its driving forces. Culture transcends nature and creates the realm of humanness according to another logic than that of the struggle for survival, namely, the logic of creating works of art, able to produce delight in the midst of a world of suffering.[39]

Burckhardt regards the natural force of the struggle for survival as the substantially "evil" nature in the human world. This struggle is a powerful drive of human political activity, and it is evil in its essence: "But power is evil in itself."[40] Culture, the heart of history, is its nonnatural quality—one can even speak of its supranatural quality—is the opposite of this power and its necessities and constraints: it is freedom and self-determination of human beings through a drive that one could call the force of freedom effective in the specificity of the power (Potenz), of a culture different from the two other powers (Potenzen), state and religion.

I have demonstrated elsewhere[41] that Burckhardt, in an astonishingly systematic way, has developed a theory of human historicity in the form of a dialectical relationship between state, religion, and culture. In this relationship of the main powers of history, culture takes the place of freedom; it transforms the natural forces of the state and its supranatural compulsive negation by religion into its opposite, the spontaneous creativity of the human mind determining the human world by itself. Burckhardt treats the Darwinist element of history in an anti-Darwinist way: certainly, he interprets history not as a realization of natural forces in human life, but as a permanent struggle in overcoming these forces in favor of cultural creations which follow a logic different from that of the natural struggle for survival.

In accordance to the idealism of the nineteenth-century historicism Burckhardt calls these cultural forces of human activity, that transform nature into history, *Geist*. But in Burckhardt's ideas we can see one decisive difference from the idealistic philosophy of history: Hegel and his reluctant followers in historicism (like Ranke and Droysen) thought that the spirit can transform nature into culture without leftovers, so that the striving forces of human nature do not have naturalistic elements: the return of the creation to God[42] or the education of humanness[43] is beyond nature. For Burckhardt nature persists, and permanently and fundamentally qualifies, challenges and destroys this realm and its creations. With Hegel, Droysen and others Burckhardt shares the idea of the human spirit constituting the specificity of history, but he does not agree with their idea that the spirit can definitely negate and overcome nature. In Burckhardt's theory of history there is a permanent antagonism of nature and culture, and it is this antagonism that makes suffering a historical category. For Hegel, the wounds the human mind receives by the temporal change of the world heal without scars; for Burckhardt, the face of humanity, which can be seen in the totality of the cultural manifestation of the human spirit in history, is full of scars.

Recognition of this feature of historical experience is itself an act of working through the many occasions of loss of humanity in the realm of historical experience. It is the realization of the fact that the loss to human self-respect in the temporal changes of history is definite. History is not the place where it can be recovered. On the contrary, history holds up the evidence of reality against the human desire for self-respect. Therefore, we have good reason to apply Freud's concept of *Trauerarbeit* to Burckhardt's way of doing history. Burckhardt himself uses the term *Arbeit* (work) in order to distinguish the efforts of historical consciousness from the wishful thinking of fictional fantasy in pleasing the human mind with the feature of its historical realization.[44]

Consolation by historical memory

This work becomes plausible as a work of mourning if Burckhardt's concept of "consolation" is taken into account systematically. He develops his concept of culture as the power of freedom amidst its involvement in the necessities of political power and religious constraints. For him the destruction of humanness by the evil forces of the struggle for power provokes a reaction in past history itself. It is a reaction in the process of change that is brought about by this struggle and its nature-like drives. He uses the term "compensation," but not in the meaning of a substitute or a replacement by something that is easier to gain than the wanted object, but in the sense of "a survival of the wounded humankind with a transfer of its centre of gravity."[45] In Burckhardt's anti-Darwinist Darwinism, history is guided by the "secret law of compensation,"[46] which constitutes the continuity of cultural creation across the discontinuities, ruptures, and destructions brought about by the evil forces of human nature in history.[47]

Because of his anti-idealistic idealism, Burckhardt insists on this surviving spirit confronting the suffering of those who are the victims of change. The latter remain *unconsoled*. But—and this brings us to the core of Burckhardt's historical thinking—afterward, in the realm of historical memory, this consolation can take place. The suffering of the people makes sense if one sets it in the framework of a comprehensive whole which is visible—but only afterwards—as the continuity of the spirit amid the uninterrupted mutations of the human world: "Only the whole speaks, in all centuries that have left us records."[48] Burckhardt transcends the experience of suffering toward an aesthetic image of the cultural development of humankind by historical memory (however limited an Eurocentric perspective). Memory represents this image as encouragement for cultural creativity. It assures the suffering people of today of their creativity and gives them the confidence in their own self-respect as humans endowed with the specific human capacity for freedom and self-determined creation of their own world.

But real life remains in the grip of suffering. Even those who realize the highest representations of freedom and creativity in real life remain subjugated to the destructive forces which imprint every cultural creation: frailty (*Hinfälligkeit*), finiteness (*Endlichkeit*), and eventually futility (*Vergeblichkeit*) thus invalidating all human creations in the course of time. Only in the realm of cognition afterward can suffering be transcended: "What had been cheers and lamentations must now be turned into cognition."[49]

It is Burckhardt's declared intention not simply to repeat the lamentations of the victims, but to transform their suffering and lamentations into a cultural form in which they could make sense: it is the form of cognition by memory, "Our task is not to bemoan the great facts and conditions, but to recognize them."[50] The mode of this recognition is contemplation beyond the constraints of practical life. Here lies the problem: contemplating the suffering means to go beyond the realm of reality within which it takes place. Historical memory leaves the place where it is rooted and where it has its cultural function, it goes into the exile of untimeliness.[51] By using the concept of "consolation" in the crisis of his time Burckhardt sees contemplation as the only place for freedom brought about by historical commemoration. "The contemplation is our freedom amidst the consciousness of enormous general constraints and the stream of necessities."[52] In this concept freedom leaves the ground to the constraining forces hostile to the force of culture.

The cold comfort of aesthetic memory

Burckhardt paid a high price for the plausibility to the opportunity for consolation: that of leaving behind the real procedures of temporal change that have been brought about by human activity, and in which the historian participates by the mere fact of his or her contemporaneity. In the realm of aesthetics, those processes are left behind. The plausibility of consolation and, accordingly, the prevention of melancholy (in the sense of Freud) is purchased at the cost of an aestheticization of historical experience,[53] which deprives it of the very gravity of real life by transforming it into a matter of art. The paradigm of Burckhardt's recognition is a theatre spectacle, in which all the true humanity in the phenomena of history is presented against a dark background of suffering and lamentation. In order to overcome the crisis of humanity in his time by means of a historical work of mourning, Burckhardt mobilizes the cultural potentials of "*Kunstreligion*." Since this mourning is bound to an aesthetization of historical experience, it comes close to melancholy and to the corresponding inability to regain the historical identity that enables people to go about their daily business. The consoling spirit of historical mourning remains exiled from the social context in which the historian would keep the cultural forces of the human mind alive through his or her work of memory.

Burckhardt places the single personality with his or her constitutive self-respect as a human being in the totality of the cultural manifestations of the human mind, of which this single person is a unique realization and representation. His anti-Darwinist idealism gives every single human being "suffering, striving, doing," a place in the universe of the spirit. Each individual has a metaphysical commitment to this totality of humanness in the course of time: "Everything singular, including ourselves, exists not for its own sake, but for the sake of the whole past and the whole future."[54] This indeed is the peak of human identity circled around the highest value of humanity and its cultural forces. But Burckhardt can conceptualize this identity only in an aesthetical dimension beyond the abyss of real word activity. In this dimension, the changing pattern of historical time is arrested in the image of its superreal totality. The sense of history—a synthesis of fact and fiction presupposed by the simple existence of human beings—breaks into pieces:[55] on the one side, the gravity of historical experience, with the crying voices of human suffering in the smoking ruins of a world set on fire by the evil force of natural human impulses; on the other side the aesthetic delight (*Genuß*) of historical memory in which humanity presents its entire spirituality in a comprehensive continuity of free cultural creation. History in the past has always synthesized fact and fiction through works of culture that purport to orient human activity in the course of time. Burckhardt can maintain this synthesis only by exiling it to the imaginary domain where meaning is generated. The consequences are obvious: history becomes dehistoricized and even remythologized, and identity, though confirmed, is depoliticized. The natural forces of human activity remain as thriving, and as evil, as ever.

This historical idea of humanity is preserved from the necessities and obligations of practical life. Burckhardt thought that his representation of the past as history would enable those who accept his vision of humanness to recognize their real duties as citizens.[56] But he could not apply his concept of the totality of history as a coherent sense-bearing and meaningful image of human culture to the demands of practical activity. His idea of universal history contains a vision of a comprehensive continuity of the human mind in its cultural creations. But one element of human activity has no place in it: the contingency of the milieu in which it occurs, which constitutes so-called real events, and which, at the same time, challenges historical consciousness. Aestheticized meaning cannot be applied to the contingency of human suffering and striving, which Burckhardt has recognized as constitutive of history. By abandoning the real life of historical societies, the spirit of cultural creativity becomes only the ghost of historical memory.

This is where I see the limits of Burckhardt's concept of historical thinking as *Trauerarbeit*.[57] But one should not forget that Burckhardt provides us with a conceptual means of making sense of the past historically through the commemorating of the sufferings of people. Those who remember identify themselves with the suffering of the remembered. They do so by mourning. In face of the catastrophes of contemporary history, the basic value of humanity, which is an essential ingredient of the historical culture of our societies, can be preserved only by an effort of cognition in which we mourn the *loss* of humanity.

Burckhardt did not speak of mourning because he was consoled by his presupposition that suffering itself is a spiritual guarantee of humanity, and thus of a corresponding continuity of culture in the midst of discontinuity. Loss of confidence in this assumption is a signature of our historical culture at the end of the millennium. This loss is an urgent reason for us to mourn beyond the possibilities that Burckhardt, "our greatest teacher" (Nietzsche[58]), disclosed to us.

Notes

1. "Don't you hear the eternal lamentation, which never will be saturated? By pains the earth has died—yet its misery has ended—but who ends the eternities?" Jacob Burckhardt, Nach dem Weltgericht, quoted in Werner Kaegi, "Die Idee der Vergänglichkeit in der Jugendgeschichte Jacob Burckhardts," *Basler Zeitschrift für Geschichte und Altertumskunde* 42 (1943), 209–43.
2. *Logik*, Einleitung, 3rd paragraph. Wilhelm von Humboldt defines "the most basic task of our lives" as "to get for the concept of humankind the biggest content as possible in our minds," (die letzte Aufgabe unseres Daseins: dem Begriff der Menschheit in unsrer Person einen so großen Inhalt, als möglich zu verschaffen. "Theorie der Bildung des Menschen," in Wilhelm von Humboldt, *Werke in fünf Bänden*, vol. 1, Darmstadt, 1960, 235.
3. E.g. Dominick La Capra, *Representing the Holocaust: History, Theory, Trauma*, Ithaca, 1994; Saul Friedländer, "Trauma, Memory, and Transference," in Geoffrey H. Hartman, ed., *Holocaust Remembrance: the Shapes of Memory*, Oxford and Cambridge, 1994, 252–63; *Mittelweg 36, Zeitschrift des Hamburger Instituts f. Sozialforschung* 1992, Heft 3; theme issue, *Trauma*.
4. Michel Foucault, *Die Ordnung der Dinge. Eine Archäologie der Humanwissenschaften*, Frankfurt am Main, 1974, 412 and 460.
5. This reconceptualization is mainly done in the discourse of metahistory, whereas practical historical research and historiography still use the presuppositions of sense, meaning, and rational argument of historical studies grounded on the anthropological paradigm. Here the distractions are limited to some general declarations or remarks at the beginning or the end of the presentation.

6. Cf. Jörn Rüsen, "Historische Sinnbildung durch Erzählen. Eine Argumentsskizze zum narrativistischen Paradigma der Geschichtswissenschaft und der Geschichtsdidaktik im Blick auf nicht-narrative Faktoren," *Internationale Schulbuchforschung* 18 (1996), 501–44.
7. Dan Diner, "Zwischen Aporie und Apologie. Über Grenzen der Historisierbarkeit des Nationalsozialismus," in idem, ed., *Ist der Nationalsozialismus Geschichte? Zu Historisierung und Historikerstreit*, Frankfurt am Main, 1987, 62–73; cf., Dan Diner, "Gestaute Zeit." Massenvernichtung und jüdische Erzählstruktur', in idem, *Kreisläufe. Nationalsozialismus und Gedächtnis*, Berlin, 1955, 125–39. Diner expresses the impossibility of giving the Holocaust a meaningful narrative with the remarkable phrase: "Der Holocaust hat eine Statistik, aber kein Narrativ" (The Holocaust has a statitics, but no narrative), 126.
8. Ibid., cf. chap. 11.
9. A theoretical exception is Walter Benjamin's philosophy of history, but it has never become fully absorbed into the established guidelines of professional historical studies. A remarkable attempt at this reception is Lutz Niethammer, *Posthistoire. Ist die Geschichte zu Ende?*, Reinbek, 1989 [Lutz Niethammer, *Posthistoire: has history become to an end?* London, 1992].
10. Cf., Hans Erich Bödeker, "Menschheit, Humanität, Humanismus," in Otto Brunner, Werner Conze, Reinhart Koselleck, eds., *Geschichtliche Grundbegriffe. Historisches Lexikon zur politisch-sozialen Sprache in Deutschland*, vol. 3, Stuttgart, 1982, 1063–128.
11. "Die Geschichte ist das γνωθι σαυτον der Menschheit, ihr Gewissen" in Droysen, *Historik*, 442.
12. Cf., Eric L. Santner, *Stranded Objects. Mourning, Memory, and Film in Postwar Germany*, Ithaca, 1990; recently Irmgard Wagner, "Historischer Sinn zwischen Trauer und Melancholie: Freud, Lacan und Henry Adams," in Klaus E. Müller and Jörn Rüsen, eds., *Historische Sinnbildung. Problemstellungen, Zeitkonzepte, Wahrnehmungshorizonte, Darstellungsstrategien*, Reinbek, 1997, 408–32. Special attention has found Alexander and Margarete Mitscherlich, *Die Unfähigkeit zu trauern. Grundlagen kollektiven Verhaltens*, 1st edn., Munich, 1967 [Alexander and Margarete Mitscherlich, *The Inability to Mourn: Principles of Collective Behavior*, New York, 1975], but it has not been applied in historical studies.
13. I suppose that the critical theory of Adorno and others can be understood as an intellectual mode of mourning.
14. Cf., Jörn Rüsen, "Auschwitz—die Symbole der Authentizität," in Rüsen, *Zerbrechende Zeit*, 181–216.
15. Cf., for instance, Micha Brumlik, "Trauerarbeit und kollektive Erinnerung," in Manuel Köppen, ed., *Kunst und Literatur nach Auschwitz*, Berlin, 1993, 197–203.
16. "Es kann sein, daß im Thukydides z.B. eine Tatsache ersten Ranges liegt, die erst in hundert Jahren Jemand bemerken wird," Burckhardt, *Über das Studium*, 252.
17. Jacob Burckhardt, "Gang der Kultur. Historische Fragmente," in idem, *Gesamtausgabe*, vol. 7; *Weltgeschichtliche Betrachtungen. Historische Fragmente aus dem Nachlaß*, ed. A. Oeri and E. Dürr, Stuttgart, 1929, 225.
18. Burckhardt, "Lebensgeschichte und Leidensgeschichte der Menschheit als eines Ganzen," in *Historische Fragmente*, 227.
19. Cf. the brilliant analysis of Friedrich Jaeger, *Bürgerliche Modernisierungskrise und historische Sinnbildung. Kulturgeschichte bei Droysen, Burckhardt und Max Weber*, Bürgertum. Beiträge zur europäischen Gesellschaftsgeschichte, vol. 5, Göttingen, 1994, 134 sqq.
20. "Das Continuum ist höchst großartig. Hier allein verwirklichen sich die Postulate des Geistes; hier allein waltet Entwicklung und kein absoluter Untergang, sondern nur Übergang," Burckhardt, *Historische Fragmente*, 225.
21. Cf. Wolfgang Hardtwig, "Jacob Burckhardt und Max Weber: Zur Genese und Pathologie der modernen Welt," in Hans R. Guggisberg, ed., *Umgang mit Jacob Burckhardt. Zwölf Studien*, Basel, 1994, 159–90.
22. A precise study about the importance of suffering for Burckhardst´s historical thought is presented by Ruth Stepper. In fact, Stepper has not analysed "suffering by history" (Leiden in der

Geschichte), but "suffering in history;" Ruth Stepper, *Leiden an der Geschichte. Ein zentrales Motiv in der Griechischen Kulturgeschichte Jacob Burckhardts und seine Bedeutung in der altertumswissenschaftlichen Geschichtschreibung des 19. und 20. Jahrhunderts*, Bodenheim, 1997. The way Burckhardt himself had come to terms with suffering, was not her question.

23. Burckhardt summarizes the paradigmatic character of the Renaissance for modernity with the words, "daß man hier zuerst die Menschen und die Menschheit in ihrem tiefsten Wesen vollständig erkannt hatte." Jacob Burckhardt, *Gesamtausgabe*, vol. 5, *Die Kultur der Renaissance in Italien. Ein Versuch*, ed., Werner Kaegi, Stuttgart, 1930, 255.

24. "… den vollständigen Menschen in seinem tiefsten Wesen wie in seinen charakteristischen Äußerlichkeiten;" Burckhardt, *Renaissance*, 220.

25. "… ungeheure Summe von Immoralität," ibid., 320.

26. "… das Verbrechen gewinnt eine eigene, persönliche Konsistenz," ibid., 321.

27. "… Ausartung des schrankenlosen Egoismus," ibid., 28.

28. Dem "moderne(n) italienische(n) Geist" war es "bestimmt," "für den Okzident maßgebendes Vorbild zu werden," Ibid., 125.

29. "… rechtlose politische Verhältnisse, die oft einem glänzenden und dauernden Siege des Bösen ähnlich sahen…," ibid., 357). In another context Burckhardt addresses politics as follows: Die "freie Behandlung der internationalen Dinge erreicht bisweilen eine Vollendung, in welcher sie elegant und großartig erscheint, während das Ganze den Eindruck eines bodenlosen Abgrundes hervorbringt." Ibid., 65.

30. Burckhardt, *Force and Freedom*, 81 sqq. "Unser Ausgangspunkt: vom einzigen bleibenden und für uns möglichen Zentrum, vom duldenden, strebenden und handelnden Menschen, wie er ist und immer war und sein wird; daher unsere Betrachtung gewissermaßen pathologisch." Burckhardt, *Über das Studium*, 226.

31. Friedrich Jaeger speaks of a "geschichtsimmanente Leidensstruktur des menschlichen Lebens," Friedrich Jaeger, *Bürgerliche Modernisierungskrise und historische Sinnbildung. Kulturgeschichte bei Droysen, Burckhardt und Max Weber*, Bürgertum. Beiträge zur europäischen Gesellschaftsgeschichte, vol. 5, Göttingen, 1994, 87.

32. "Es gibt schon in den alten Zeiten ein entsetzliches Bild, wenn man sich die Summe von Verzweiflung und Jammer vorstellt, welche das Zustandekommen z.B. der alten Weltmonarchien verlangte und voraussetzte." Burckhardt, *Über das Studium*, 41.

33. "… lauter entsetzliche letzte Kämpfe, von denen wir nichts mehr wissen. Haben sie umsonst gekämpft?" Ibid., 241.

34. … die "rauchenden Ruinen der Welt," ibid., 241.

35. "Ihre Missetaten schrien laut…," Burckhardt, *Renaissance*, 4.

36. An example is his interpretation of the early European colonization: "Beginning of the subjugation of the inferior human races, especially the red ones…" (Beginn der Unterwerfung der inferioren Menschenrassen, besonders der Roten), quoted in Werner Kaegi, *Jacob Burckhardt. Eine Biographie*, vol. 5, *Das neuere Europa und das Erlebnis der Gegenwart*, Basel, 1973, 68; Kaegi refers to Burckhardt's relationship to Darwin ibid., 281 sqq., 286 sqq.

37. "Die Naturgeschichte zeigt einen angstvollen Kampf ums Dasein; dieser nämliche Kampf erstreckt sich weit in Menschenleben und Geschichte hinein." Burckhardt, *Über das Studium*, 169.

38. "Es ist die Gewalt, das Recht des Stärkeren über den Schwächeren, vorgebildet schon in demjenigen Kampf ums Dasein, welcher die ganze Natur, Tierwelt wie Pflanzenwelt, erfüllt, weitergeführt in der Menschheit durch Mord und Raub in den frühern Zeiten, durch Verdrängung resp. Vertilgung oder Knechtung schwächerer Rassen, schwächerer Völker innerhalb derselben Rasse, schwächerer Staatenbildungen, schwächerer gesellschaftlicher Schichten innerhalb desselben Staates und Volkes." Ibid., 240.

39. Therefore I doubt that Kaegi is right when he states that "Darwin has definitely won over Hegel and Herder" ("Darwin so eindeutig über Hegel und Herder gesiegt hat"), Werner Kaegi, *Jacob Burckhardt. Eine Biographie*. vol. 6, *Weltgeschichte—Mittelalter—Kunstgeschichte. Die letzten Jahre 1886—1897*, Basel, 1977, 70.

40. "Die Macht aber ist schon an sich böse," Burckhardt, *Über das Studium*, 328. A precise analysis of the evil character of power would bring about that it cannot be sufficiently described with the concept of nature. Burckhardt himself attributes "goodness" to nature, since she guarantees across the discontinuity of culture the connexion of human life and its ability of creating culture. "But humankind is not determined to fall, and nature creates as benignantly as ever." ("Aber zum Untergang ist die Menschheit noch nicht bestimmt, und die Natur schafft so gütig wie jemals"), Burckhardt, *Historische Fragmente*, 269. Concerning the metanatural status of the evil of power cf., Wolfgang Sofsky, *Die Ordnung des Terrors: Das Konzentrationslager*, Frankfurt am Main, 1997. Sofsky describes the concentration camps as "the extremest form of power and modern organization" (17). The specificity of the concentration camp consists of "absolute power" as a principle of social life (19). No natural purpose can be found in this manifestation, and that is true for the Darwinistic struggle for survival as well. If there is any telos of power, than it is not life, but death. Even death is no objective; because realizing absolute power is not centered around death but around the pure activity of killing. "Absolute power does not obey the paradigm of activity intending results. It is aimless, negative 'praxis', not 'poesis'." (33) With its aimlessness this practice is not determined by sense—a hole of senselessness in the texture of history.
41. Rüsen, *Konfigurationen des Historismus*, 300 sqq.
42. Droysen, *Historik*, 294, 411.
43. "… in der Herbeiziehung der verschiedenen Nationen und Individuen zur Idee der Menschheit und der Kultur ist der Fortschritt ein unbedingter." Leopold von Ranke, *Über die Epochen der neueren Geschichte*, ed. T. Schieder and H. Berding, *Aus Werk und Nachlaß*, vol. 2, Munich, 1971, 80.
44. Burckhardt, *Über das Studium*, 255.
45. "Ein Weiterleben der verletzten Menschheit mit Verlegung des Schwerpunkts," Burckhardt, *Über das Studium*, 242.
46. "Das geheimnisvolle Gesetz der Kompensation," ibid., 242.
47. Klaus Große Kracht has brought to our attention the hitherto neglected importance of this idea: "'Das Weiterleben der verletzten Menschheit'—Kultur und Kompensation bei Jacob Burckhardt', *Storia della Storiografia* 30 (1996), 125–33. He has already treated the issue of mourning in his MA-Thesis, Bielefeld, 1996, on "Trauer und Melancholie. Historiographische Verlustverarbeitung bei Jules Michelet und Jacob Burckhardt." I have learned a lot from him.
48. "Nur das Ganze spricht, in allen Jahrhunderten, die uns Zeugnisse hinterlassen." Burckhardt, *Historische Fragmente*, 226.
49. "Was Jubel und Jammer war, muß nun Erkenntnis werden." Ibid., 168–69.
50. "Unsere Aufgabe ist nicht: die großen Tatsachen und Zustände zu bejammern, sondern sie zu erkennen." Ibid., 158—The elimination of grieving, however, robs historical cognition of the character of mourning.
51. Ibid., Cf. chap. 7.
52. "Die Kontemplation ist unsere Freiheit mitten im Bewußtsein der enormen allgemeinen Gebundenheit und des Stromes der Notwendigkeiten." Ibid., 166.
53. Cf. John R. Hinde, "Jacob Burckhardt and the Art of History," *Storia della Storiografia* 30 (1996), 107–23. Hinde strictly separates Burckhardt from the tradition of German historicism and its approach to make history a science. He overlooks the insight into the constructive mode of history realized by Droysen and others, thus pretending that one has only to choose between a reifying objectivism on the one hand, and an aestheticism of history on the other hand, which creates the meaning of the past only by its representation. This alternative lets us overlook the element of experience in Burckhardt's concept of history: the experience of suffering, only dimly covered by aesthetic contemplation.
54. "Alles Einzelne aber, und wir mit ihm, ist nicht nur um seiner selbst, sondern um der ganzen Vergangenheit und um der ganzen Zukunft willen vorhanden." Burckhardt, *Über das Studium*, 237 sqq.

55. Cf. Jörn Rüsen, "Geschichte als Sinnproblem," in Rüsen, *Zerbrechende Zeit*, 7–42.
56. "... seine wahre Bürgerpflicht ermitteln," Burckhardt, *Über das Studium*, 117.
57. This critique comes close to the fourth type of problematic mourning presented by Irmgard Wagner who applied Freud's and Lacan's theory of mourning to history; Irmgard Wagner, 'Historischer Sinn zwischen Trauer und Melancholie: Freud, Lacan und Henry Adams," in Klaus E. Müller and Jörn Rüsen, eds., *Historische Sinnbildung. Problemstellungen, Zeitkonzepte, Wahrnehmungshorizonte, Darstellungsstrategien*, Reinbek, 1997, 408–32, 415 sqq.
58. Friedrich Nietzsche, "Brief an Burckhardt, 4 January 1889," in *Werke in drei Bänden*, ed., Karl Schlechta. vol. 3, Munich, 1956, 1350.

Chapter 10

Historizing Nazi-Time: Metahistorical Reflections on the Debate Between Friedländer and Broszat

> After all, life consists of nothing but hazy images. When the haze is lifted, a person dies of sheer horror.
> Peter Handke[1]

> History always tells us how to die, never how to live.
> Jules Michelet[2]

> The taboo that lies upon Auschwitz for us will not begin to be loosened until we are ... prepared to relinquish all the internal resistance we feel against acknowledging the full magnitude of those nameless atrocities. And against the fact that these were acts committed by Germans... We have to turn our historical memory into historical consciousness.
> Christian Meier[3]

Stating the problem

The debate on the historization of National Socialism has raised substantial theoretical problems that need further elucidation. The thrust of the *Historikerstreit* was largely political, which meant that fundamental questions on the nature of historical knowledge inherent in that dispute went unseen; they were generally not touched upon or figured only on the periphery. But the exchange of letters between Martin Broszat and Saul Friedländer prompted by the formers provocative "plea" was different.[4] It also addressed political constellations in German historical culture, and National Socialism's place in German memory. Yet it differed from the historians' debate in several ways: the two conversants approached one another with a welcome and salutary sense of

---

Notes for this section begin on page 185.

objectivity, and their dialogue was imbued with a tenor of fairness. Most importantly, though, the exchange brought to light the basic contours of an underlying problem that is characteristic of historical thought in its cultural and social functions and in the discourse of the discipline.

Saul Friedländer was able to show quite convincingly that Broszat's plea for a historization of National Socialism confronted contemporary history with one of the most crucial questions for both theory and method.[5] I agree, and believe that this is true not just for the historiography of National Socialism, but has far more fundamental importance. The historization of National Socialism acts as a prism, bringing into sharper analytical focus diverse features of the tasks, achievements, and limits of historical thought at the end of the twentieth century. In the following, I will attempt to pry loose the problem of historization from the constrictions imposed by scholars of contemporary history, and from its moorings in the dynamic of generational succession, in order to consider its unsettling and controversial features, with reference to presentday historical culture as a whole.

At first glance, it might appear that the problem of historization only arises when subjects are existentially involved in the nexus between past and present, and this charged bond takes on a manifestly historical perspective as the past recedes. The present immediacy of this past dissolves, becoming a temporal distance that can now be freshly reinterpreted in an existentially less burdensome form. Simultaneously, it is accorded another place and function in present-day historical culture. The attempt to historicize National Socialism appeared so problematic to the two disputants because they were operating on the basis of an uninterrogated assumption that the historization of the other past, preceding National Socialism, was unproblematic and self-evident. Yet that unstated assumption needs to be queried. The mass of difficulties thrown up by the historical interpretation of National Socialism appears to call into question all previous modes of dealing "historically" with the past more generally, in any past. These interpretive strategies appear more difficult and problem laden than the public, and even professional historians, have generally realized. After all, the basic challenge for historical thought arising from the historization of National Socialism is that, unlike all earlier eras in "normal" historical thought, this particular past cannot and will not pass away. Until now, the problem seemed to be that the one past was transitory, the other abiding. But how about the reverse case?

In the following, therefore, I intend to shift the problem of historization into the frame of basic thinking on the nature of historiography. In that context, of course, the subfield of contemporary history has always been connected with the broader debate on historization. The status of contemporary history in the discipline has largely revolved around the question of whether (and if so, how) its object's proximity in time led to a basic diminishment of historical cognition, a lack of objectivity springing from inadequate temporal detachment. An underlying assumption was that temporal distance in itself opened a door to objectivity that contemporary history, by its very nature and nearness, could not pass through.

That same question is broached in the debate on historization, but in a more pointed form. Increasing distance in time is indeed viewed as a window opening onto new possibilities for insight. At the same time, however, time's steady lapse appears to harbor a potential risk: a possible diminution in the significance of the ever-receding recent past for the present's self-interpretation. Greater knowledge appears to be determined by less current relevance. But it is precisely that mutual determinancy that we should interrogate. To see the historical character of the past solely in terms of its temporal difference to the present is an oversimplification. The past's historicity would then increase in direct proportion to its distance from the present. Yet a past is not historical simply by dint of its pastness, its remove from the present, but also because of its meaningful link with the present. Moreover, that distance does not necessarily entail a loss in meaningfulness, on the contrary, it can enhance meaning. In terms of the theory of history, it makes good sense to say that only a past that cannot and will not pass away is and remains history.

The overriding problem at the nub of the debate on historization is the historical place of the Holocaust. Quite obviously it constitutes a boundary experience of what is historical, with primal import for how we understand and conceptualize history and historicity. The Holocaust calls into radical question the very character of what is historical. It cannot be incorporated within the representational confines of a usual research object for historical inquiry. Rather, in recoil, it exerts a metahistorical impact on the very way in which the methods and categories of research are constituted. Thus, the debate on historization broaches several questions central to historical theory.

First, what is the relation between morality and historicity? This queries the plane on which historical thinking is constituted, the level that for Droysen hinges on the question of how everyday dealings (*Geschäfte*) become history (*Geschichte*).[6] Is our relation to National Socialism, and thus to the Holocaust, to be de-moralized, divested of moral dimensions? That is the searching question posed by the ever increasing distance between the present and National Socialism, and the consequent and unavoidable historization of our relation to it.

Broszat's "plea" is propelled by his repeated assertion that moral condemnation acts as a blockade to knowledge. Friedländer did not dispute the necessity of a historization that can serve to open up such windows on new knowledge. Yet he clearly saw the concomitant danger: the historical experience of National Socialism—and the Holocaust in particular—could forfeit the very quality which is at the core of their special historical significance. Broszat addressed these concerns in elaborating a more complex argument as to the moral dimension of the historical relation to National Socialism. Though he continued to maintain that a present-oriented moralism threw up an undesirable barrier to knowledge, he was clear and unequivocal in stressing that the historization he envisioned would not divest the terrain of moral questions; rather, it constituted a new, more knowledgeable and persuasive infusion of our historical relation to that past with moral constituents.

What he meant exactly has remained unclear. On the one hand, he contended that a moral perspective acts as an impediment to knowledge. Yet Friedländer's probing questions and arguments induced Broszat to describe "the now widely accepted evaluation of the basic political–moral character of Nazi rule" as a foundation of historization.[7] I think that is an inconsistency on his part, although one that can be clarified and surmounted if we analyze how historical thought is constituted. The immediate beneficiaries of Broszat's inconsistency were those who interpreted his plea primarily as a call for a more distanced and detached objectivity, a bid to "de-moralize" the German relation to National Socialism and the Holocaust.[8] Broszat's remark that historization in respect to the Nazi period should be conceived as "anti-thetical"—that is, a synthesis of distancing objectivization and subjective appropriation, of judgment (*Urteil*), and understanding (*Verstehen*)[9]—needs to be fleshed out and anchored in basic historical theory. After all, this antitheticality applies more broadly, not just to our historical relation to National Socialism, but in a primary sense to the bonds of significance between past and present more generally, the reticulation we are wont to call history.

This broaches a second complex of problems, one whose explosiveness also springs from the imbrication of existential involvement as contemporaries of that era on the one hand, and a historical perspective on the past's special character on the other: namely, the way in which what is historical is constituted in memory. The category of remembrance and cultural memory attempts to name and analyze a relation to the past lacking certain key elements and factors regarded by the discipline as typical of any reasoned relation to the past, such as methodical rationality, progress in knowledge through research, strict controls on experience, and historical interpretations that are theoretically consistent. Yet remembrance has always stood for the past's vividness and vitality in the cultural orientations of one's concrete life-world. Remembrance does not permit the past to pass away (though admittedly at the cost of a diminished experiential fink and an enhanced normative bond).

Just the opposite appears to be the case when professional historians tackle the past. In their discourse and praxis, "historicizing" National Socialism means transforming that past from a mode of memory-based remembrance into one of scientific knowledge. If one takes what was long regarded as a self-evident given—namely the antithesis between memory and history—then this transformation is indeed the transposition of a dearth of experience replete with (normative) meaning into a meaninglessness rich with experience. That extreme formulation serves to make clear that the postulated contrast is unpersuasive and, indeed, acts to obscure the constitutive link between memory and historical knowledge.

Broszat placed special emphasis on a specific quality of experience that he claimed was excluded by the moralism of an undistanced "presentizing" of National Socialism: namely the "authenticity" of the past.[10] He urged that this authenticity be guaranteed by means of hermeneutic knowledge and narrative procedures of representation. In so doing, he was sanctioning and promoting the general trend in the discipline that favors new hermeneutic methods to deal with contemporary history. On the other hand—and this became quite obvious as a result of Friedländer's critique and probing questions—his plea for authenticity also disclosed an open, unprotected flank in this hermeneutical thrust, namely an unclarified relation to the criteria of meaning and significance that the present constitutionally infuses into the historical relation to the past.

Broszat left no doubt that his plea for the historization of National Socialism was unabashedly political and didactic in its aims. Yet that was possible to overlook because he had championed the need for heightened historical knowledge and authenticity against the alternative of a political and didactic treatment of the period. Thus, the impression could arise that historization itself helped to reduce the political and pedagogical tensions engendered by the experience of National Socialism—at least for that group of contemporaries who had an objective genealogical link with the perpetrators and their victims. Broszat's concern was to unshackle National Socialism from the moralistic and political anathema of a past that deserved total rejection and negation so that it could become a historical experience anchored in an identity-shaping nexus between past and present.

In raising the topic of historization, Broszat broaches the question of identity. This is not a bid to "deactualize" this past, to render it more distanced. One could say that this past has to pass away and become history precisely so that it can then be internally appropriated—and thus made living and vital—within the cultural processes of identity formation. In his view, the objective genealogy that connects us as later generations with this past should become part of our own subjectivity by our sloughing off an abstract–negative moral relation to that past. By historicizing National Socialism, Broszat wishes to overcome the historical estrangement of Germans and their identity in relation to that era. Friedländer interrogates this project, wondering whether a normalization in the historical patterns of German identity can only be achieved at the cost of neglecting the special quality of National Socialism in historical perception.[11]

In the Broszat–Friedländer dispute, this special dimension was termed the "category of the mythical." This category refers to those features in the historical experience of National Socialism, culminating in the Holocaust, by dint of which it arches beyond the status or boundaries of a concrete past subject to inquiry and interpretation—as a primary precondition for the possibility of its representation in the present. The "mythical" component intrinsic in the relation to National Socialism is precisely what is assumed to determine the fundamental and constitutive meaningful nexus between past and present—a relation in which the past becomes history for the present, and in whose alembic the present processes the experience of the past to be better equipped for dealing with life in the here and now. The counterpositioning of myth and knowledge marks and highlights the character of the Holocaust as a boundary experience. At the same time, however, this opposition, which Friedländer does not dispute, obscures various problems in meaning generated by the experience of the Holocaust, not only for contemporary history, but for historical thinking more generally. There is a basic, intrinsic, problem of historical knowledge here which cannot be sidestepped if historical thinking intends in some sense to be objective, that is if it wishes to do justice to the significance of the Holocaust as a boundary experience of the historical as such. One can also say that although the counterpositioning of knowledge and myth proceeds from a historical processing of the Holocaust experience, it ultimately intersects with that mode of historical thinking that seeks to operate on the level of experience and interpretation—a level perceived objectively in relation to the Holocaust as provocative.

Historicity and its dimensions

Not every relation to the past is historical per se. Only after the past is infused with a definite quality of pastness—and its pastness related to the present by a special cognitive operation of historical consciousness—can we speak of a "specifically historical" relation to the past.[12] This remove of the past as a necessary (though not sufficient) condition for historicity is generally operative on the plane of individuals' life-worlds whenever an attempt is made to reach into the past over and beyond the boundaries of personal (autobiographical) remembrance in order to interpret one's present circumstances and forge plans for future action. A past is historical when it lies beyond the boundaries of an individual's own memorable lifespan. Yet reminiscences conjunctive with events in one's own life can be historical when they are endowed with a significance usually accorded only that other "more past" era.

It is precisely this definition of the historical via a "past" past that underlies the concept of historization. National Socialism is part of the solid stock of memories of its contemporaries; it then moves with the succession in generations into a temporal distance beyond the lifespans of those dealing with the era. At this distance, the past assumes certain qualities that make it simultaneously past and present. This historical character unfolds in differing dimensions and is realized via different principles, criteria, and cognitive operations. If we wish to clear up misconceptions surrounding the concept of historization in the discussion on contemporary history, and clarify its basic features, it is useful to make this differentiation explicit to the extent that it is relevant to its need for interpretation.

For what follows, I propose an operative distinction between a constitutive or foundational level on the one hand, and a functional, developmental, plane on the other. It is my intention to analyze the historization as problematic in its specific constitution. Pivotal at the level of constitution are ultimate criteria for meaning and meaningfulness in dealing with the past, and the fundamental way human subjectivity interweaves into that process. On the developmental or functional level, historical thinking is differentiated into a complex manifold of criteria for meaning, patterns of interpretation, methodological strategies, normative factors, aesthetic elements, and an array of effects that the historically internalized past has within the orientation systems of concrete lifeworlds and their praxis.

On the level of constitution, historical consciousness and historical thinking are rooted in memory, and memory is a primary constituent of human subjectivity.[13] It is on this plane that we find what Broszat and Friedländer term the "mythical." Here, the past, prior to any determination of its historical character, is always contemporary. Here, it has preinscribed itself in the subjectivity of the rememberers. Here, human praxis is always temporally oriented—before this orientation unfolds into a reflexive cultural effort (on the part of historical thought). And it is precisely here that we can find that "authenticity" of the past that Broszat reclaims for the historization of National Socialism.

As history is not an attribute of the past inherent in it as an objective given property, something that can be simply read off, as it were, from elements of that past still empirically present (by whatever methodological operations), it would be a serious error to regard this past—present in empirically given remains and reports—as truly "authentic." It only acquires authenticity at the constitutive or foundational level alluded to here. The past is authentic as history when, in its pastness, it is at the same time present and alive in the living presence of human subjects who remember it. Authenticity is an existential quality of remembrance. By means of that authenticity, the past has always inscribed itself as precedent into the present, a unique and unsurpassable imprint, by means of reflexive and methodologically ordered operations carried out by historical consciousness. Therein lies the dignity and value of praehistorical memory.

It would be misguided to conceive its prae-historical tenor as something that dissipates in proportion to temporal distance and the necessary concomitant historization. On the contrary, this existential quality of meaning intrinsic to memory unfolds into historization and manifests itself there, though changing its character in the process. It flows into reflexivity and the particular operations of historical consciousness. That "ingressiveness" is addressed in the debate on historization pivoting on the respective perspectives of the perpetrator and the victim, and points up an internal genealogical nexus between National Socialism's past and the rememberers' present (or that of those grappling with that past historically). And that ligature is more than a merely subjective construct. Here, in this perspective, radical subjectivity and equally radical objectivity are identical. The psychological findings in the first and second generation after the perpetrators and victims offer clear evidence to support this unity of the subjectivity and objectivity of historical memory persisting through successive generations.[14]

This authenticity overarches time and is prae-historical in that it still does not evince the temporal difference constitutive for the historical character of the past. Yet it enters as a constitutive factor into the historicity of the relation to the past because it can fulfill the necessary precondition for this historicity, namely the capacity to bridge over the temporal difference between past and present (in terms of narrative).[15] It can do so precisely by creating the coherent meaning in and by which the past as past is history. The authenticity of constitutive memories that is particularly allowed to the survivors is a metahistorical dimension. This metahistoricity is expressed in and through the concept of the mythical. However, since mythical is understood in everyday discourse as tantamount to nonhistorical, the term is misleading. This authenticity is prae-historical, but not nonhistorical. On the contrary, as a necessary element of the formation of historical meaning, it directly enters historicity itself.

Broszat had a different notion of authenticity in historical relation to National Socialism. What he had in mind was the attribute that the past takes on under the category of the historical as a differential determination from the present. Authenticity stands for "alterity," in a quite specific feature, namely, in regard to the acting and suffering subjects of this period, the subjective "inside" of this era in German history. This authenticity is indebted to a process of subjective transfer: the subjectivity of the rememberers is extrapolated to the subjectivity of those whose actions and sufferings are the content of memory. Indeed, Broszat "historicizes" the constitutive subjectivity of the rememberers in their historical bond with the others whom they remember. Thus, the genealogical nexus with the perpetrators and their victims comes into view, as well as the power of historical identity formation by means of memory with which that nexus is infused.

This brief excursion to the constitutive level of what is historical should make it clear that historization is quite different from demoralization. On the contrary, if morality addresses the existential inside the relation to the past, a relation in which subjects—via remembrance—are themselves the past before its temporal distancing, then historization should be understood as the unfolding of morality into the temporal distance of the past. This means that the moral "loadings" that the contents of memory always has as constituents of one's own personal identity is transposed, so to speak, into temporal distance as this past wings on out of the present. It is manifest as a factor of meaning and signification in the relation that has now turned specifically historical. In the constitutive nexus of historical thinking, morality does more than simply block access to the past. It also underpins history by infusing the experiential contents of the past with the significational dimensions of temporality. And solely by dint of these meaning-laden aspects do those contents become distinctively "historical."

Broszat repeatedly marshalled the so-called blockade argument in support of his contentions.[16] It is absolutely pivotal in his plea for historization. Yet I regard that argument, in the way he presents it, as untenable (in respect to the constitutive level of what is historical). Broszat thematizes the plane of highly differentiated thought, in particular that which is discipline specific. Nonetheless, he calls attention to a salient issue: namely, the moral "loading" of the Nazi era. That loading acts as a brake on the transformation of moral immediacy into a nexus of historical meaning and significance. Unfortunately, Broszat provides little more than hints as to what he really means, giving no concrete examples that can be analyzed in detail.

In order to get to grips better with the question, I propose to distinguish here between two cognitive operations which impede or block the process whereby the moral element unfolds into and infuses that which is historical. On the one hand, there is the authenticity of the memory of the survivors; that is, the still present past of National Socialism in the trauma of psychological constellations reaching on down into the present via the genealogy of the perpetrators and their victims. This blockage in historization disappears in the natural course of the biological succession of generations. The other phenomenon is quite different and involves a moral condemnation with which the Nazi past is kept alive and present in counterpointed tension—as the negative counterimage of a current political and existential value system, though devoid of any genealogical intermediating link. Genealogy is supplanted by moral condemnation, thus disencumbering individual subjectivity from the heavy burden of its inner link with this past.[17] It is this defensive appropriation in negative moralism that acts to impede a historization on the constitutive level of historical consciousness. And it is this constitutive nexus that Broszat has in mind when he wishes to nullify the moralism of defensive condemnation, transforming it into the knowledge of "authentic" historical experience.[18]

The debate on the historical place and function of Auschwitz is conducted on the same plane. When Broszat claims that "the role of Auschwitz in the original historical context of action" was "significantly different from its subsequent importance in terms of later historical perspective,"[19] he is calling attention to a "blindness" of historical vision that has a similar blocking effect on knowledge to that of condemnatory moralism. Auschwitz distorts present-day sight to such an extent that those previous times can no longer be perceived as they appeared to most contemporaries at the time. In order to render this "authenticity" plausible, Broszat points to a basic difference, noting that the era of National Socialism can be viewed retrospectively, from its catastrophic end backward. Auschwitz then becomes the "decisive measuring rod for the historical perception of this period."[20] One could also develop an approach that proceeds from the perspective of the time.[21] He amplifies this difference as an exaggerated "contrast between authentic historical reconstruction" on the one hand, and its use "for pedagogical purposes" on the other, leaving no doubt which is the sole plausible alternative.[22]

However, this contrast does not exist, for the authenticity of a historical insight is inconceivable without retrospective elements. The logic of historical explanation as explicated by Arthur Danto (1968) frames the "prospection" (in his neologism) of the progression from earlier to later as an answer to a question that is prompted by what comes later, by the "end" or, more precisely, by a difference between earlier and later that poses a challenge to historical thinking.[23]

So where does the problem lie? The difficulty is that the chain of events lifted from experience—an explanatory, narrative sequence—always extends its reach into the present, at least when questions of identity are at stake. So the Holocaust and the "German catastrophe" are indeed not the terminus of contemporary history, but constitute one link in a longer temporal chain. Then prospection over time must be organized according to a line of development that reduces the catastrophe to being one constituent in an overarching whole—not its end to which everything leads. This "reduction" of the Holocaust to the status of a single link in a temporal chain of events leading to the present or, more precisely, streaming into the self-concept, the self-interpretation of those who must remember the Holocaust in order to understand who they are, constitutes the real nub, the primal problem of historization.

This is the basis for Friedländer's objections to Broszat: he argues against this "reduction" of the Holocaust, marshalling reasons rooted in the constitutive ligature of this history itself, in the authenticity of its precedent presentness. The Holocaust resists such incorporation into overarching lines of development. Indeed, one can formulate it even more radically: it explodes any conception of such a nexus. Dan Diner has been the most vigorous proponent of this thesis.[24]

The metahistorical significance of the Holocaust

Broszat and Friedländer concur that the significance of the Holocaust for remembrance, memory, and historical knowledge rules out any attempt to assimilate it qua historical experience into the customary templates of historical interpretation. Broszat severs this significance from the specificity of what is historical, relegating it to the plane of the mythical. He downscales its meaning to the point that the Holocaust appears compatible with a temporal progression that reincorporates the Nazi era into an overarching, identity-forming temporal nexus with the present. The "metahistorical event"[25] can only be historicized at the cost of its metahistorical quality. Friedländer is vehement in rejecting this, arguing that the Nazi period cannot be treated like any other history (for example, sixteenth-century France).[26]

To my mind, that line of argument is invalid. It seizes on the authentic character of Holocaust memory (as delineated above) and transports it to the plane of developed historical thought. In that move, however, something occurs to the special quality of this prae-historical authenticity. It is marshalled as an operative factor of historical knowledge, moral and political judgment and aesthetic representation, transformed into a catalyst for "normal" historical thought. It dissolves in this normality, thereby paradoxically gaining significance. Only when the Holocaust is treated as any other normal span of history does it take on its own distinctive historical contours, just as its singularity can only be made plausible by means of cognitive comparison.

Friedländer is quite correct in characterizing the Holocaust as a "historical 'boundary event'," viewing this as an "unresolved theoretical aspect" of historization.[27] The crux of the theoretical problem is that the patterns for interpretation cannot simply be applied to the facts of the past *after* they have been determined by historical inquiry. Rather, in the prae-historical presence of the past, the facts themselves play a role in the very formation of these interpretive patterns.[28] Naturally, what is central to this precedent impact of the past on the present, as it seeks to discover that past historically, is not the multiplex of facts quarried by research, but rather the quality of memory of what inquiry explores. That dimension is already manifest prior to any and all research in the shaping of meaningful perspectives that guide inquiry. One might call this an intangible theoretical quality of historical experience. That is, what is implied by the statement that the Holocaust cannot be confined to the plane of an object for research. In principle, however, that holds true for every possible historical experience, not just the Holocaust, insofar as it has previously entered historical memory and generates meaning there or, more precisely, itself acts as a vessel of significance, a preformed conception of possible historical meaning.

Naturally, this does not mean to say that the operational procedures of historical knowledge simply have to conform to these dicta, have only to give them their cognitive stamp of approval. On the contrary, the cognitive procedures of historical knowledge are well able to develop a basic critical view regarding the central meanings of the past inscribed in remembrance and collective memory. Memory's prae-historical constitutive attribution of meaning to the past has to prove itself, as it were, on the testing ground of the operations of historical consciousness, where it is often significantly emended as a result of memory's workings and those operations. That also holds for the Holocaust. But it is precisely on this "testing ground" that the Holocaust realizes its metahistorical meaning, as its factuality is subjected to the rational critique of knowledge anchored in experience, formulated in concepts, and methodically ordered. To put it more paradoxically: if one wishes to treat the Nazi period like sixteenth-century France, then historical inquiry will come up with facts that are critical of the heuristically preconceived interpretations themselves. Interpretive approaches and attempts can be criticized, modified, and (of course) also falsified by historical experience. That is especially true in the case of the Holocaust. In its sheer facticity, and the dearth of facts yielded by the extant sources, it resists bids to make sense of it.

Another way to formulate this is to say that historical experience has a say in its own interpretation because it already bears within itself (however mediated) intrinsic elements of the very significance that a historical interpretation arrives at in retrospect. This is precisely what the hermeneutics of the historical method is grounded on.

Dan Diner has categorized this metahistorical dimension of the Holocaust as a "break with civilization."[29] What he means is that the elements of interpretation of self and the world, constitutive of modern civilization and society, were negated by the Holocaust. But since the patterns of historical interpretation are themselves components of this civilization, not only can they not be used to interpret the Holocaust, but the hiatus renders them nugatory. Now negated, they lie riven within the ambit of an interpretation organized around the criteria of openness to experience and the experiential monitoring of historical thought. Even if one does not agree with the specific configuration of Diner's thesis, the logic of his argument is compelling. Precisely to the extent that one wishes to interpret the Holocaust historically, the Holocaust must be comprehensible within a temporal sequence of events in which human life is acted out—a train of events stamped and determined by human subjectivity. Understanding here means comprehending the chain of occurrences by grasping the intentions and interpretations of their participants. In this bid, the viewpoints authoritative for historical interpretation (a complex mix of criteria governing rationality, on the plane of meaning and of rational action) enter into an internal relation to the analogous complex of criteria of the perpetrators and victims in the past. Only when this internal relation achieves a certain coherence is it possible to speak of history as a meaning-saturated nexus between past and present.

But it is precisely this coherence that becomes precarious in reference to the Holocaust. That is, its metahistorical character, and by dint of it the Holocaust is indeed the "hub of happening,"[30] though not in the sense that Broszat rejects, namely, an event toward which all others in the chronology have to be causally or teleologically aligned. Rather, it is an event whose cultural significance and negative meaningfulness, figures as a factor in the interpretive organization of the chain of occurrences itself.

What is historical authenticity?

Broszat believes that a general moralistic condemnation of National Socialism acts as an impediment to historical authenticity. Only when National Socialism becomes "authentic" can it be integrated into German history as an era and become a historical experience that the Germans can really include in their self-understanding, in the notion of their historical identity.

Broszat thus views authenticity as a necessary precondition for historical appropriation and processing. Friedländer objects to this attempt to impute an authentic quality to National Socialism. In his eyes, this is a stratagem serving solely to normalize National Socialism, in a backhanded manner and contrary to the intention of achieving critical appropriation. It is divested of its specific historical hallmark, and its criminality then becomes one more "feature" among others. Yet the ultimate objective here, Friedländer contends, is indeed to center on these other, more "normal" features, in order to arrive at historical experience that is truly amenable to internal appropriation.

Both conversants focus on the same phenomenon: the subjectivity of those who lived under Nazi rule and their historical nexus with the subjectivity of those engaged in the recollection of National Socialism—especially, though not exclusively, the Germans. Broszat criticizes the previous moralistic approach in dealing with National Socialism, categorizing it as a mode of subjectivity of the observers, one which ignores the subjectivity of the observed. For the sake of moralism, the observed are silenced ex post facto. To counteract this, Broszat proposes that hermeneutically they be given back their voices. They should then be taken seriously as participants in the hermeneutic production of historical meaning within the historical time-link with the present. Friedländer attaches a condition to this internal, subjective, identity generating nexus between then and now: in this bond, the Holocaust as theme should be speakable, an object of discourse; the moral negativity of the Holocaust should be as much a part of the internal, subjective dimension of National Socialism's contemporaries as it is of this era's appropriation today. Is such comprehension really possible, and can it enable National Socialism to be internally appropriated when "right from the outset, it was criminal to the core?"[31]

In their debate on the achievements of and limits to any hermeneutic approach to National Socialism, Friedländer and Broszat agree on two points: both reject the historicist principle of understanding (to understand the past only within its own horizon); both concur that understanding demands the inclusion—not exclusion—of criticism, from a moral perspective as well. We can regard that repudiation of the concept of historicist understanding as a special problem in the history of historiography and leave it aside. However, the fact should not be overlooked that the notion of authenticity Broszat employs is the heir (in the history of science) to historicism's concept of individuality and development.[32] One can concur regarding the other point—the unity of understanding and criticism—on the level of a methodological basic premise, but it is not clear what that means in specific terms. Moral criticism should be tied concretely to the empirically determined attitudes of those affected by the Nazi regime, to the objectives that guided their actions, their situated interpretations. Such critique should no longer be "from the outside" but internal. If one really takes this perspective seriously, the postulate of historization takes on a surprising new form and a sharpened normative edge: on the one hand, hermeneutics demands that the attempt be made to transpose oneself into the horizon of perception and interpretation of past actors, artificially bracketing all knowledge about what happened later. On the other hand, the call for criticism (with its intrinsic normative criteria) while holding any knowledge of later consequences in abeyance cannot be as vigorous and resolute as it must be today in the light of the monstrous crimes that this past enfolds.

The contemporaries of the Nazi past were historically blind compared with later generations. But this blindness cannot be elevated to the paramount principle of a hermeneutics geared to "historical interconnections," not just single isolated situations.[33] On the other hand, in reconstructing horizons of perception, interpretation, and orientation, hermeneutics precludes utilizing perspectives that are simply assumed retrospectively to be part of the given time and then imputed to it. The imputation that actors were capable of criticism (or in need of it) must be demonstrated and made plausible in reference to the subjective factors of these horizons themselves. Of course, it would be totally unhistorical to proceed by simply applying the same yardstick, such as an unchanging human moral nature, as a criterial scheme for historical judgment right across the temporal board, disregarding time differences. For their part, the normative perspectives used to arrive at historical judgment in appropriating the past must be integrated into an internal temporal bond with the normative viewpoints that shaped human action and suffering in that past itself. Such a nexus does not preclude the possibility that later generations may apply normative standpoints that differ from those of the earlier generation(s) they are attempting to understand. But it is absolutely crucial that those perspectives be capable of being rendered plausible to those they are propounded to (in a virtual dialogue over time), utilizing knowledge of the outcomes of action and suffering as guided by those earlier viewpoints.

"Empathy" with the subjects in the past would be badly unhistorical were it not propelled by questions as to the how and why of what happened. In their light the contours emerge of a subjectivity that is anything but "normal." The question itself, of course, is quite standard in historical terms. So I would disagree with Friedländer and contend that a "normal historical empathy" with the Nazi period is certainly necessary. But the aim of that empathy should not be a backhanded bid to divest the era of its horror and domesticate it as one among many on the historical shelf. Rather, just the opposite: the goal should be genuine insight ("authentic," if you will) into the era's special tenor, precisely by entering into the distinctive configurations of its contemporaries' subjectivity.

What does "normality" signify? If we are talking about the mass of contemporaries, "simple people" and their lives, widely shared and deeply rooted views, motivations, anxieties, and hopes, then it is something empirical, not normative. However, the concept becomes highly problematic in a double sense if normality refers to a mode of subjectivity within large sections of the population "unmarked" by their objective contemporaneity with the Holocaust, and who fully share the same value system with us (who radically condemn the Holocaust). On the one hand, as Friedländer fears, there is the danger that everything that made them willing or unwilling accomplices of the system precisely in the ways they organized their concrete lives, and in the configurations of their subjectivity, will indeed be obliterated from the everyday-life worlds of the masses. At the same time, however—and I think this has been largely overlooked in the debate—the category of normality presupposes a certain distance from the Holocaust. Due to that distance, its shadow no longer extends into the present—as if there were no continuity in structural- historical terms, a continuity that several necessary (though naturally not sufficient) conditioning factors underlying the Holocaust point to.

Subjective appropriation of the Nazi past is also a question of historical representation. Broszat makes a plea for historical narration;[34] this is the only means of expressing the subjective quality of the experience of National Socialism, the only way it can be appropriated intellectually. Indeed, narration is a cognitive operation that can incorporate experienced time into the internal organization of current self-understanding and existential orientation. Narration processes the experience of the past, preparing it for infusion into the cultural frames of orientation operative in contemporary practical life. This is true no matter how diverse the forms of historical narration. Of course, one of the reasons that the Holocaust is a historical boundary experience is because it also demarcates the boundaries of historical narration. Friedländer notes that it is impossible to render the crime of the Holocaust comprehensible through narration, since it exceeds the powers of human imagination, lacks narrativity. Rather he suggests, "One may wish merely to produce the documentation."[35]

But what is meant by saying that the Holocaust is not narratable? The contention is certainly not that, as processed historical experience, it should not become part of the cultural frame of orientation of current social praxis. Lack of narrativity entails a divestment: we have a situation where previously customary modes for processing temporal experiences in narrative strip the Holocaust of precisely that crucial experiential quality, the present, due to its objective link with this experience. What is at issue here is not the "mythical" quality of the weight of its remembrance, for that is precisely the quality that emerges from narration, particularly from the authentic narratives of those directly affected by the Holocaust. Rather, it is necessary to seize on the specific features that the receding Holocaust assumes and inject them as an experiential quality into its narrative processing. That experiential quality calls into question previous forms of narrative processing of historical experience, provoking new modes. The Holocaust thus requires, as Friedländer correctly notes, "a new style ... for the purpose of historical description," one that "we have not yet encountered very much in historiographical work."[36]

Narration has quite definite limits when it comes to the Holocaust if it is only conceived as a mode of narrative representation of the past temporally conjunct with the present and associated with a "vivid, plastic" description that is internally meaningful and linked with concrete human subjects and conceivable series of events. Those limits are palpable when the past's imaginative present, realized by means of narration, takes on the form of a coherent configuration, a comprehensible image, a meaningful unit situated in time. The Holocaust bursts asunder these forms and their shells of meaning. If one is really prepared to deal with the Holocaust as a real event—most certainly when it comes to the subjective experience of both its victims and perpetrators—then both cases involve a clear and demonstrative negation of meaning (one in the magnitude of suffering, the other in the extent of dehumanization). This negation blocks coherent configurations, imaginative unity and integration into overarching historical developments. Such a blockage can and must be expressed in narrative form, thereby altering the mode of narration, and losing those features that Broszat stresses.

Continuity and Appropriation

By means of historization, Broszat wants to release National Socialism from the status of erratic blockage and transform it into one more era of German history among others. Within that history's span, National Socialism appears together with periods before and after, in an overarching continuity of development—one in which the Germans are able to rediscover their historical identity. Broszat's aim is nothing less than an "original authentic continuum" of German history.[37] The "most profoundly depraved chapter in German history" should become "capable of reintegration as part of our national history."[38] Authenticity and narrative representation help to render the historical experience of National Socialism more malleable for integration. A temporal span linking the era of National Socialism with preceding and, in particular, subsequent periods, endows it with a decidedly historical physiognomy. The standard term for this is "continuity."[39] Naturally, this refers to an internal genetic nexus in which National Socialism is incorporated as one epoch within an overarching span of history, in which it finds its distinctive historical signature and impact on German historical self-understanding. Here, continuity has nothing to do with specific patterns of social life (or at least elements of such patterns) that can be connected with earlier or later periods.

Broszat touches only very briefly on the notion of continuity he regards as valid. He refers at one point to "a social-historical theory of modernization"[40] and points to Nazi social policies as an illustrative example. Those policies show that there were formative elements of social life in the Nazi era that can be connected with what transpired before and after. Given such facts, the 1933–1945 boundaries of the era become more porous.

One cannot deny the utility of such an approach grounded in modernization theory for interpreting National Socialism, nor the relevance of the specific example. However, Friedländer raises a question that goes to the very heart of the theoretical concept and the historical understanding of the example cited: in this theoretical approach and its empirical concretization, where are the specific features of the Nazi regime, its murderous, inhumane policies, its mobilization of all resources to implement these policies? To put it more pointedly, do not the constraints of the prism provided by modernization theory marginalize these aspects? Are they not peripheralized and thus downgraded into elements that have little to do with the real (that is, connectible) core of this era? Continuity, whether conceived in terms of modernization theory or otherwise, highlights factors in everyday living persisting through different periods. In their concrete manifestations they can be identified as being the same within the ongoing change, so that their present-day form appears as the product of some process of development that in retrospect can be perceived as having a definite direction. There are numerous such phenomena in all domains of everyday praxis. Now if their change from period to period is to be (re)presented as a process of extended duration, so to speak, a mode of permanence projectable into the future as a perspective guiding action, then National Socialism indeed becomes a kind of ensemble of temporal circumstances that has little to do with its core, its paramount historical meaning. That is the point Friedländer raises: does not this approach (however inadvertently) divest National Socialism of its very essence?[41]

This differentiation can also be made by means of the conceptual dyad structural/contingent. In this light, National Socialism appears accidental: a contingent constellation in an overarching structural line of development that would have taken a different direction given other external circumstances. This continuity appears plausible since the contingent circumstances by which the overarching structures had been perverted by National Socialism cannot be detected either in the present or the foreseeable future. From this perspective, National Socialism becomes an accident, a monstrous mishap within general developmental tendencies found in modem societies. The contingency of the circumstances responsible for this perversion plays no decisive role when it comes to appropriating, adopting, continuing, and even altering the persisting patterns and factors of social life. Contrasted with their continuity, National Socialism becomes contingent—and thus a thing of the past—no longer present in the internal intellectual appropriation of the past as a historical process that flows into the present and plunges on into the future.

This conceptualisation is unpersuasive on two counts. First of all, it postulates contingency as a mere externality of structural developments, overlooking the fact that these developments themselves have a contingent nature, and that contingency is an essential element of structural developments themselves. It simply hangs on too simplistic an interpretation of contingency, the vital elixir of what is historical. Second, it does not provide any cognitive basis for locating the genealogy of the perpetrators and victims—and the genealogy of the nexus between them—in the timespan that begins before the Nazi era and issues into our own. The strands of perpetration and victimization reach back into times prior to National Socialism and flow on cognitively over generations down to the present. Using theoretical concepts and experiential contents of genetic continuity, that specific cognitive nexus should be fleshed out in historical terms, to the extent that the various elements (in a certain sense, the "neutral" ones) in everyday social life render National Socialism connectible in the historical orientation of the present. How can one do the one and not the other? Friedländer has pointed out that these "neutral" factors in continuity were so affected by the Nazi period that their contextualization with it constitutes the essential difference.[42] They simply cannot be "neutralized," or isolated, they cannot pass through the terrain of 1933 to 1945 and emerge unscathed. On the other hand, it is hard to make a plausible case that this fundamental difference makes it impossible to discern any continuity at all.

So there is a constellation of both continuity and connectibility on the one hand, radical discontinuity and critical distance on the other. Whether—and if so, how—these two poles can be reconciled depends on the "choice of focus."[43] Can the epoch of National Socialism be integrated historically in such a manner that the crimes mark a sharp line of discontinuity, while elements and factors of its context point to the very opposite? There is no logical contradiction here, and in categorial terms there are a number of possibilities for conceptualising this difference as a dimension of a historical nexus, and bringing it to bear while working on an interpretation.

There is a multiplicity of perspectives in which connectibility and discontinuity can be discussed, and a high degree of complexity of historical experience interpretively processed. Yet this notion of differing perspectives provides no answer to a key question: what standpoint of coherence can be applied to interrelate these various and diverse perspectives, if they are not totally arbitrary in their differentiation (which would indeed make it difficult to appropriate the era as a whole)? Thus, only one other avenue remains open: to integrate divergence, ambivalence and contrariness into the concept of an overarching whole, to include it in the category of development or continuity itself.[44] Yet this nullifies a premise that Broszat appears to use in his argument: that it is only possible to appropriate National Socialism by historicizing it, by mobilizing an overarching conception of time span—which has the logical character of what I would term an inner-temporal extension of meaning.

I am not advocating here that this category be replaced by one of inner-temporal senselessness, since this would mean that there would no longer be any intellectual appropriation of historical experience whatsoever. Rather, I believe it is necessary to jettison the equivalence of external temporal nexus and internal meaning, now a traditional commonplace in modern historical thought. It should be supplanted by a more complex conception in which the disappearance, negation, and absence of historical meaning become the instrument of historical thought itself in the developmental context of the changing times. Continuity can then be conceived as partly contrafactual and applied heuristically, so that radical discontinuities can also be identified and interpreted—without having in principle to relinquish the precondition of a meaningful bond between past and present.

In the discourse of historical theory there was the possibility that the Holocaust would acquire a solid place in the concept of an appropriable past framed in terms of development, and that the contingency of its realization would be included in the distinctive signature of historical time. This would burden the category of modernization with a dialectic that contains the contextualized "essential difference," alluded to above, as a categorial element. Horkheimer and Adorno attempted to constitute such a difference even in specific anthropological terms in their *Dialektik der Aufklärung*. But their dialectics lacked a temporal specificity that could have transformed it into a category of historical thought. Such a historization is long overdue. It would concretize the difference between National Socialism and the preceding and subsequent historical epochs other than by mere periodization and disintegration. National Socialism would appear as the chrono-dynamic product of a constellation of contingent circumstances and systemic preconditions for action, also to be found in other configurations, both earlier and later. The overarching development could be conceived as a schematism of this configuration with differing manifestations at different times. An additional feature here would be a direction of development relevant to the individual factors at play (such as technical options for action, ideological formations, techniques of dominance, possibilities for manipulation, etc.). Such a direction would serve to keep the path open for a fundamental contingency, thus allowing catastrophic events of monstrous proportion to appear possible, even as a result of elements of one's own world.

In such a perspective, the Holocaust would not forfeit its singularity, but rather would derive it from the very contingency of its genesis. Yet at the same time it would be historicized, its inception would be traced back in terms of the genesis of the individual factors of the contingent constellation that gave rise to it, as well as in terms of other contingent constellations that might emerge in the future.

But this conceptualising is only meaningful if at the same time, and in a similar configuration, elements and factors of everyday human life capable of continuity that make the Holocaust appear avoidable are underscored, or at least demystify its image as an ineluctable mythical fate. Operating from such a historical orientation, historical self-understanding in the present could be burdened with the experience of the Holocaust. This would set free and foster possibilities for action that could generate another future in the interplay of contingencies—different from the one projectable on the basis of a historicized conception of the Holocaust.

German identity

Only with the Holocaust can the Nazi era be appropriated intellectually. This proviso, which is obvious from the point of view of the perpetrators, cannot be directly transposed to the plane where Martin Broszat wishes to render National Socialism amenable to historical appropriation. Friedländer's understanding but persistent questioning as to what place the Holocaust will have in the way later generations of Germans view the Nazi era has underscored that the Holocaust retains a "blocking" and "erratic" place in the overarching temporal nexus within which National Socialism is integrated. Since it does not appear plausible to permit the mythical quality of authentic remembrance to stand alongside the historicizing appropriation of National Socialism—or even just to grant that mythic dimension the status of a vital source of strength in the perspective of the victims—this blockade is loaded with an additional unmitigated horror in the face of a past reality that must be processed into the present. That horror must be acknowledged and withstood precisely at the locus where the appropriated past is inscribed into the contours of present historical identity. In the process of historical appropriation, the Nazi era can only become relevant for identity if the Germans define themselves within the frame of a continuity containing within itself a genealogical nexus with the perpetrators. Ultimately, the entire debate really hinges on this perspective of the perpetrators: without this perspective National Socialism cannot be historicized, and only with this perspective can National Socialism as a historical era be distanced and at the same time remembered, with understanding and judgment. What does this imply for the contours of historical identity of those tied genealogically to the perpetrators?

If historical identity is based largely on a process whereby experiential components of the past with which one can identify in a positive sense (victories, deeds and exploits, primary foundational acts with traditional relevance for longer periods) are imputed to the present temporally and historically, then the intellectual appropriation of the Holocaust by historicizing National Socialism can indeed only act to confound identity formation. Thus, among those with an objectively genealogical link with the Holocaust, the psychological ability to survive depends on how well they dissociate from it mentally—either through the outright nonidentification of moral condemnation or by establishing absolute temporal discontinuity between that past and our present.

Yet such a "positivistic" historical identity remains problematic. It is based on a cultural practice of constructing belongingness according to the laws of exclusion: all elements of historical experience standing in the path of such a positive identification have to be shunted aside and integrated into the alterity of the others, from whom one has to be distinguished in order to become oneself. Those are elements, for example, that do not buttress the nonempirical identity one wants to imagine for oneself. Goldhagen's interpretation of the Holocaust exemplifies such a strategy of identity formation, via dichotomising exclusion.[45] Since the Holocaust is simply the "other" of our own self, it cannot be appropriated; it can only be understood and interpreted as part of the other. Who is to serve as this other? That remains an open question with diverse answers. This alterity can be an existent subject (such as communism in the interpretive scheme of totalitarianism theory) or some phantasm like the "demonic powers." In the self-understanding of Germans in the immediate post-war period, those fantasized fiendish forces had to serve as an excuse for exterritorializing complicity in the crimes of National Socialism, deporting them from their own subjectivity.

However, the logic of historical identity formation by means of exterritorializing has become increasingly more problematic. National Socialism owes its aggressiveness to that logic, and this was the cultural helm that guided its genocidal practice. It reached its most radical form in the Holocaust. Intellectual appropriation of the Holocaust means overcoming this logic of exclusion. In terms of identity theory, it means that the exterritorialized difference must be reabsorbed into one's own subjectivity. Then the alterity of the other becomes an inner precondition for one's own selfhood. Such an identity concept opens up new possibilities and modes of communication. Now you can see yourself in the other, and vice versa. At the same time, hand in hand with the acknowledgment of difference, something like a notion of human existence overarching all difference is inscribed as a cultural element in social life.

Translated into historical thought, such an identity concept permits one to see the reflection of one's own subjectivity in the dark glass of National Socialism's crimes; this sounds more astounding than it is. The "ordinary men" Christopher Browning describes constitute just such a reflection.[46] Within that mirroring, the crimes are still viewed as morally reprehensible, but condemnation takes on a genuinely historical dimension. Moral evaluation no longer centers on the past of the Nazi era, but on the temporal dynamics in which this era shuttles back and forward in time (running, so to speak, on the track of normality that made these people into murderers). The moralism intrinsic to the condemnation of past acts is transformed into a historical insight of a potentiality spanning the decades as an ever-present danger. This does not blur in any way the historical differences between the potentiality and actuality of inhumanity; rather, they are now perceived in the light of contingency. At the same time, the rigid focus on a temporally limited piece of the past dissolves and is amplified to encompass the perception of dynamic processes vaulting through the present on into the future.

Within the frame of such a conception of historical identity, what becomes of the perpetrators' authenticity? Like the suffering of the victims, it cannot be situated in a space of mythical presence displaced from historical consciousness. On the contrary, it must be taken seriously and brought to bear as a challenge of historical experience precisely at that site where the historical appropriation of the era intersects the innermost core of one's subjective being, one's "identity." It would appear as though there was only a fundamental act of nonidentification here, of unmitigated discontinuity and unmediated rupture. But then the moralism that obstructs the historical appropriation of this past would be ensconced in the very core of historization itself.

Yet there is another way to interpret complicity, one in which one's own subjectivity enters in some way into the perpetrators' brain, simultaneously reaching out beyond its perimeter. What constitutes the crime's historical particularity? To what extent does that particularity strike at the innermost core or foundation of the identity of those born after? The Holocaust constituted the most radical negation of an elementary normative dimension of being human—let me call it humanness (*Menschheitlichkeit*). At the same time, it shattered the conviction that humanness, imbued with a quasi-natural, fundamental and universal self-evidence, has a normative character and paramount inner value. It is this humanness that later generations, engaged in the identity-crucial process of historical understanding, must ascribe fundamentally to the subjects of the past (otherwise there would be nothing to understand). This applies likewise to the perpetrators. With their deeds, they also murdered their own humanness—and thus, in a certain way, humanity as a whole. It is here that the monstrousness of the Holocaust lies, an enormity that does not permit its inclusion in a continuity of historical developments that could serve as a positive fulcrum for appropriation.

But so conceptualized, does it not also destroy the basis of one's own humanness? Of course not. Yet it does reveal a basic truth: that the normative quality of humanness, one's own and at the same time universal *Menschheitlichkeit,* is itself contingent. It was murdered in the Holocaust. Those who recall the Holocaust in historical imagination must view this death as the loss of an essential part of their own selves. Yet in historical retrospect, this loss can be simultaneously perceived and overcome.

The psychological process required for that is mourning. Mourning has to be viewed as a cognitive achievement, its political significance realized. And it must be made concrete and palpable in the symbolic representation of the past.[47] My suggestion is that the thrust of the arguments in the debate between Broszat and Friedländer should be so interpreted that the plea for the historization of National Socialism issues in a corollary appeal: we must learn how to mourn historically.

This chapter was translated from the German by William Templer.

Notes

1. Peter Handke, in an interview with André Müller, *Die Zeit*, 3 March 1989, 77.
2. Jules Michelet, *Oeuvres complètes* 21, Paris, 1982, 462.
3. Christian Meier, *Vierzig Jahre nach Auschwitz: Deutsche Geschichtserinnerung heute*, 2nd edn. Munich, 1990, 10.
4. Martin Broszat, "A Plea for the Historization of National Socialism (1985)," translated in Peter Baldwin, ed., *Reworking the Past: Hitler, the Holocaust, and the Historians' Debate*, Boston, 1990, 77–87 (hereafter Broszat, "Plea"); Martin Broszat and Saul Friedländer, "A Controversy about the Historization of National Socialism," in ibid., 102–34.
5. Friedländer, "Reflections," pp. 88–101.
6. See Droysen, *Historik*, 69.
7. Martin Broszat, "Was heißt Historisierung des Nationalsozialismus?," *Historische Zeitschrift* 247 (1988), 5 (my emphasis).
8. Cf., e.g., Uwe Backes, Eckhard Jesse, Rainer Zitelmann, "Was heißt 'Historisierung' des Nationalsozialismus?," in idem, eds., *Der Schatten der Vergangenheit: Impulse zur Historisierung des Nationalsozialismus*, Frankfurt am Main, 1990, 25–57. The authors do not reject the idea of a moral evaluation of National Socialism, but fail to explore the question at least broached by Broszat regarding the impact of historization on the mode of normative evaluation of National Socialism. For them, historization means distancing and objectivizing, and no more, conceptualized as an uncoupling of historical thought from moral questions and perspectives. They do not inquire whether (and to what extent) such an uncoupling is even feasible epistemically. Rather, they justify it, and indeed assume it to be self-evident, invoking a common educational bugbear in support: the need to deal with the Nazi period in the framework of "popular education."
9. Broszat, "Historisierung," 2–3.
10. Brozat and Friedländer, "Controversy," 126.
11. Ibid., 132–33 and passim.
12. See Rüsen, *Historische Orientierung*.
13. The discourse on memory that takes its cue from Halbwachs makes a fundamental distinction between memory and history. The latter is conceptualized as the proper sphere of the historical sciences and regarded as an objective complex of facts, while memory is conceived as being subjectively constituted in its entirety. Friedländer follows this distinction, cf his *Memory, History and the Extermination of the Jews of Europe* Bloomington, 1993, viii. But he points out that memory and history are interconnected, and both are conveyed via the instrumentality of historical consciousness. Paul Ricoeur takes a similar tack in his "Gedächtnis-Vergessen-Geschichte," in Klaus E. Müller and Jörn Rüsen, eds., *Historische Sinnbildung. Problemstellungen, Zeitkonzepte, Wahrnehmungshorizonte, Darstellungsstrategien*, Reinbek, 1997.
14. A few representative studies: Nicolas Abraham, "Aufzeichnungen über das Phantom: Ergänzungen zu Freuds Metapsychologie," *Psyche* 45 (1991), 691–98; Bar-On, Dan, *Legacy of Silence: Encounters with Children of the Third Reich*, Cambridge, 1989; Werner Bohleber, "Das Fortwirken des Nationalsozialismus in der zweiten und dritten Generation nach Auschwitz," *Babylon* 4 (1990), 70–83.
15. On this complex constitutive nexus, see Jörn Rüsen, "Historisches Erzählen," in Rüsen, *Zerbrechende Zeit*, 43-106.
16. For example, Brozat, "Plea", 77 and 79; Brozat and Friedländer, "Controversy," 113; Broszat, "Historisierung," 3.
17. Of course, what remains as identity-shaping nexus is the ability to use general principles in moral and political evaluation beholden to the thought pattern of exemplary signification.
18. Yet one should not overlook the fact that this moralism too is historical in a substantive sense-only "exemplary" interpretive pattern that is too narrow for the present historical culture. Naturally, the Holocaust can be interpreted as an example, as an instance of human barbarism or

the like. In this interpretation, it forfeits its singularity (to be understood only genetically) and at the same time, as noted, its genealogical place and function. For an application of the typology of the traditional, exemplary, critical, and genetic as categories of the Holocaust, see Saul Friedländer, "The 'Final Solution': On the Unease in Historical interpretation," *History and Memory* 1.2 (1989), 61–73, esp. 72. Cf., my remarks on this in "Über den Umgang mit den Orten des Schreckens-Überlegungen zur Symbolisierung des Holocaust," in Detlef Hoffmann, ed., *Vergegenständlichte Erinnerung*, Frankfurt am Main, 1997, 26.

19. Brozat and Friedländer, "Controversy," 116.
20. Ibid.
21. Brozat, "Plea", 82.
22. Ibid., 85.
23. See on this Rüsen, *Rekonstruktion der Vergangenheit*, 37 sqq.
24. Dan Diner, "Between Aporia and Apology: On the Limits of Historicizing National Socialism," in P. Baldwin, ed., *Reworking the Past: Hitler, the Holocaust, and the Historians' Debate*, Boston, 1990, 135–45.
25. Martin Broszat, *Nach Hitler: Der schwierige Umgang mit unserer Geschichte*, Munich, 1988, 345.
26. Friedländer, "Reflections," 98.
27. Brozat and Friedländer, "Controversy," 133.
28. Christian Meier has remarked that the mythical quality which Broszat accords the memories of the victims "adheres to the event itself." See Christian Meier, "Der Historiker Martin Broszat," in Klaus-Dietmar Henke and Claudio Natoli, eds., *Mit dem Pathos der Nüchternheit. Martin Broszat, das Institut für Zeitgeschichte und die Erforschung des Nationalsozialismus*, Frankfurt am Main, 1991, 31.
29. Dan Diner, "Between Aporia and Apology: On the Limits of Historicizing National Socialism," 143.
30. Broszat, "Historisierung," 13.
31. Friedländer, "Reflections," 94.
32. If what is meant by the concept of historicist understanding is that National Socialism should be grasped within the purview of its own ideology, then it is correct to reject it. But historicism was not so stupid. Rather, a legacy of historicism here is the subjective quality of historical knowledge that is utilized hermeneutically.
33. Brozat, "Plea", 78.
34. Ibid.
35. Broszat and Friedländer, "Controversy," 132.
36. Ibid., "Description" is probably not meant here to be a concept counterposed to "narrative," unless conceived in terms of a narrow traditional notion of narration, a telling that reveals in vivid form the meaning of what is narrated via the chain of events described.
37. Ibid., 127.
38. Brozat, "Historisierung," 6.
39. See, for example, Broszat and Friedländer, "Controversy," 132. The expression "continuity" has categorial meaning. Cf., Hans Michael Baumgartner, *Kontinuität und Geschichte: Zur Kritik und Metakritik der historischen Vernunft*, Frankfurt am Main, 1972; Rüsen, *Historische Orientierung*,160 sqq.
40. Brozat and Friedländer, "Controversy," 125–26.
41. Friedländer later stated that German reunification "restored national continuity to German history" and reduced the Nazi period to a closed chapter, since its worst consequence for the Germans, namely the division of Germany, had now been ended; see his "Martin Broszat und die Historisierung des Nationalsozialismus," in Klaus-Dietmar Henke and Claudio Natoli, eds., *Mit dem Pathos der Nüchternheit. Martin Broszat, das Institut für Zeitgeschichte und die Erforschung des Nationalsozialismus*, Frankfurt am Main, 1991, 155–71, here 159. Yet this does not resolve the issue of continuity in the form of that basic problem for historical theory, namely, the question of historization as it emerges from the

arguments put forward by Broszat and Friedländer. How indeed can National Socialism have acquired in retrospect the attribute of connectible continuity in conjunction with patterns of social life, as a result of reunification? Moreover, the genealogy of the perpetrators has been reinforced in the wake of reunification, not attenuated.
42. Friedländer, "Reflections," 93.
43. Ibid.
44. Wolfgang Welsch has impressively demonstrated that this is a mode of reason; see: *Vernunft: Die zeitgenössische Vernunftkritik und das Konzept der transversalen Vernunft*, Frankfurt am Main, 1996.
45. Cf. Jörn Rüsen, "Goldhagens Irrtümer," in Rüsen, *Zerbrechende Zeit*, 263–78.
46. Christopher R. Browning, *Ordinary Men: Reserve Police Battalion 101 and the Final Solution in Poland*, New York, 1992.
47. Cf. Jörn Rüsen, "Trauer als historische Kategorie: Überlegungen zur Erinnerung an den Holocaust in der Geschichtskultur der Gegenwart," in Hanno Lowey, ed., *Erinnerung, Gedächtnis, Sinn: Authentische und konstruierte Erinnerung*, Frankfurt am Main, 1996, 57–78; also idem, "Auschwitz—die Symbole der Authentizität," in Rüsen, *Zerbrechende Zeit*, 181–216.

Chapter 11

Holocaust-Memory and German Identity

> Hätte ich doch unbekannte Worte, fremde Sprüche, in neuer Sprache, die noch nicht entstanden ist, ohne Wiederholung—keine Sprüche der Vergangenheit, die schon die Vorfahren gesagt haben.
> Doctrine of Chacheperresenub, 2nd Millenium BC[1]

> Statt des Schlafes tropft vor das Herz
> schwer die Erinnerung und ihre Qual, und
> ob der Sinn sich auch sträubt, es kommt
> die Erkenntnis.
> Aischylos[2]

> Denn da wir nun einmal die Resultate früherer Geschlechter sind, sind wir auch die Resultate ihrer Verirrungen, Leidenschaften und Irrtümer, ja Verbrechen; es ist nicht möglich, sich ganz von dieser Kette zu lösen.
> Friedrich Nietzsche[3]

A borderline experience

The Holocaust is the most radical experience of crisis in history. It is unique in its genocidal character and its radical negation and destruction of the basic values of modern civilization. As such it negates and destroys even the principles of its historical interpretation.

It has often been characterized as a "black hole" of meaning, that dissolves every concept of historical interpretation. It occludes construction of a meaningful narrative connection between the time before and after it. It is a "borderline-experience" of history, which doesn't allow its integration into a coherent narrative. It makes every attempt to apply comprehensive concepts of historical development fail.

Notes for this section begin on page 203.

Nevertheless it is necessary to recognize the Holocaust as a historical event and to give it a place in the historiographical pattern of modern history, within, which we understand ourselves, express our hopes and threats for the future, and develop our strategies of communication with others. If we placed the Holocaust beyond history by giving it a "mythical" significance it would lose its character of a factual event with empirical evidence. At the same time historical thinking would be limited in its approach to the experience of the past. This contradicts the logic of history. So the Holocaust represents a "borderline event," the importance of which consists in its transgression of the level of the subject matter of historical thinking and reaching into the core of the mental procedures of historical thinking itself.[4]

It is the intention of this chapter to analyze this "borderline" character of the Holocaust in respect to the role historical thinking plays in the process of building collective identity. I will deal mainly with problems of German identity after the end of the Second World-War, but I think that these problems include elements of identity formation, that can be found in many other societies as well.

In order to clarify this specific case I would like to discuss the issue against the background of a general theory of historical consciousness and its cultural function.

Crisis, history, identity

A crisis is nothing special and peculiar in the realm of historical consciousness. On the contrary, crises constitute historical consciousness, so one can say that there is no historical consciousness without crises. By "crises" I mean a certain experience of temporal change: that of contingency. It evokes the human mind in its conceptualization of the relationship between human activity and suffering and the change of the human world in the course of time. This course of time always has a "critical" character: it cannot be sufficiently understood as the result of change brought about by human activities along the line of deliberate intentions. On the contrary, it happens against intended objectives, or at least deviates from them. There is no human life without this experience of disturbing temporal changes against expectation and intention. This specific time experience of rupture and discontinuity is what is meant by "contingency."

Historical consciousness is the mental answer to the challenge of contingency.[5] Since contingency disturbs pregiven orientations of human life in the course of time, it has the ontological status of a "crisis" related to the fundamental pattern of significance, that orients human activities in such a way that people can pursue and realize their objectives. The security of human life in the relationship between objectives, means, and realizations of actions is permanently and fundamentally irritated by the experience of things, that are relevant for these actions happening in a way, that cannot be understood within the instrumental rationality of human activity. By this I mean that the temporal change of the world in general cannot be understood along the line of causality by intention (something happened because somebody wanted it to happen and pursued his or her will).

In order to meet this distraction of security the human mind has to establish patterns of meaning and significance, following another logic than the logic of instrumental rationality. It is the logic of telling a story, that makes sense of the contingent events not subjugated under the notion of realizing objectives by changing the pregiven situation of human life. Historical narratives put the temporal change of these situations into an order in which the crisis of contingency is dissolved into a sense and meaningful concept of temporal change of the human world. This is what I meant when I said that crisis constitutes historical consciousness.

The interpretative work of historical consciousness is a procedure of identity building. This is true for individuals as well as for groups. Identity is a concept of the coherence of oneself in relationship to others and to oneself as well. This coherence has a synchronic and a diachronic dimension. Synchronically identity integrates the different relationships of an individual or collective "self" to others into a unit in which the self is aware of itself. It "reflects" (bends back)* the relationship to others back to the self and gives it an internal unity in the variety of its manifold relations to others. Diachronically this self-reflectedness is related to the change of the self and its relationships to others in the course of time. In this respect identity is a concept of continuity of the sameness of oneself in the changes that every person and group have to undergo in the course of their lives.

In my further considerations I will neglect the relationship between the synchronic and diachronic dimension of identity and deal only with the diachronical dimension. Here I will focus on two issues: the intergenerational extension of identity and its grounding on events of the past kept present by causal consequences and by memory.

The temporal coherence of the human self is not limited by the lifespan of individuals. Social units of individuals that form a collective identity tend to extend their temporal self-awareness and self-relationship into an intergenerational duration and continuity. Belonging to such a self furnishes the individual members with an awareness of an eternity-like duration; they transform the biological chain of generations within which they live into a cultural unit of time which comprehends past, present, and future beyond their individual life span. It is this temporal unit which they feel and think of as being their collective self, beyond the limits of their births and deaths, defining the cultural nature of their social relationship. Brought about by historical consciousness,

---

*latin *reflectere* = to bend back

this temporal unit of a collective self consists in a synthesis of experiences of the past and expectations of the future. In this synthesis the past is present as a mentally moving force loaded with the entire powers with which the human mind is directed toward the future. It is the force of memory which shapes the features of identity and makes the past a projection of the future.

So memory and historical consciousness are closely interrelated, but they are not the same. Historical consciousness is grounded on the mental forces of memory, but it transgresses memory in a decisive step: it keeps, or makes, the past alive where it lies beyond the memory of the social unit concerned. It even influences and shapes the memory of the people with conceptualized experiences they themselves did not have. Historical consciousness enlarges the temporal extension of memory into an intergenerational continuity and duration of the collective self. The idea of this continuity, that meets the desire of transgressing birth and death, moves the cultural procedures and practices in which a society thematizes and confirms its togetherness and its difference from others.

Identity by events

In these procedures and practices historical events play a decisive role. They are commemorated and represented in a way that their contingency stands for the peculiarity and uniqueness of the self. These philosophical terms describe very familiar phenomena: Marriage, for example, is an element of social identity and it is grounded and constituted on a single event, the ceremony in which a man and a woman become husband and wife. Human life is full of these constitutive events: baptizing makes a person a Christian; in early societies every socially important stage in the human life cycle was done in a ceremony which constituted an element of the individual's identity. By memory these events are kept alive and with this life the constituted identity is kept up and permanently confirmed in the interaction and communication where identity is intensively discussed or only mentioned.

The same is true for the temporal realm of historical consciousness beyond the limits of personal and generational memory. Here, events play a constitutive role in shaping collective identity. Historical consciousness furnishes and moulds them by the mental force of norms and values that regulate human activities with cultural orientations and impulsions and objectives of will.

The social group concerned, relates itself to events in the past beyond the lifespan of its members. They feel themselves committed to them in a certain way: they use them in order to formulate, express, activate, and confirm the cultural pattern of their self, of their togetherness and their difference to others. So in the realm of religious identity, for example, Christians are fundamentally related to the events that happened with and by Jesus. In the same way Muslims are related to the events of Mohammed's life. So events constitute identity in the realm of historical consciousness. If the constitution is related to the social world in general, the constituting event takes place beyond the horizon of this world in the experience of its people. In this case the event has a "mythical" character. But this does not mean that the people think it did not really happen. On the contrary, the reality of this event is estimated as being higher, or more real, than the so-called real world.

The term "historical" covers the whole realm of this constitutive commemoration of events. In a more narrow sense it means that the constitutive event is of the same nature as the events within the horizon of experience of the people who rely on it.

It is not always a single event, of course, that constitutes identity, mainly it is an event in a temporal connection with other events in which it has its specific importance, its constitutive power. There is always a chain of events which combines the present-day situation with the very event on which the people rely in order to explain themselves, and the others they live together with; to explain who they are, what the order of their lives is, and how they understand the otherness of the others. "History" as a subject matter of historical consciousness is this temporal chain of events. It has the cultural power of shaping identity. It is a power that can be described with the Hegelian term of "causality of fate" (*Kausalität des Schicksals*). It is a decision about the peculiarity of one's own self as a cultural framework of life, (not at all constructed), by those who were defined by it, but constructing them in their peculiarity and distinction from others.

So historical identity is shaped by the representation of historical events continued by the chain of generations. These events lie at different levels of importance concerning their power of identity formation. In an ideal typological way one can distinguish three possibilities.

Events with a positive founding or constituting function

Well known examples are the Declaration of Independence for the political identity of the citizens of the United States, the resurrection of Christ for the Christians; and the exodus from Egypt for the Jews.

Events constituting identity in a negative way

In this case identity is built against the importance of events for the identity of others against whom one's own identity has to be conceptualized. For a long time this has been, for example, the case of Germany. German identity in its modern national form was shaped against the model of national identity in the Western (mainly the French) type. The Germans focused their obligatory political value system against the "ideas of 1789." They claimed for a German *"Sonderweg"* defined by its deviation from the Western way of modernization.[6] During the history of German nationalism there was no one single decisive event which had the normative character of constituting the German national self-understanding. But in most cases the historical events which served as a focus of national self-understanding (like the Reformation, the war of liberation against the French, the victory over France 1870/71, the national enthusiasm of August 1914—"Die Ideen von 1914") were conceptualized against another idea of national identity, mainly the French one with its universalistic dimension, including human and civil rights.

EVENTS, OR CHAINS OF EVENTS

Such events that change older concepts of collective identity into newer ones, were seen as being more convincing according to the present-day situation of the people and their future expectations. An example of such a change could be a process of secularization which changed a religious identity into a nonreligious one (then called "cultural"), or the replacement of an old constitution by a new one. For the current German national identity, such a chain of events can be shortly described as a sequence: defeat of the Nazi regime; a new constitution in West Germany; and unification. In the last case it is remarkable, and belongs to the specificy of the topical concept of national identity in Germany, that there was no "founding" or "constituting" activity of unification: so objectively, the new Germany is only an enlargement of the old West Germany, whereas subjectively it might be different. This difference causes problems of German identity today.

This character of events which are remembered as decisive steps of a historical process in the concept of collective identity can furthermore be distinguished by the following types:

- Events as turning points. Here the German unification can serve as an example. It has turned German 'national' identity into a new form, from an unclear feeling of togetherness, comprehending the Federal Republic and the Democratic Republic and weakened by an emerging West-German East-German identity, into a clear national dimension of political identity. Other turning points influencing the German identity are the events of the European unification.
- Events revoking hitherto valid patterns of collective identity, for example, the German defeat in 1945.
- Events which renew valid patterns of collective identity, for example, the American civil war.

This enumeration is not complete and can be further developed and differentiated. For the purpose of my argument it is sufficient, because it shows that those historical events which focus collective identity can do this focussing in highly different ways. There is not only one mode of presenting historical events with the normative power of forming collective identity with the causality of fate.

Depending upon and working about the past

Collective identity is rooted in the presentation of events. They play their role as roots in the form of "historical events." "Historical" means that the events have a specific meaning and significance in the life orientation of the people who rely on them when they reflect about who they are, and when they characterize the otherness of the others. So a "historical" event is a synthesis of factuality based on experience on the one hand and intentionality (traditionally called "spirituality" and today mainly called "fictionality") based on the creative forces of the human mind, on the other hand. These two elements should be carefully distinguished in analyzing the process of identity building by historical consciousness. To distinguish them is an artificial act, but it is necessary, as the dynamics of identity building are constituted in a mental process in which an event becomes historical, and in which the experience of the past is moulded into a meaningful history by interpretation and representation.

Dependence upon the past means that historical consciousness takes place in a context where the past has brought about conditioning presuppositions for the mental activities of remembering it. These presuppositions are not freely disposable, but they have to be recognized in order to pursue their mental procedures and to fulfill the orienting function of historical consciousness. They are the result of developments in the past which determine the lives of the people in the present, and are looked upon by them as being fateful. So the dependence concerned can be characterized in Hegel´s (1955) words as "causality by fate." "Causality" can be concretized as a place in a chain of generations, aside from and independent of the awareness and the deliberate relationship to the past of those who have to live their lives in this place of time. They were bound into this specific link of the chain of generations. Here the past has grown into the external and internal circumstances of present-day life, without, and sometimes even against, the will of those who have to come to terms with them. In this perspective historical consciousness depends upon the past, which it has to transform into sense- and meaningful history.

This "causal" or "fateful" relationship is not limited to external conditions of human life, but includes its internal conditions as well, the mental preformations and possibilities in culturally dealing with the past when making history out of it. The fateful generational chain has a mental dimension effective in traditions, prejudices, resentments, threats, hopes, value systems, basic convictions, and—not to forget—the forces of subconscious attitudes and instincts guided by suppressive forgetfulness.

In the other perspective the past becoming history depends upon the mode of those for whom it has the meaning and relevance of history. Now the events are, so to speak, raw material, which has to be formed into a concept of temporal change with which topical human activity and suffering can be oriented toward the future. The burden of the past pressing human identity into the responsibility for things and events that happened without their participation, has now changed into the creativity of the human mind. It shapes the past into a perspective of a development, that ends in the projection of the future bearing the identity of the people along the lines of their self-esteem. Fateful causality is replaced by value-guided commitment, deliberately related to the events of the past. They are treated as if they had to be redeemed in the future course of temporal change of the human world.

In the frame of this tension between fateful causality and value-guided commitment, historical consciousness pursues its operations of identity building.

A catastrophic root of German identity

In most perspectives of historical consciousness the Holocaust constitutes German identity by a catastrophe. As a pregiven event to be dealt with, the Holocaust belongs to those events of the past which have determined the life situation of Germany today. It is a part of a history which led to a complete defeat of the nation and to a destruction of large parts of the country, to the political division of Germany; to a loss of land and the expulsion of its people; and to a mental burden of guilt, responsibility, shame, horror, suppression, and trauma. The pregiven temporal chain of generations is the channel through which this event is related to the external and internal circumstances under which the Germans have to live. It would be misleading to look at this channel as one single string combining the Nazi past with the Germany of today. In fact, it is a very complex texture of threads knitting together, through different knots, different parts of the German people. The historical perspective which comprehends this texture is a complex mixture of subperspectives in which different groups of Germans today are related to different groups of Germans and non-Germans in the past. Concerning the people, the activities and sufferings of which constituted decisive elements of the fateful dependence, one

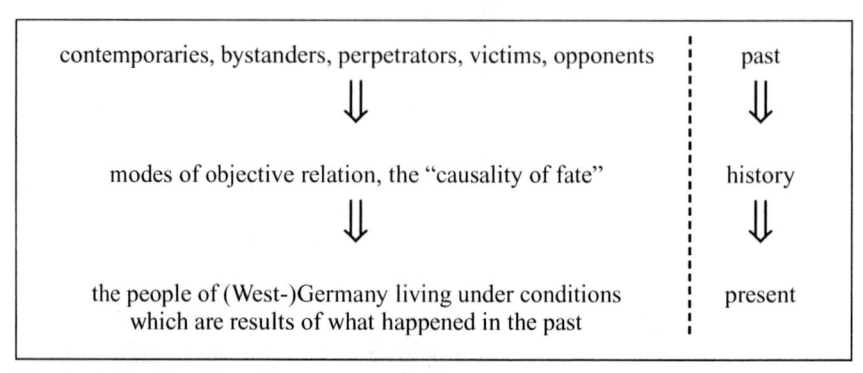

contemporaries, bystanders, perpetrators, victims, opponents	past
⇓	⇓
modes of objective relation, the "causality of fate"	history
⇓	⇓
the people of (West-)Germany living under conditions which are results of what happened in the past	present

FIGURE 11.1 THE PAST CONDITIONS THE PRESENT

can distinguish different groups: the contemporaries, bystanders, perpetrators, victims, and opponents. There is no clear and evident historical relationship between these groups of Germans in the Nazi period to specific groups of the German people of today. The majority may be objectively related to bystanders and perpetrators, but one should not overlook that a notable part of the victims and opponents were Germans as well. This is even true for a part of the Jewish victims who considered themselves as being Germans.

Through this network of generational relationship the specific German fateful tie to the Holocaust can be typologically differentiated into four classes of determinations.

1. The consequences of Nazi period inbuilt in the life conditions of the German people of today. I have already mentioned some of the consequences (e.g. division of the nation), but here I have to add two more: it is a rupture in the genealogical chain caused by the high death rate of soldiers and civilians due to the events of the war, and the disappearance of influential Jewish elements in German culture.
2. Mentally there can be observed a "silent continuity" of attitudes, including a change in at least some parts of these attitudes (e.g. authoritarian personality, a certain kind of work ethics, power-protected inwardness (*machtgeschützte Innerlichkeit*), anti-Western resentments. It is not so much the single attitude which combines the generations, but it is a certain mode of realization and its relationship to others which characterizes German identity and its alteration. The historical character of its relationship between past, present, and future is a synthesis of continuity and change, caused by the change in the life circumstances of the people.
3. A specific element of these continuous attitudes, mentioned separately, consists of different kinds of traumatic transference, the heritage of the victims as well as that of the perpetrators, handed down to their children and grandchildren (at least to a part of them).
4. Finally, the memory of those who participated in the Holocaust is a determining factor of historical consciousness. This memory changed in the course of time according to new experiences, such as the Cold War, and new interpretations that changed the content and the patterns of significance of the memory of the Holocaust. But this memory (including a suppressive forgetfulness) remained the most important representation of the Holocaust as an event of central importance for German identity.

All of the factors together form the "starting point" of historical consciousness in Germany. It is initiated by these pregiven circumstances, initiated so far as future-directed intentions and pregiven reality structurally differ and have to be bridged. Historical consciousness has to work through these circumstances in presenting them as an end of historical development which

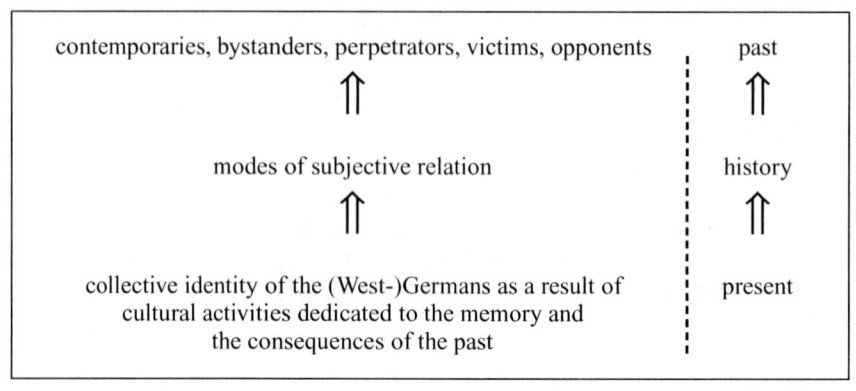

```
┌─────────────────────────────────────────────────────────────────────┐
│   contemporaries, bystanders, perpetrators, victims, opponents  ┊  past      │
│                              ⇑                                  ┊   ⇑        │
│                   modes of subjective relation                  ┊  history   │
│                              ⇑                                  ┊   ⇑        │
│   collective identity of the (West-)Germans as a result of      ┊  present   │
│   cultural activities dedicated to the memory and               ┊            │
│   the consequences of the past                                  ┊            │
└─────────────────────────────────────────────────────────────────────┘
```

FIGURE 11.2 THE PRESENT CONDITIONS THE PAST

started in, or at least passed, the Nazi period and which will lead into a different future. Bridging the gap between the conditioning past and the intended future, historical consciousness changes the fateful dependence into a value-guided acceptance or legitimacy of identity. In this transformation the experience of catastrophe remains a decisive point. On the intentional level it works as a normative factor, that decides about the interpretation by which the past becomes history for the present. Catastrophe here works as a negative evaluation which structures the decisive events in the narrative flow of historical arguments that shape German self-awareness, their idea of collective identity and their distinction of otherness.

The Holocaust has not always been the decisive event of the Nazi period in respect to which the Germans related themselves to this period. On the contrary; the post-wardevelopment of German historical consciousness is characterized by an increasing importance of the Holocaust with the growing temporal distance to it. Since this distance brings about the already mentioned difference between memory and historical consciousness one can say that the Holocaust gained its historical significance in the transforming process by which the memory of Nazi period develops the features of historical consciousness.

Concealment

In the last part of the chapter I would like to propose an outline of the development of German historical consciousness, and its related concept of collective identity, according to the catastrophical feature of Nazi period and the Holocaust.

I would like to characterize the very complex development of post-war German identity in an ideal typological way distinguishing three main stages. It would be misleading to understand this distinction of three stages as if they replaced each other. In fact, they coexist and form different constellations and mixtures. But logically, and even in respect to temporal sequences, they can clearly be distinguished.

In the first one the crime of the Nazi era remained, of course, in the minds of the perpetrators and the victims who still lived in Germany, and of those who knew about them. As such it had the importance of an event against which identity was shaped, or at least the importance of an event which changed the collective identity substantially. The Germans entered the postwar era with a feeling of a collective catastrophe, a complete defeat. This catastrophe was also seen as a rupture of identity, which radically weakened the hitherto strong nationalism. Self-esteem, which belongs to traditional nationalism, had become impossible vis-à-vis its role in the Nazi period. Only a certain manifestation of it could survive: the self-esteem of being industrious and effective in work.[7]

For the purpose of mental survival the Germans had to bridge the rupture within their historical identity and to overcome its fundamental crisis. The answer to the challenge of rupture was—at least on the level of the intellectual debate and the education system—a revocation of national traditions, that could be interpreted as opposed to the Nazi ideology. Friedrich Meinecke, for example, recommended Goethe as a renovating historical element of German identity.[8] Events from a long way back, or historical elements of German history where collective identity can be positively rooted, had bypassed Nazi-time, and especially the Holocaust. The Holocaust was not a historical element that fitted into the realm of "our" history. If it had an identity-building role at all (on the level of deliberate mental activity and not in the unconscious) it indicated and manifested "otherness."

The crisis of collective identity was overcome by leaving aside if not suppressing the memory of the Holocaust and related crimes in the realm of public discussion and political activity. The new West German democracy became very successful, and one condition for this success was the integration of the largest part of the elite of the Nazi system into the new republic. This integration had a mental dimension, for there was an unspoken agreement not to deal with the far-going entanglement in the Nazi system.[9] In the mental strategy of identity building the threatening features of the Nazi period were projected into the otherness of the perpetrators, beyond the limits of one's own self. The Nazis were demonized and exterritorialized into a realm beyond the main lines of German history. Nazism and Nazi dictatorship shrank into an invasion of a relatively small group of political gangsters coming out of nowhere and occupying Germany.[10] The "ordinary" Germans—and that meant those who had to come to terms with their own past—were characterized as victims of a devilish Nazi seduction.[11] The psychological strategy of this kind of moulding of collective memory in order to get rid of the burden of one's own entanglement is described as the procedure of "reversing" in psychoanalysis. It can be observed even in the subtlety of academic discourse.[12]

The concept of totalitarianism later on confirmed this exterritorialization: now during the cold war period "the others" could be identified beyond the iron curtain, and the burdening experience of Nazism could be inscribed into the face of the common enemy, the Communists. So a collective conviction could be brought about: not we, but the others were guilty.[13]

Later on this strategy of public silence and exterritorialization has been criticized as a mental failure, a structural deformation of the German mind. This criticism was the consequence of a new moralistic approach to the Nazi period, which constitutes the second period. This criticism, the most prominent document of which is Alexander and Margarete Mitscherlich's "Die Unfähigkeit zu trauern,"[14] overlooked the limited possibilities of mental survival and the function of forgetfulness in overcoming a deep identity crisis by a rupture of historical continuity.

The only line of continuity, which went through the Nazi period bound it to the real German history, and therefore what was publicly commemorated was the German opposition to Hitler (except for its Communist branch).

Moralization

The second stage came along with the next generation of Germans who had to gain their own concept of collective identity by struggling with their parents. Their concept is characterized by its relationship to the Holocaust by two tensional intentions. The first is to remember the Holocaust and give it a historical relevance and importance for German collective memory. Now, for the first time, it got its place in a historical perspective that ended in the mental field of historical German self-understanding. It was not especially the Holocaust, but the Nazi period in general, that played a new role in building collective identity. Now it was used as a counterevent, constituting German identity in a negative way. In this negative way the Nazi period became an integral part of German history.

The new generation grounded its self-esteem in a strictly moralistic criticism of this period, using universal standards of political culture which had become valid in their political socialization. In its most elaborated form this negative constitutive role was confirmed and realized by an identificatory step into the period of Nazism: selfness got its moralistic power by an identification with the victims. The others were the perpetrators and bystanders. Otherness now lost its transhistorical status and became a part of German history itself, against which the new Germany was placed.

What were the consequences of this integration of the Holocaust into German history for the concept of collective identity? In respect to its peculiarity it lost the features of an obligatory tradition. Tradition was replaced by universalistic values and norms. This universalism has now become a constitutive factor for reshaping German identity. It has got its mental power and the strength of its conviction by the negative historical experience of Nazi history. Brought into the horizon of German self-awareness it pushed the new generation into the mental attitude of standing for its contrary, and of placing itself strictly beyond any historical relationship reaching into the centre of oneself. By this approach otherness has become a part of one's own history: now it is manifest in the past of one's own people but in a way that it is excluded from the realm of oneself.

This relationship of German identity to the Nazi period shows a fragile mixture of a metahistorical universality of norms and values, and historical experience, mediated by contradiction and still prevailing with many Germans. The next step is dedicated to the task to overcome the fragility of this mixture into an entire historization of the Nazi past, including the Holocaust.

Historization

The third stage has just started and it is an open question whether it will come to a particular new form of collective identity; but there are clear indications of it. The decisive new element reshaping German identity is an opening of the German mind to the genealogical relationship to the perpetrators. The moralistic criticism of the Holocaust, accompanied by an identification with the victims, kept this relationship outside the constitutive historical elements of the Germans' self. The growing distance of generational change enables the Germans to bridge the mental gap which separated them from their fathers and grandfathers in the historical perspective of their self-awareness. Those who perpetrated the Holocaust, were "the others." But these "others" were, at the same time, Germans like those who could not mediate themselves with them along the line of temporal change in German history. Now this mediation takes place: prominent historians start to say "we" to the perpetrators.[15]

This indicates a challenging need for reconceptualizing German identity. The objectively pregiven genealogical chain of generations now has become a structural element of the historical perspective within which German identity is shaped. The Germans start to define themselves as a result of a historical transformation, in which the perpetrators and bystanders become integral parts of the historical experience, moulding the feature of German peculiarity as a mirror of self-reflection. The a-temporal moral distance of the second stage is transformed into a specifically "historical" distance. The Holocaust is about to obtain a place in the chain of events by which the shape of German identity is constituted. In this "historical" place the Holocaust, of course, has not lost its character as the contrary of any valid system of values which the Germans feel collectively committed to. The point is that this otherness is now a part of a person's own self.

It is not yet clear what this means in respect to the symbolic order of historical experience as a feature of the collective self of the Germans. Such a feature always needs a certain coherence in arranging the events of the past into a concept of temporal order, that can function as a pattern of selfunderstanding and of cultural orientation. Coherence gives constitutive values a legitimatory role. For the Germans the Holocaust can never serve as a legitimation of their peculiarity as a nation. The reason is complex. Certainly there is a genealogical line between the Germans today and the perpetrators, but this line doesn't exclusively combine them with the perpetrators, since a part of the victims and of the opponents were Germans as well. On the other hand, this line is so strong that any legitimatory approach to the Holocaust would put the Germans of today into the role of the successors of the perpetrators, which strictly contradicts the universalistic values which were deeply rooted in the German political culture and a constitutive element of their collective identity. As long as the perpetrators were integrated into a common "Germanhood," that is, as long as they were recognized as Germans, German collective identity is featured by a negative constituting event as an inclusive part of their own history.

This inclusion of the otherness of the Holocaust requires a new logic of historically shaping collective identity: the strict exclusion of negative elements in the horizon of historical experience related to one's own people has become impossible. The temporal chain of events constituting historically collective identity includes the Holocaust with its negative meaning and significance. This significance prevents any form of coherence in the historical feature of oneself, which is brought about by an entire positive identification with the past. The historical feature of oneself has become fragmented and loaded with tensions and even contradictions. As long as this fragmentary character and negativity is conceptualized with a principle of historical sense it can serve as a reliable cultural frame of orientation and identity building. "Sense"[16] in this respect means an essential openness of the temporal dimension of historical identity, a contrafactual validity of fundamental regulative ideas, placing the collective self just on the borderline between past and present, where the transformation of pregiven circumstances takes place. Here an essential insufficiency of historical origin ends in the projective force of the human mind, which discloses creative chances of change. Identity—whether it is a personal or a collective one—is always a synthesis of what one has been and of what one would like to become. In respect of this tensional synthesis the constitutive force of the Holocaust in the historical perspective of German identity evokes its complement as a projection of a future, which is committed to the categorical consequence of the Holocaust which Adorno has stated as a general principle of human thinking: that it should never happen again.[17]

Within this new feature of collective identity the relationship of crisis and identity has essentially changed. In traditional cultural procedures of commemoration, identity has overcome the crisis: the discontinuity and rupture caused by contingency is transformed by historical consciousness into a new meaningful coherence in the temporal connection of past, present, and future.

Now crisis has become an element of identity itself. This means that the people cannot rely on a deep conviction that their form of life is fundamentally legitimated and they can rely on the permanence of their life form at least in its essential elements. An inbuilt "critical" element in this feature furnishes this permanence and legitimacy with projective elements with regulative ideas of practical reason. They are permanently generated and pushed forward by the sting of memory that keeps the Holocaust present. The memory of the Holocaust has been transformed into a historical consciousness, which relativates one's self-esteem with a character of imperfectability, and this imperfectability can be realized as a chance for practical activities.

Concerning this third stage, one can only observe indications and starting points. So it is an open question whether and how this new logic of identity building by the Holocaust memory will bring about a new relationship between German national identity and the Holocaust, and a new structure in the concept of collective identity, where otherness and selfness will have a new mediation beyond the cultural logic and practice of identity building by exclusion of otherness.

Notes

1. (That I had unknown words, strange sayings in a new language, not yet born and unprecedented, no sayings from the past which the forefathers have already used.) Wolfgang Helck, "Ägypten im frühen Neuen Reich. Grundzüge einer Entwicklung," in Arne Eggebrecht, ed., *Ägyptens Aufstieg zur Weltmacht*, Mainz, 1987, 11.
2. (Instead of sleep memories and their pain heavily drip to the heart and with the sense resisting cometh cognition.) Agamemnon, 177f.
3. (Since we are the results of former generations we also are the results of their aberrations, passions and errors, even their crimes; it is impossible to completely sever from this chain.) Friedrich Nietzsche, "Vom Nutzen und Nachteil der Historie für das Leben (Unzeitgemäße Betrachtungen, zweites Stück)," in idem, *Sämtliche Werke*, Kritische Studienausgabe in 15 Einzelbänden, vol. 1, Munich, 1988, 270.
4. Cf. chap. 10.
5. Cf. Rüsen, *Historische Orientierung*, 3 sqq, "Was ist Geschichtsbewußtsein? Theoretische Überlegungen und heuristische Hinweise."
6. Bernd Faulenbach, *Ideologie des deutschen Weges. Die deutsche Geschichte in der Historiographie zwischen Kaiserreich und Nationalsozialismus*, Munich, 1980.
7. Frank Trommler has described this nationalism and its origin in the late nineteenth century. Frank Trommler, "Arbeitsnation statt Kulturnation? Ein vernachlässigter Faktor deutscher Identität," in *Akten des VII. Internationalen Germanistenkongreß*, vol. 9, Göttingen, 1985.
8. Friedrich Meinecke, *Die deutsche Katastrophe*, 2nd edn., Wiesbaden, 1946.
9. This is the famous thesis of Hermann Lübbe that originally caused much emotional contradiction, but in the meantime has got widespread acceptance: "Der Nationalsozialismus im deutschen Nachkriegsbewußtsein," *Historische Zeitschrift* 236 (1983), 579–99.

10. An example for this exterritorialization is the inaugural speech of Leopold von Wiese at the first post-war meeting of German sociologists: "Die Pest kam über die Menschen von außen, unvorbereitet, als ein heimtückischer Überfall. Das ist ein metaphysisches Geheimnis, an das der Soziologe nicht zu rühren vermag" (The plague came upon the unprepared people from the outside. This is a metaphysical secret, not to be touched by a sociologist). Leopold von Wiese, 'Die gegenwärtige Situation, soziologisch betrachtet', in *Verhandlungen des Achten Deutschen Soziologentages vom 19. bis 21. September 1946 in Frankfurt am Main*. Tübingen, 1948, 29.
11. A rather late example for this presentation of the Nazi period is the film, *Hitler—eine Karriere*, directed by Christian B. Herrendörfer and Joachim Fest, 1976.
12. So, for example, Ernst Nolte's argument that the Zionist world congress had declared war on Nazi Germany, so Hitler was legitimized at least to intern the Jews. Ernst Nolte, "Zwischen Geschichtslegende und Revisionismus?" in *"Historikerstreit:" Die Dokumentation der Kontroverse um die Einzigartigkeit der nationalsozialistischen Judenvernichtung*, Text von Augstein, Munich, 1987, 13–35.
13. This again can be exemplified by Nolte's thesis that Nazidictatorship was only a reaction to Bolshevism and the Holocaust only an answer to a "more original" event, namely the October Revolution and the crimes of the Bolsheviks (see fn. 12).
14. Alexander Mitscherlich und Margarete Mitscherlich, *Die Unfähigkeit zu trauern. Grundlagen kollektiven Verhaltens*. 1st edn. Munich 1967, reprinted Leipzig, 1990; Alexander and Margarete Mitscherlich, *The Inability to Mourn. Principles of Collective Behavior*, New York, 1975.
15. Christian Meier, *Vierzig Jahre nach Auschwitz. Deutsche Geschichtserinnerung heute*, Munich, 2nd edn, 1990, for example argues in favor of the integration of the Holocaust into the identity building perspective of German history. In his foreword of the new edition of 1990 he clearly speaks of a "hypothecial attempt, to include the Germans from 1933 till 1945 into a historical 'We'" (10). Meier himself did the step from hypothesis to positive assertion in an article, published in *Die Zeit*, 11th April 1997, 48, commenting the controversial debate about a Holocaust memorial in Berlin. He speaks of the Holocaust and uses the words "our crimes" (unsere Verbrechen). Another finding: Reinhart Koselleck, "Vier Minuten für die Ewigkeit," *Frankfurter Allgemeine Zeitung*, 9 January 1997. Some further observations: "Als Deutscher stehe ich unvermeidlich auf der Seite der Täter ... Wenn ich mich in meinem Land verwurzelt fühlen möchte, muß ich mich auch in die Geschichte seiner Menschen hineinversetzen. So werde und bleibe ich verantwortlich verbunden mit dem, was Deutsche getan haben" Thomas Auchter, "Jenseits des Versöhnungsprinzips. Die Grenzen des Erinnerns," *Universitas* 52 (1997), 230–40, cit. 231.
16. More details of this principle were discussed in Rüsen, *Zerbrechende Zeit*, chaps. 1 and 2.
17. Theodor W. Adorno, "Erziehung nach Auschwitz," in idem, *Stichworte. Kritische Modelle 2*, Frankfurt am Main, 1969, 85–101, cit. 85.

Bibliography

Abraham, Nicholas (1991) "Aufzeichnungen über das Phantom: Ergänzungen zu Freuds Metapsychologie," *Psyche* 45:691–98.
Adorno, T.W. (1969) "Erziehung nach Auschwitz," in idem *Stichworte. Kritische Modelle 2*, Frankfurt am Main.
Aischylos (1976) *Die Orestie des Aischylos,* trans. Dietrich Ebener, Berlin.
Angvik, M. and Borries, Bodo von (eds.) (1997) *Youth and History: A Comparative European Survey on Historical Consciousness and Political Attitudes among Adolescents*, Hamburg.
Ankersmit, Frank R. (1983) *Narrative Logic. A Semantic Analysis of the Historian's Language*, The Hague.
Ankersmit, Frank R. (1986) *Denken over Geschiedenis. Een Overzicht van Moderne Geschiedfilosofische Opvattingen*, 2nd edn, Groningen.
Ankersmit, Frank R. (1994) *History and Tropology: The Rise and Fall of Metaphor*, Berkeley.
Ankersmit, Frank R. (2001) "The sublime dissociation of the past: or how to be(come) what one is no longer," *History and Theory* 40:295–323.
Ankersmit, Frank R. and H. Kellner (eds.) (1995) *A New Philosophy of History*, Chicago.
Appleby, Joyce, Hunt, Lynn and Jacob, Margaret (1994) *Telling the Truth about History,* New York.
Aristotle (1982) *Poetik. Griechisch/Deutsch,* trans. and ed. Manfred Fuhrmann, Stuttgart.
Arthur C.D. (1968) *Analytical Philosophy of History*, Cambridge.
Asthana, Pratima (1992) *The Indian View of History*, Agra.
Auchter, Thomas (1997) "Jenseits des Versöhnungsprinzips. Die Grenzen des Erinnerns," *Universitas* 52:230–40.
Backes, U., Jesse, E. and R. Zitelmann (1990) "Was heißt 'Historisierung' des Nationalsozialismus?", in *Der Schatten der Vergangenheit: Impulse zur Historisierung des Nationalsozialismus*, ed. idem, Frankfurt am Main, 25–57.
Bann, Stephen (1990) "Analysing the Discourse of History," in idem *The Inventions of History: Essays on the Representation of the Past*, Manchester, 33–63.
Bar-On, D. (1989) *Legacy of Silence: Encounters with Children of the Third Reich*, Cambridge.

Baumgartner, H.M. (1972) *Kontinuität und Geschichte. Zur Kritik und Metakritik der historischen Vernunft*, Frankfurt am Main.
Beasley, William G. and Pulleyblank, Edward G. (eds.) (1961) *Historians of China and Japan*, London.
Becher, Ursula A.J. and Rüsen, Jörn (eds.) (1988) *Weiblichkeit in geschichtlicher Perspektive*, Frankfurt am Main.
Benhabib, Seyla (1986) "The Generalized and the Concrete Other: Visions of the Autonomous Self," *Praxis International* 5.4:402–24.
Benjamin, Walter (1991) "Über den Begriff der Geschichte," in idem *Gesammelte Schriften*, vol. I, 2, Frankfurt am Main, 691–704.
Berding, Helmut (1971) "Leopold von Ranke," in *Deutsche Historiker*, vol. 1, ed. Hans-Ulrich Wehler, Göttingen, 7–14.
Berding, Helmut (1977) *Bibliographie zur Geschichtstheorie*, Göttingen.
Berger, P.L. and Luckmann, T. (1966) *The Social Construction of Reality*, Garden City.
Bergman, K., Kuhn, A., Rüsen, Jörn and Schneider, G. (eds.) (1985) *Handbuch der Geschichtsdidaktik*, 5th edn, Düsseldorf; Seelze-Velber, 1997.
Berlin, Isaiah (1966) "The Concept of Scientific History," in *Philosophical Analysis and History*, ed. W.H. Dray. New York, 5–53.
Bevir, M. (1994) "Objectivity in History," *History and Theory* 33:328–44.
Blanke, Horst Walter (1991) *Historiographiegeschichte als Historik* (*Fundamenta Historica*, vol. 3), Stuttgart/Bad Cannstatt.
Blanke, Horst Walter (2000) "Zum Verhältnis von Historiographiegeschichte und Historik—Eine Analyse der Tagungsbände Theorie der Geschichte und Geschichtsdiskurs," *Tel Aviver Jahrbuch für deutsche Geschichte* 29:55–84.
Blanke, Horst Walter and Fleischer, D. (eds.) (1990) *Theoretiker der deutschen Aufklärungshistorie*, 2 vols (*Fundamenta Historica*, vol. 1), Stuttgart/Bad Cannstatt.
Blanke, Horst Walter and Fleischer, D. (eds.) (1991) *Aufklärung und Historik. Aufsätze zur Entwicklung der Geschichtswissenschaft*, Kirchengeschichte und Geschichtstheorie in der deutschen Aufklärung, Waltrop.
Blanke, Horst Walter, Fleischer, D. and Rüsen, Jörn (1984) "Theory of History in Historical Lectures: The German Tradition of Historik 1750–1900," *History and Theory* 23:331–56.
Blanke, Horst Walter and Rüsen, Jörn (eds.) (1984) *Von der Aufklärung zum Historismus. Zum Strukturwandel des historischen Denkens* (Historisch-politische Diskurse, vol. 1), Paderborn.
Bödeker, Hans E. (1982) "Menschheit, Humanität, Humanismus," in *Geschichtliche Grundbegriffe. Historisches Lexikon zur politisch-sozialen Sprache in Deutschland*, vol. 3, eds. O. Brunner, W. Conze and R. Koselleck, Stuttgart, 1063–128.
Bohleber, Werner (1990) "Das Fortwirken des Nationalsozialismus in der zweiten und dritten Generation nach Auschwitz," *Babylon* 4:70–83.
Borries, Bodo von (1995) *Das Geschichtsbewußtsein Jugendlicher. Eine repräsentative Untersuchung über Vergangenheitsdeutungen, Gegenwartswahrnehmungen und Zukunftserwartungen von Schülerinnen und Schülern in Ost- und Westdeutschland*, Weinheim.

Borries, Bodo von (1998) "Forschungsprobleme einer Theorie des Geschichtsbewußtseins. Am Beispiel einer Studie zum empirischen Kulturvergleich," in *Dimensionen der Historik. Geschichtstheorie, Wissenschaftsgeschichte und Geschichtskultur heute. Jörn Rüsen zum 60. Geburtstag,* eds. H.-W. Blanke, F. Jaeger and T. Sandkühler. Köln, 139–52.

Borries, Bodo von (1999) *Jugend und Geschichte. Ein europäischer Kulturvergleich aus deutscher Sicht,* Opladen.

Borries, Bodo von, Pandel, H.-J. and Rüsen Jörn (eds.) (1991) *Geschichtsbewußtsein empirisch,* Pfaffenweiler.

Borries, Bodo von, Rüsen, Jörn et al (eds.) (1994) *Geschichtsbewußtsein im interkulturellen Vergleich. Zwei empirische Pilotstudien,* Pfaffenweiler.

Borries, Bodo von and H.-J. Pandel (eds.) (1994) *Zur Genese historischer Denkformen. Qualitative und quantitative Zugänge* (Jahrbuch für Geschichtsdidaktik 4, 1993/94), Pfaffenweiler.

Brecht, Bertolt (1967) "Geschichten vom Herrn Keuner," in idem *Gesammelte Werke,* vol.12, Frankfurt am Main.

Breisach, Ernst (1983) *Historiography—Ancient, Medieval, and Modern,* Chicago.

Broszat, Martin (1988) *Nach Hitler: Der schwierige Umgang mit unserer Geschichte,* Munich.

Broszat, Martin (1988) "Was heißt Historisierung des Nationalsozialismus?", *Historische Zeitschrift* 247:1–14.

Broszat, Martin (1985) "A Plea for the Historization of National Socialism," trans. in *Reworking the Past—Hitler, the Holocaust, and the Historians' Debate,* ed. P. Baldwin, Boston, 1990: 77–87.

Broszat, Martin and Friedländer, S. (1990) "A Controversy about the Historization of National Sozialism," in *Reworking the Past: History, the Holocaust and the Historians' Debate,* ed. P. Baldwin, Boston, 102–34.

Brown, Donald E. (1988) *Hierarchy, History and Human Nature: The Social Origins of Historical Consciousness,* Tucson.

Browning, Christopher R. (1992) *Ordinary Men: Reserve Police Battalion 101 and the Final Solution in Poland,* New York.

Brumlik, Micha (1993) "Trauerarbeit und kollektive Erinnerung," in *Kunst und Literatur nach Auschwitz,* ed. M. Köppen, Berlin, 197–203.

Burckhardt, Jacob (1943) *Force and Freedom. Reflections on History,* New York.

Burckhardt, Jacob (1929) "Gang der Kultur. Historische Fragmente," in idem *Gesamtausgabe,* vol. 7. *Weltgeschichtliche Betrachtungen. Historische Fragmente aus dem Nachlaß,* ed. A. Oeri and E. Dürr, Stuttgart.

Burckhardt, Jacob (1929) "Weltgeschichtliche Betrachtungen," in idem "Gesamtausgabe" vol. 7. *Weltgeschichtliche Betrachtungen. Historische Fragmente aus dem Nachlaß,* ed. A. Oeri and E. Dürr, Stuttgart.

Burckhardt, Jacob (1930) *Gesamtausgabe,* vol. 5. *Die Kultur der Renaissance in Italien. Ein Versuch,* ed. W. Kaegi, Stuttgart.

Burckhardt, Jacob (1955) *The Letters,* selected, ed. and trans. A. Dru, New York.

Burckhardt, Jacob (1959) *Judgements on History and Historians,* trans. H. Zohn, London.

Burckhardt, Jacob (1982) *Über das Studium der Geschichte. Der Text der 'Weltgeschichtlichen Betrachtungen' auf Grund der Vorarbeiten von Ernst Ziegler nach den Handschriften*, ed. P. Ganz, Munich.
Burke, Peter (ed.) (1989) *New Perspectives on Historical Writing*, Cambridge.
Carr, David (1986) *Time, Narrative and History: Studies in Phenomenolgy and Existential Philosophy*, Bloomington, 2nd ed., 1991.
Danto, Arthur (1968) *Analytical Philosophy of History*, Cambridge.
Davis, Natalie Z. (1983) *The return of Martin Guerre*, Cambridge, MA.
Devahuti, D. (ed.) (1979) *Problems of Indian Historiography*, Delhi.
Diner, Dan (1955) "Gestaute Zeit. Massenvernichtung und jüdische Erzählstruktur," in idem, *Kreisläufe. Nationalsozialismus und Gedächtnis*, Berlin, 125–39.
Diner, Dan (1990) "Between Aporia and Apology: On the Limits of Historicizing National Socialism," in *Reworking the Past: Hitler, the Holocaust, and the Historians Debate*, ed. P. Baldwin, Boston, 135–45.
Diner, Dan (1987) "Zwischen Aporie und Apologie. Über Grenzen der Historisierbarkeit des Nationalsozialismus," in *Ist der Nationalsozialismus Geschichte? Zu Historisierung und Historikerstreit*, ed. idem, Frankfurt am Main, 62–73.
Dray, William H. (ed.) (1966) *Philosophical Analysis and History*, New York.
Droysen, J.G. (1893) *Outline of the principles of History*, Boston, 1893, Reprint New York, 1967.
Droysen, J.G. (1977) *Historik. Historisch-kritische Ausgabe*, vol. 1, ed. P. Leyh, Stuttgart/Bad Cannstatt.
Duby, George (1988) *Der Sonntag von Bouvines*, Berlin.
Dunk, H. von der (1988) "Die historische Darstellung bei Ranke: Literatur und Wissenschaft," in *Leopold von Ranke und die moderne Geschichtswissenschaft*, ed. W.J. Mommsen, Stuttgart, 131–65.
Dürr, E. (1937) *Jacob Burckhardt als politischer Publizist: Mit seinen Zeitungsberichten aus den Jahren 1844/45*, Zürich.
Extrême-Orient/Extrême-Occident, 9 (1986) *La référence à l'histoire*, Paris.
Faulenbach, Bernd (1980) *Ideologie des deutschen Weges. Die deutsche Geschichte in der Historiographie zwischen Kaiserreich und Nationalsozialismus*, Munich.
Fletcher, Roger (1984) "Recent developments in West German historiography: The Bielefeld School and its Critics," *German Studies Review* 7:451–80.
Foucault, Michael (1974) *Die Ordnung der Dinge. Eine Archäologie der Humanwissenschaften*, Frankfurt am Main.
Friedländer, Saul (1989) "The Final Solution: On the Unease in Historical interpretation," *History and Memory* 1(2):61–73.
Friedländer, Saul (1990) "Reflections on the Historization of National Socialism," in *Reworking the Past: History, the Holocaust and the Historians' Debate*, ed. P. Baldwin, Boston, 88–101.
Friedländer, Saul (1991) "Martin Broszat und die Historisierung des Nationalsozialismus," in *Mit dem Pathos der Nüchternheit*, K.-D. Henke and C. Natoli, eds., Frankfurt am Main, 155–71.
Friedländer, Saul (1993) *Memory, History and the Extermination of the Jews of Europe*, Bloomington.

Friedländer, Saul (1994) "Trauma, Memory, and Transference," in *Holocaust Remembrance: The Shapes of Memory*, ed. Geoffrey H. Hartman, Oxford and Cambridge, 252–63.
Friedländer, Saul (1997) "Über den Umgang mit den Orten des Schreckens-Überlegungen zur Symbolisierung des Holocaust," in *Vergegenständlichte Erinnerung*, ed. D. Hoffmann, Frankfurt am Main.
Friedländer, Saul (ed.) (1992) *Probing the limits of representation: Nazism and the 'Final Solution'*, Cambridge.
Furet, François (1971) "Quantitative History," *Daedalus* 100:151–67.
Furth, Hans G. (1969) *Piaget and Knowledge: Theoretical Foundations*, Englewood Cliffs, NJ.
Füßmann, Klaus (1994) "Historische Formungen. Dimensionen der Geschichtsdarstellung," in *Historische Faszination. Geschichtskultur heute*, eds. K. Füßmann, H.T. Grütter and Jörn Rüsen, Köln, 27–44.
Galtung, Johan (1996) "Six Cosmologies: an Impressionistic Presentation," in idem *Peace by Peaceful Means*, London, 211–22.
Galtung, Johan (1997) "Die 'Sinne' der Geschichte," in *Historische Sinnbildung. Problemstellungen, Zeitkonzepte, Wahrnehmungshorizonte, Darstellungsstrategien*, eds. K.E. Müller and Jörn Rüsen, Reinbek, 118–41.
Gardner, Charles S. (1961) *Chinese Traditional Historiography*. Cambridge.
Gatterer, Johan Christoph (1767) "Vom historischen Plan und der darauf sich gründenden Zusammenfügung der Erzählung," in *Allgemeine Historische Bibliothek*, 1:15–89. Reprinted in H.W. Blanke and D. Fleischer (eds.) *Theoretiker der deutschen Aufklärungshistorie*, vol. 2 Stuttgart and Bad Cannstatt (1990) 621–62.
Geertz, Clifford (1973) "Thick Description: Toward an Interpretative Theory of Culture," in idem *The Interpretation of Cultures: Selected Essays*, New York, 3–30.
Gervinus, Georg Gottfried (1837) "Gründzüge der Historik," in *Schriften zur Literatur*, ed. G. Erler, Berlin, 49–103 (1962).
Ginzburg, Carlo (1980) *The Cheese and the Worms*, Baltimore.
Gossman, L. (1990) *Between History and Literature*, Cambridge.
Gottlob, Michael (1995) "Writing the History of Modern India historiography," *Storia della Storiografia* 27:123–44.
Groethuysen Bernard (1995) "Introduction à la pensée philosophique allemande depuis Nietzsche," in idem *Philosophie et histoire,* ed. B. Danoism, Paris, 91–143.
Große Kracht, K. (1996) "Das Weiterleben der verletzten Menschheit—Kultur und Kompensation bei Jacob Burckhardt," *Storia della Storiografia* 30:125–33.
Große Kracht, K. (1996) "Trauer und Melancholie. Historiographische Verlustverarbeitung bei Jules Michelet und Jacob Burckhardt," MA dis., University of Bielefeld.
Hallam, R.N. (1970) "Piaget and Thinking in History," in *New Movements in the Study and Teaching of History*, ed. M. Ballard, London, 162–78.
Han, Yu-sha (1995) *Elements of Chinese Historiography*, Hollywood.
Handke, P. and Müller, A. (1989) "Interview," *Die Zeit* (March):77.
Hao, Chang (1987) *Chinese Search for Order and Meaning 1890–1911*, Berkeley.

Hardtwig, Wolfgang (1974) *Geschichtsschreibung zwischen Alteuropa und moderner Welt: Jacob Burckhardt in seiner Zeit*, Göttingen.
Hardtwig, Wolfgang (1994) "Jacob Burckhardt und Max Weber: Zur Genese und Pathologie der modernen Welt," in *Umgang mit Jacob Burckhardt. Zwölf Studien*, ed. H.R. Guggisberg, Basel, 159–90.
Haupt, H.-G. and J. Kocka (eds.) (1996) *Geschichte und Vergleich. Ansätze und Ergebnisse international vergleichender Geschichtsschreibung*, Frankfurt am Main.
Hegel, G.W. (1955) *Ästhetik*, ed. F. Bassenge, Berlin.
Heimrod, U. (ed.) (1999) *Der Denkmalsstreit—das Denkmal? Die Debatte um das "Denkmal für die ermordeten Juden Europas." Eine Dokumentation*, Berlin, 881–82.
Helck, Wolfgang (1987) "Ägypten im frühen Neuen Reich. Grundzüge einer Entwicklung," in *Ägyptens Aufstieg zur Weltmacht*, ed. A. Eggebrecht, Mainz.
Hempel, Carl G. (1942) "The Function of General laws in History," *Journal of Philosophy* 39:35–48.
Henke, Klaus-Dietmar and Claudio Natoli (eds.) (1991) *Mit dem Pathos der Nüchternheit. Martin Broszat, das Institut für Zeitgeschichte und die Erforschung des Nationalsozialismus*, Frankfurt am Main.
Herder, J.G. (1952) "Auch eine Philosophie der Geschichte zur Bildung der Menschheit," in idem *Zur Philosophie der Geschichte. Eine Auswahl in zwei Bänden*, vol. 1, *Abhandlungen, Fragmente, Notizen*, Berlin.
Hinde, John R. (1996) "Jacob Burckhardt and the Art of History," *Storia della Storiografia* 30:107–23.
Hu, Changtze (1983) *Deutsche Ideologie und politische Kultur Chinas. Eine Studie zum Sonderwegsgedanken der chinesischen Bildungselite 1920–1940*, Bochum.
Huang, Chun-chieh (1995) "Historical Thinking in Classical Confucianism—Historical Argumentation from the Three Dynasties," in *Time and Space in Chinese Culture*, eds. C. Huang, and E. Zürcher, Leiden, 72–85.
Hughes, Henry S. (1965) *History as Art and as Science: Twin Vistas on the Past*, New York.
Humboldt, Wilhelm von (1960) "Betrachtungen über die bewegenden Ursachen der Weltgeschichte," in idem *Schriften zur Anthropologie und Geschichte*, ed. A. Flitner and K. Giel, Darmstadt, 578–84. Akademieausgabe 2: 360–66.
Humboldt, Wilhelm von (1960) "Theorie der Bildung des Menschen," in idem *Schriften zur Anthropologie und Geschichte. Werke in fünf Bänden,* vol. 1, ed. A. Flitner and K. Giel, Darmstadt, 234–40.
Humboldt, Wilhelm von (1960) "Über die Aufgabe des Geschichtschreibers," in idem *Schriften zur Anthropologie und Geschichte*, Werke in fünf Bänden, ed. A. Flitner, K. Giel, Darmstadt, 585–606. [Akademieausgabe 4: 35-56], English translation in *History and Theory* 6:57–71 (1967); and in Ranke, L. von, *The Theory and Practice of History*, ed. G.G. Iggers, and K. Moltke. Indianapolis, 5–23 (1973).
Iggers, George G. (1984) *New Directions in European Historiography*, rev. ed., Middletown, CT.
Iggers, George G. (1993) *Geschichtswissenschaft im 20. Jahrhundert. Ein Überblick im internationalen Zusammenhang*, Göttingen.

Iggers, George G. (1985) "Introduction," in *The Social History of Politics: Critical Perspectives in West German Historical Writing since 1945*, ed. idem, Leamington Spa.
Iggers, George G. and Parker, H.T. (eds.) (1979) *International Handbook of Historical Studies. Contemporary Research and Theory*, Westpoint, CT.
Iggers, George G. and Rüsen, Jörn (1986) "Historicism (A Comment)," *Storia della Storiografia* 10:112–52.
Imdahl, Max (1980) *Giotto. Arena-Fresken. Ikonographie, Ikonologie, Ikonik*, Munich.
Jaeger, Friedrich (1992) "Der Kulturbegriff im Werk Max Webers und seine Bedeutung für eine moderne Kulturgeschichte," *Geschichte und Gesellschaft* 18:371–93.
Jaeger, Friedrich (1994) *Bürgerliche Modernisierungskrise und historische Sinnbildung. Kulturgeschichte bei Droysen, Burckhardt und Max Weber* (Bürgertum. Beiträge zur europäischen Gesellschaftsgeschichte, vol. 5), Göttingen.
Jeismann, K.-E. (1978) "Didaktik der Geschichte: Das spezifische Bedingungsfeld des Geschichtsunterrichts," in *Geschichte und Politik. Didaktische Grundlegung eines kooperativen Unterrichts*, eds. G.C. Behrmann, K.-E. Jeismann and H. Süssmuth, Paderborn, 50–108.
Jeismann, K.-E. (1985) "Geschichtsbewusstsein," in *Handbuch der Geschichtsdidaktik*, eds. K. Bergman, A. Kuhn, Jörn Rüsen and G. Schneider, Düsseldorf, 40–44.
Jeismann, K.-E. (1985) *Geschichte als Horizont der Gegenwart. Über den Zusammenhang von Vergangenheitsdeutung, Gegenwartsverständnis und Zukunftsperspektive*, Paderborn.
Johnson, Samuel (1971) *A Journey to the Western Islands of Scotland*, New Haven and London.
Kaegi, Werner (1943) "Die Idee der Vergänglichkeit in der Jugendgeschichte Jacob Burckhardts," *Basler Zeitschrift für Geschichte und Altertumskunde* 42:209–43.
Kaegi, Werner (1973) *Jacob Burckhardt. Eine Biographie*. vol. 5, *Das neuere Europa und das Erlebnis der Gegenwart*, Basel.
Kaegi, Werner (1977) *Jacob Burckhardt. Eine Biographie. Weltgeschichte—Mittelalter—Kunstgeschichte. Die letzten Jahre 1886–1897*, vol. 6, Basel.
Kant, Immanuel (1784) "Idee zu einer allgemeinen Geschichte in weltbürgerlicher Absicht," in *Schriften zur Anthropologie, Geschichtsphilosophie, Politik und Pädagogik. 1. Teil* (Werke in 10 Bänden, vol. 9.) ed. W. Weischedel, Darmstadt (1968).
Kao, G. ed. (1982) *The Translation of Things Past. Chinese History and Historiography*, Hong Kong.
Kessler, Echard (1971) *Theoretiker humanistischer Geschichtschreibung*, Munich.
Kessler, Echard (1982) "Das rhetorische Modell der Historiographie," in *Formen der Geschichtsschreibung* (Beiträge zur Historik, vol. 4), eds. R. Koselleck, H. Lutz and Jörn Rüsen, Munich, 37–85.
Klotz, V. (1972) "Erzählen als Enttöten. Notizen zu zyklischem, instrumentalem und praktischem Erzählen," in *Erzählforschung. Ein Symposion*, ed. E. Lämmert, Stuttgart, 319–34.
Kocka, J. (1975) "Sozialgeschichte—Strukturgeschichte—Gesellschaftsgeschichte," *Archiv für Sozialgeschichte* 25:1–42.

Kocka, J. (1975) "Theorien in der Sozial- und Gesellschaftsgeschichte. Vorschläge zur historischen Schichtungsanalyse," *Geschichte und Gesellschaft* 1:9–42.

Kocka, J. (1986) *Sozialgeschichte, Begriff—Entwicklung—Probleme*, 2nd edn, Göttingen.

Kocka, J. (1982) "Theorieorientierung und Theorieskepsis in der Geschichtswissenschaft," *Historical Social Research* 23:4–19.

Kocka, J. (1986) "Theory Orientation and the New Quest for Narrative. Some Trends and Debates in West Germany," *Storia della Storiographia* 10:170–81.

Kocka, J. (2000) "Historische Sozialwissenschaft heute," in *Perspektiven der Gesellschaftsgeschichte*, eds. P. Nolte, M. Hettling, F.-M. Kuhlemann and H.-W. Schmuhl, Munich, 5–24.

Kocka, J. (ed.) (1986) *Max Weber, der Historiker*, Göttingen.

Kocka, J. and T. Nipperdey (eds.) (1979) *Theorie und Erzählung in der Geschichte* (Beiträge zur Historik, vol. 3), Munich.

Kohlberg, L. (1974) *Zur kognitiven Entwicklung des Kindes*, Frankfurt am Main.

Kölver, B. (1993) *Ritual und historischer Raum. Zum indischen Geschichtsverständnis*, Munich.

Koselleck, Reinhart (1979) "Historia magistra vitae. Über die Auflösung des Topos im Horizont neuzeitlich bewegter Geschichte," in idem *Vergangene Zukunft. Zur Semantik geschichtlicher Zeiten*, Frankfurt am Main, 29–94.

Koselleck, Reinhart (1979) *Vergangene Zukunft. Zur Semantik geschichtlicher Zeiten*, Frankfurt am Main.

Koselleck, Reinhart (1997) "Vier Minuten für die Ewigkeit," *Frankfurter Allgemeine Zeitung* (January).

Koselleck, Reinhart (ed.) (1978) *Historische Semantik und Begriffsgeschichte*, Stuttgart.

Koselleck, Reinhart, Mommsen, W.J. and Rüsen, Jörn (eds.) (1977) *Objektivität und Parteilichkeit in der Geschichtswissenschaft* (Theorie der Geschichte. Beiträge zur Historik, vol. 1), Munich.

Kühnhardt, L. (1987) *Die Universalität der Menschenrecht. 2. Studie zur Ideengeschichtlichen Schlüsselbestimmung eines politischen Schlüsselbegriffs,* Munich.

Küttler, W., Rüsen, Jörn and Schulin, E. (eds.) (1993) *Geschichtsdiskurs*, vol. 1: *Grundlagen und Methoden der Historiographiegeschichte*, Frankfurt am Main.

Küttler, W., Rüsen, Jörn and Schulin, E. (eds.) (1994) *Geschichtsdiskurs*, vol. 2: *Anfänge modernen historischen Denkens*, Frankfurt am Main.

Küttler, W., Rüsen, Jörn and Schulin, E. (eds.) (1996) *Geschichtsdiskurs*, vol. 3: *Die Epoche der Historisierung*, Frankfurt am Main.

Küttler, W., Rüsen, Jörn and Schulin, E. (eds.) (1997) *Geschichtsdiskurs*, vol. 4: *Krisenbewußtsein, Katastrophenerfahrungen und Innovationen 1880–1945*, Frankfurt am Main.

Küttler, W., Rüsen, Jörn and Schulin, E. (eds.) (1999) *Geschichtsdiskurs*, vol. 5: *Globale Konflikte, Erinnerungsarbeit und Neuorientierungen*, Frankfurt am Main.

Kuhn, Thomas S. (1962) *The Structure of Scientific Revolution*, Chicago.

Kung-yang chuan, Ch'un-ch'iu (1980) *Shh-san-ching chu-shu [fu chiao-k'an chi]*, Nd. in 2 Bde., Peking, 28/2354a.

La Capra, Dominick (1985) *History and Criticism*, Ithaca.

La Capra, Dominick (1994) *Representing the Holocaust: History, Theory, Trauma*, Ithaca.
Le Goff, Jacques and Pierre, Nora (eds.) (1974) *Faire de l'histoire: Nouveaux problemes*, Paris.
Leicht, R. (1998) "Nur das Hinsehen macht frei," *Die Zeit* (December):1.
Lorenz, Chris (1987) *De Constructie van het Verleden. Ee Inleiding in de Theorie van de Geschiedenis*, Amsterdam.
Lorenz, Chris (1994) "Historical Knowledge and Historical Realitity: A Plea for 'Internal Realism'," *History and Theory* 33:297–327.
Lorenz, Chris (1997) *Konstruktion der Vergangenheit. Eine Einführung in die Geschichtstheorie* (Beiträge zur Geschichtskultur, vol. 13), Köln.
Lübbe, Hermann (1983) "Der Nationalsozialismus im deutschen Nachkriegsbewusstsein," *Historische Zeitschrift* 236:579–99.
Lüdtke, Alf (1993) *Eigen-Sinn. Fabrikalltag, Arbeitserfahrungen und Politik vom Kaiserreich bis in den Faschismus*, Hamburg.
Lukian (1965) *Wie man Geschichte schreiben soll*, ed. H. Homeyer, Munich.
Marx, Karl (1964) "Zur Judenfrage," in Marx, Karl and Engels, F., *Werke 1*, Berlin.
Medick, Hans (1984) "Missionare im Ruderboot? Ethnologische Erkenntnisweisen als Herausforderungen an die Sozialgeschichte," *Geschichte und Gesellschaft* (March):295–319.
Megill, Allan (1989) "Recounting the Past: Description, Explanation and Narrative in Historiography," *American Historical Review* 94:627–53.
Megill, Allan (ed.) (1994) *Rethinking Objectivity*, Durham. (Originally appeared in *Annals of Scholarship*, vol. 8, no. 3–4 (1991); vol. 9, no. 1–2 (1992).)
Meier, Cristian (1973) "Die Entstehung der Historie," in *Geschichte—Ereignis und Erzählung* (Poetik und Hermeneutik 5), eds. R. Koselleck and W.-D. Stempel, Munich, 251–306.
Meier, Cristian (1990) *Vierzig Jahre nach Auschwitz. Deutsche Geschichtserinnerung heute*, 2nd edn, Munich.
Meier, Cristian (1991) "Der Historiker Martin Broszat," in *Mit dem Pathos der Nüchternheit. Martin Broszat, das Institut für Zeitgeschichte und die Erforschung des Nationalsozialismus*, eds. K.-D. Henke and C. Natoli, Frankfurt am Main.
Meier, Cristian (1997) *Die Zeit* (11 April):48.
Meier, Cristian and Rüsen, Jörn (eds.) (1988) *Historische Methode* (Beiträge zur Historik, vol. 5), Munich.
Meinecke, Friedrich (1946) *Die deutsche Katastrophe*, 2nd edn, Wiesbaden.
Mencius (1893–1895) in *The Works of Mencius. The Chinese Classics*, vol. 2, ed. J. Legge, Oxford; Hong Kong (1960).
Meran, Josef (1985) *Theorien in der Geschichtswissenschaft. Die Diskussion über die Wissenschaftlichkeit der Geschichte*, Göttingen.
Michelet, Jules (1982) *Oeuvres complètes*, vol. 21, Paris.
Mitscherlich, Alexander and Mitscherlich, Margarete (1975) *The Inability to Mourn. Principles of Collective Behavior*, New York.
Mitscherlich, Alexander and Mitscherlich, Margarete (1967) *Die Unfähigkeit zu trauern. Grundlagen kollektiven Verhaltens*, 1st edn, Munich, reprinted Leipzig, 1990.

Mittelweg 36 (1992), Zeitschrift des Hamburger Instituts f. Sozialforschung Heft 3: theme issue: trauma.

Müller, Klaus E. and Rüsen, Jörn (eds.) (1997) *Historische Sinnbildung. Problemstellungen, Zeitkonzepte, Wahrnehmungshorizonte, Darstellungsstrategien*, Reinbek.

Negt, Oskar and Kluge, Alexander (1981) *Geschichte und Eigensinn*, Frankfurt am Main.

Niethammer, Lutz (1989) *Posthistoire. Ist die Geschichte zu Ende?* Reinbek; English trans. *Posthistoire: Has History Come to an end?* London, 1992.

Nietzsche, Friedrich (1956) "Brief an Burckhardt 4 January 1889," in *Werke in drei Bänden*, vol. 3, ed. K. Schlechta, Munich, 1350.

Nietzsche, Friedrich (1983) "On the Uses and Disadvantages of History for Life," in *Untimely Meditations*, trans. R.J. Hollingdale, Cambridge, 83–100.

Nietzsche, Friedrich (1985) *The Use and Abuse of History*, trans. Adrian Collins, New York.

Nietzsche, Friedrich (1988) "Vom Nutzen und Nachteil der Historie für das Leben (1874)," in *Sämtliche Werke. Kritische Studienausgabe, vol. 1*, ed. G. Colli, and M. Montanari, Munich, 243–334; English trans. *On the Advantage and Disadvantage of History for Life*, trans. P. Preuss. Indianapolis, 1980.

Nietzsche, Friedrich (1988) "Zur Genealogie der Moral (1887)," in idem, *Sämtliche Werke. Kritische Studienausgabe,* vol 5, ed. G. Colli and M. Montanari, Munich, 245–412.

Nolte, Ernst (1987) "Zwischen Geschichtslegende und Revisionismus?" in *"Historikerstreit" Die Dokumentation der Kontroverse um die Einzigartigkeit der nationalsozialistischen Judenvernichtung*, Texte von Augstein, Munich, 13–35.

Novick, Peter (1988) *That Noble Dream. The "Objectivity-Question" and the America Historical Profession*, New York and Cambridge.

Oehler, K. (1989) *Geschichte in der politischen Rhetorik. Historische Argumentationsmuster im Parlament der Bundesrepublik Deutschland* (Beitrage zur Geschichtskultur, vol. 2), Hagen.

Olabarri, Ignacio (1995) "'New' history: a longue durée structure," *History and Theory* 34:1–29.

Osterhammel, Jürgen (1996) "Sozialgeschichte im Zivilisationsvergleich. Zu künftigen Möglichkeiten komparativer Geschichtswissenschaft," *Geschichte und Gesellschaft* 22:143–64.

Owen, S. (1990) "Place: Mediation on the Past at Chin-ling," *Harvard Journal of Asiatic Studies* 56:417–57.

Piaget, Jean (1973) *Das moralische Bewußtsein beim Kinde*, Frankfurt am Main.

Piaget, Jean (1974) *Die Bildung des Zeitbewußtseins beim Kinde*, Frankfurt am Main.

Pigulla, A. (1996) *China in der deutschen Weltgeschichtsschreibung vom 18. bis zum 20. Jahrhundert*, Wiesbaden.

Quirin, Michael (1987) *Liu Zhiji und das Chun Qiu*, Frankfurt am Main.

Ranke, Leopold von (1867) *Deutsche Geschichte im Zeitalter der Reformation*, (Sämtliche Werke, vol. 1), Leipzig.

Ranke, Leopold von (1874) *Die römischen Päpste in den letzten vier Jahrhunderten*, (Sämtliche Werke, vol. 38), Leipzig.

Ranke, Leopold von (1874) *Geschichten der romanischen und germanischen Völker von 1494 bis 1514*, 2nd edn (Sämtliche Werke 33/34), Leipzig.
Ranke, Leopold von (1874) *Zur Kritik neuerer Geschichtsschreiber* (Sämtliche Werke, vos. 33-34), Leipzig.
Ranke, Leopold von (1877) *Englische Geschichte vornehmlich im 17. Jahrhundert*, vol. 2 (Sämtliche Werke, vol. 15), Leipzig.
Ranke, Leopold von (1877) *Über die Verwandtschaft und den Unterschied der Historie und der Politik* (Sämtliche Werke, vol. 24), Leipzig, 280–93.
Ranke, Leopold von (1975) "Idee der Universalgeschichte," in idem *Vorlesungseinleitungen*, 72, ed. V. Dotterweich and W.P. Fuchs (Aus Werk und Nachlaß, vol. 4), Munich.
Ranke, Leopold von (1896) *Weltgeschichte*, vol. I,1. 4th edn, Leipzig.
Ranke, Leopold von (1971) *Über die Epochen der Neueren Geschichte*, ed. T. Schieder and H. Berding (Aus Werk und Nachlaß, vol. 2), Munich.
Ranke, Leopold von (1973) *The Theory and Practice of History*, ed. Georg G. Iggers and K. von Moltke, Indianapolis.
Ranke, Leopold von (1975) *Vorlesungseinleitungen* (Aus Werk und Nachlaß. Bd. 4), ed. V. Dotterweich and W.P. Fuchs, Munich.
Reill, Peter H. (1973) "History and Hermeneutics in the Aufklärung: The Thought of Johann Christoph Gatterer," *Journal of Modern History* 45:24–51.
Reill, Peter H. (1975) *The German Enlightenment and the Rise of Historicism*, Berkeley.
Reill, Peter H. (1986) "Science and the Science of History in the Spätaufklärung," in *Aufklärung und Geschichte. Studien zur deutschen Geschichtswissenschaft im 18. Jahrhundert*, ed. H.E. Bödeker, Göttingen, 430–51.
Ricoeur, Paul (1984–1988) *Time and Narrative*, 3 vols, Chicago.
Ricoeur, Paul (1997) "Gedächtnis—Vergessen—Geschichte," in *Historische Sinnbildung—Problemstellungen, Zeitkonzepte, Wahrnehmungshorizonte, Darstellungsstrategien*, eds. K.E. Müller and Jörn Rüsen, Reinbek.
Rieß, Peter (1985) *Footnotologie: Towards a theory of the footnote*, Berlin.
Roetz, Heiner (1995) *Konfuzius*, Munich.
Rosenthal, Franz (1968) *A History of Muslim Historiography*. 2nd rev. edn, Leiden.
Rossi, Pietro (ed.) (1987) *Theorie der modernen Geschichtsschreibung*, Frankfurt am Main.
Röttgers, K. (1982) "Geschichtserzählung als kommunikativer Text," in *Historisches Erzählen. Formen und Funktionen*, eds. S. Ouandt and H. Süssmuth, Göttingen, 29–48.
Rüsen, Jörn (1972) "Jacob Burckhardt," in *Deutsche Historiker*, vol. 3, ed. H-U. Wehler, Göttingen, 7–28.
Rüsen, Jörn (1976) *Ästhetik und Geschichte. Geschichtstheoretische Untersuchungen zum Begründungszusammenhang von Kunst, Gesellschaft und Wissenschaft*, Stuttgart.
Rüsen, Jörn (1976) "Historismus und Ästhetik: Geschichtstheoretische Voraussetzungen der Kunstgeschichte," in idem *Ästhetik und Geschichte*, Stuttgart, 89–95.
Rüsen, Jörn (1977) "Unzeitgemäßer Gegenwartsbezug im Geschichtsdenken Jacob Burckhardts," *Philosophisches Jahrbuch* 84:433–43.

Rüsen, Jörn (1983) *Historische Vernunft. Grundzüge einer Historik I: Die Grundlagen der Geschichtswissenschaft*, Göttingen.
Rüsen, Jörn (1986) "Narrative und Strukturgeschichte im Historismus," *Storia della Storiografia* 10:112–52.
Rüsen, Jörn (1986) *Rekonstruktion der Vergangenheit. Grundzüge einer Historik II: Die Prinzipien der historischen Forschung*, Göttingen.
Rüsen, Jörn (1987) "The Didactics of History in West Germany: Towards a New Self-Awareness of Historical Studies," *History and Theory*, 26:275–86.
Rüsen, Jörn (1987) "Historical narration: foundation, types, reason," *History and Theory*, 26:87–97.
Rüsen, Jörn (1987) "The Representation of Historical Events," *History and Theory*, Beiheft 26:87–97.
Rüsen, Jörn (1988) "New Directions in Historical Studies," in *Miedzy Historia a Teoria. Refleksje nad Problematyka Dziejow Historycznej*, ed. M. Drozdowski. Warsaw, 340–55.
Rüsen, Jörn (1989) "Historical Enlightenment in the light of Postmodernism: History in the Age of the 'New Unintelligibility'," *History and Memory* 1:109–29.
Rüsen, Jörn (1989) "Narrative competence: on the ontogeny of historical and moral consciousness," *History and Memory* 1(2):35–60.
Rüsen, Jörn (1989) *Lebendige Geschichte. Grundzüge einer Historik III: Formen und Funktionen des historischen Wissens*, Göttingen.
Rüsen, Jörn (1990) "Rhetoric and aesthetics of history: Leopold von Ranke," *History and Theory* 29:190–204.
Rüsen, Jörn (1990) *Zeit und Sinn. Strategien historischen Denkens*, Frankfurt am Main.
Rüsen, Jörn (1990) "Geschichtsschreibung als Theorieproblem der Geschichtswissenschaft. Skizze zum historischen Hintergrund der gegenwärtigen Diskussion," in idem *Zeit und Sinn. Strategien historischen Denkens,* Frankfurt am Main, 135–52.
Rüsen, Jörn (1990) "Die vier Typen des historischen Erzählens," in idem *Zeit und Sinn*, 153–230.
Rüsen, Jörn (1990) "Historische Aufklärung im Angesicht der Post-Moderne: Geschichte im Zeitalter der 'Neuen Unübersichtlichkeit'," in idem *Zeit und Sinn. Strategien historischen Denkens*, Frankfurt am Main, 231–51.
Rüsen, Jörn (1993) *Konfigurationen des Historismus. Studien zur deutschen Wissenschaftskultur*, Frankfurt am Main.
Rüsen, Jörn (1993) "Bemerkungen zu Droysens Typologie der Geschichtsschreibung," in idem *Konfigurationen des Historismus*, 267–75.
Rüsen, Jörn (1993) "Der ästhetische Glanz der historischen Erinnerung—Jacob Burckhardt," in idem, *Konfigurationen des Historismus*, 276–330.
Rüsen, Jörn (1993) "Der Historiker als 'Parteimann des Schicksals'—Georg Gottfried Gervinus," in idem, *Konfigurationen des Historismus*, 157–225.
Rüsen, Jörn (1993) "Theorien im Historismus," in idem, *Konfigurationen des Historismus*, 69–82.
Rüsen, Jörn (1993) "Von der Aufklärung zum Historismus. Idealtypische Perspektiven eines Strukturwandels," in idem, *Konfigurationen des Historismus*, 29–94.

Rüsen, Jörn (1993) "Human Rights from the Perspective of a Universal History," in *Human Rights and Cultural Diversity. Europe—Arabic—Islamic World—Africa—China*, ed. W. Schmale, Frankfurt am Main, 28–46.
Rüsen, Jörn (1993) "Vom Umgang mit den Anderen—Zum Stand der Menschenrechte heute," *Internationale Schulbuchforschung* 15:167–78.
Rüsen, Jörn (1993) *Studies in Metahistory*, Pretoria.
Rüsen, Jörn (1993) "Historical enlightenment in the age of postmodernism: history in the age of the 'new unintelligibility'," in idem *Studies in Metahistory*, 221–39.
Rüsen, Jörn (1994) "Historical studies between modernity and postmodernity," *South African Journal of Philosophy* 13:183–89.
Rüsen, Jörn (1994) "Theorie der Geschichte," in Richard van Dülmen, ed., *Fischer Lexikon Geschichte*, vol. 2, Frankfurt am Main, 32–52.
Rüsen, Jörn (1994) *Historische Orientierung. Über die Arbeit des Geschichtsbewußtseins, sich in der Zeit zurechtzufinden*, Köln.
Rüsen, Jörn (1994) "Was ist Geschichtsbewußtsein? Theoretische Überlegungen und heuristische Hinweise," in idem *Historische Orientierung*, 3–24.
Rüsen, Jörn (1994) "Der Teil des Ganzen—über historische Kategorien," in idem *Historische Orientierung*, 150–67.
Rüsen, Jörn (1994) "Die Individualisierung des Allgemeinen—Theorieprobleme einer vergleichenden Universalgeschichte der Menschenrechte," in idem *Historische Orientierung*, 168–87.
Rüsen, Jörn (1994) "Schöne Parteilichkeit, Feminismus und Objektivität in der Geschichtswissenschaft," in idem *Historische Orientierung*, 130–67.
Rüsen, Jörn (1994) *Historisches Lernen. Grundlagen und Paradigmen*, Köln.
Rüsen, Jörn (1996) "Trauer als historische Kategorie: Überlegungen zur Erinnerung an den Holocaust in der Geschichtskultur der Gegenwart," in H. Lowey, ed. *Erinnerung, Gedächtnis, Sinn: Authentische und konstruierte Erinnerung*, Frankfurt am Main, 57–78.
Rüsen, Jörn (1996) "Historische Sinnbildung durch Erzählen. Eine Argumentationsskizze zum narrativistischen Paradigma der Geschichtswissenschaft und der Geschichtsdidaktik im Blick auf nicht-narrative Faktoren," *Internationale Schulbuchforschung* 18:501–44.
Rüsen, Jörn (1997) "Über den Umgang mit den Orten des Schreckens—Überlegungen zur Symbolisierung des Holocaust," in Detlef Hoffman, ed., *Vergegenständlichte Erinnerung*, Frankfurt am Main, 330–43.
Rüsen, Jörn (2001) "History: Overview," in N.J. Smelser, and P.B. Baltes, eds., *International Encyclopedia of the Social & Behavioral Sciences*, Amsterdam.
Rüsen, Jörn (2001) *Zerbrechende Zeit. Über den Sinn der Geschichte*, Köln.
Rüsen, Jörn (2001) "Auschwitz—die Symbole der Authentizität," in idem *Zerbrechende Zeit*, 181–216.
Rüsen, Jörn (2001) "Goldhagens Irrtümer," in idem *Zerbrechende Zeit*, 263–78.
Rüsen, Jörn (2001) "Geschichte als Sinnproblem," in idem *Zerbrechende Zeit*, 7–42.
Rüsen, Jörn (2001) "Historisches Erzählen," in idem *Zerbrechende Zeit*, 43–106.
Rüsen, Jörn, Fröhlich, K., Horstkötter H. and Schmidt, H.-G. (1991) "Untersuchungen zum Geschichtsbewußtsein von Abiturienten im Ruhrgebiet," in *Geschichtsbewußtsein empirisch*, eds. B. von Borries, H.-J. Pandel and Jörn Rüsen, Pfaffenweiler, 221–344.

Rüsen, Jörn, Große-Kracht, K., Hanenkamp, B. and Schmidt, H.-G. (1994) "Geschichtsbewußtsein von Schülern und Studenten im internationalen und interkulturellen Vergleich," in *Geschichtsbewußtsein im interkulturellen Vergleich. Zwei empirische Pilotstudien*, eds. Bodo von Borries and Jörn Rüsen, Pfaffenweiler, 79–206.

Rüsen, Jörn (ed.) (1975) *Historische Objektivität. Aufsätze zur Geschichtstheorie*, Göttingen.

Rüsen, Jörn, and Süssmuth, H. (eds.) (1980) *Theorien in der Geschichtswissenschaft*, Düsseldorf.

Santner, Eric L. (1990) *Stranded Objects. Mourning, Memory, and Film in Postwar Germany*, Ithaca.

Schlaffer, H. and Schlaffer, H. (1975) "Jacob Burckhardt und das Asyl der Kulturgeschichte," in idem *Studien zum ästhetischen Historismus*, Frankfurt am Main, 72–111.

Schleier, H. (1986) "Narrative und Strukturgeschichte im Historismus," *Storia della Storiografia* 10:112–52.

Schlözer, August Ludwig (1772) *Vorstellung einer Universalhistorie*, Göttingen, reprint, ed. H.W. Blanke, Hagen, 1990.

Schmidt, Hans-Günter (1987) "Eine Geschichte zum Nachdenken. Erzähltypologie, narrative Kompetenz und Geschichtsbewußtsein: Bericht über einen Versuch der empirischen Erforschung des Geschichtsbewußtseins von Schülern der Sekundarstufe I (Unter- und Mittelstufe)," *Geschichtsdidaktik* 12:28–35.

Schulin, Ernst (1979) "Rankes Erstlingswerk oder Der Beginn der kritischen Geschichtsschreibung über die Neuzeit," in idem *Traditionskritik und Rekonstruktionsversuch. Studien zur Entwicklung von Geschichtswissenschaft und historischem Denken*, Göttingen, 44–46.

Schütz, Alfred, Berger, Peter L. and Luckmann, Thomas (1966) *The Social Construction of Reality*, Garden City.

Sofsky, Wolfgang (1997) *Die Ordnung des Terrors: Das Konzentrationslager*, Frankfurt am Main.

Stepper, R. (1997) *Leiden an der Geschichte. Ein zentrales Motiv in der Griechischen Kulturgeschichte Jacob Burckhardts und seine Bedeutung in der altertumswissenschaftlichen Geschichtschreibung des 19. und 20. Jahrhunderts*, Bodenheim.

Stone, Lawrence (1979) "The Revival of Narrative. Reflections on a new old History," *Past and Present* 85:3–24.

Sybel, Heinrich von (1863) "Über den Stand der neueren deutschen Geschichtsschreibung (1856)," in idem, *Kleine historische Schriften*, Munich, 343–59.

Taylor, Charles (1993) *Multikulturalismus und die Politik der Anerkennung*, Frankfurt am Main.

Topolski, Jerzy (ed.) (1990) *Narration and Explanation: Contributions to the Methodology of Historical Research*, Amsterdam.

Trauzettel, R. (1984) "Die chinesische Geschichtsschreibung," in, Debon, G., ed. *Ostasiatische Literaturen*, Wiesbaden, 77–90.

Trommler, Frank (1985) "Arbeitsnation statt Kulturnation? Ein vernachlässigter Faktor deutscher Identität," in *Akten des VII. Internationalen Germanistenkongre*, vol. 9, Göttingen.

Viperano, G.A. (1967) *De poetica libri tres* (Poetiken des Cinquecento 10), Munich.
Voltaire (1878) *Oeuvres complètes*, vol. II, ed. L. Moland, Paris.
Wagner, Irmgard (1997) "Historischer Sinn zwischen Trauer und Melancholie: Freud, Lacan und Henry Adams," in *Historische Sinnbildung. Problemstellungen, Zeitkonzepte, Wahrnehmungshorizonte, Darstellungsstrategien*, eds. K.E. Müller and Jörn Rüsen, Reinbek, 408–32.
Weber, Max (1949) *The Methodology of the Social Sciences*, trans. and eds. E.A. Shils and H.A. Finch, New York, 1949.
Weber, Max (1968) *Gesammelte Aufsätze zur Wissenschaftslehre*, 3rd edn, ed. J. Winckelmann, Tübingen, 475–88.
Weber, Max (1994) "'Objectivity' in Social Science," in idem *Sociological Writings*, (The German Library, vol. 60), ed. W. Heydebrand, New York, 248–59.
Weber, Max (1994) *Sociological Writings*, ed. W. Heydebrand, New York.
Weber, W. (1987) *Priester der Clio. Historisch-sozialwissenschaftliche Studien zur Herkunft und Karriere deutscher Historiker 1800–1970*, 2nd edn, Frankfurt am Main.
Wehler, Hans-Ulrich (1973) *Geschichte als historische Sozialwissenschaft*, Frankfurt am Main.
Wehler, Hans-Ulrich (1984) "Historiography in Germany Today," in *Observations on The Spiritual Situation of the Age*, ed. J. Habermas, Cambridge, 221–59.
Wehler, Hans-Ulrich (1986) "Sozialgeschichte und Gesellschaftsgeschichte," in *Sozialgeschichte in Deutschland*, vol. 1, eds. W. Schieder and V. Sellin, Göttingen, 33–52.
Wehler, Hans-Ulrich (2001) *Historisches Denken am Ende des 20. Jahrhunderts. 1945-2000* (Essener kulturwissenschaftliche Vorträge, vol. 11), Göttingen.
Welsch, Wolfgang (1996) *Vernunft. Die zeitgenössische Vernunftkritik und das Konzept der transversalen Vernunft*, Frankfurt am Main.
Wenzel, J. (1967) *Jacob Buckhardt in der Krise seiner Zeit*, Berlin.
White, Hayden (1973) *Metahistory. The Historical Imagination in Nineteenth Century Europe*, Baltimore.
White, Hayden (1978) *Tropics of Discourse. Essays in Cultural Criticism*, Baltimore.
White, Hayden (1980) "Droysen's Historik." *History and Theory* 19:73–93.
White, Hayden (1987) *The Content of the Form. Narrative Discourse and Historical Representation*, Baltimore.
Wierling, Dorothy (1991) "Keine Frauengeschichte nach dem Jahr 2000!" in *Geschichtswissenschaft vor 2000. Perspektiven der Geschichtstheorie, Historiographiegeschichte und Sozialgeschichte*, Festschrift für Georg Iggers zum 65. Geburtstag (Beiträge zur Geschichtskultur, vol. 5), eds. K. Jarausch, Jörn Rüsen and H. Schleier, Hagen, 440–56.
Wiese, Leopold von (1948) "Die gegenwärtige Situation, soziologisch betrachtet," in *Verhandlungen des Achten Deutschen Soziologentages vom 19. bis 21. September 1946 in Frankfurt am Main*, Tübingen.
Windschuttle, Keith (2000) *The Killing of History: How Literary Critics and Social Theorists are Murdering our Past*, New York.
Zemlin, Michael-Joachim (1988) *Geschichte zwischen Theorie und Theoria. Untersuchungen zur Geschichtsphilosophie Rankes*, Würzburg.

Ziegler, E. (1974) *Jacob Burckhardts Vorlesung über die Geschichte des Revolutionszeitalters. In den Nachschriften seiner Zuhörer. Rekonstruktion des gesprochenen Wortlautes*, Basel and Stuttgart.

Index

A

Adorno, T.W. 181
Aischylos 189
Augustine 120

B

Bancroft, George 15
Benjamin, Walter 138
Braudel, Fernand 95
Broszat, Martin 163, 164, 165, 166, 167, 169,
　170, 171, 172, 174, 175, 177, 178, 180, 182,
　184
Browning, Christopher 183
Burckhardt, Jacob 15, 85, 147, 150, 151, 152,
　153, 154, 155, 156, 157, 158

D

Danto, Arthur 172
Darwin, Charles 153, 154, 155, 157
Davis, Natalie 139
Diner, Dan 148, 172, 174
Droysen, Johann Gustav 12, 64, 79, 84, 86, 119,
　149, 154, 155, 165

E

Engels 85

F

Foucault, Michel 148
Freud, Sigmund 152, 155, 156
Friedländer, Saul 147, 163, 164, 165, 166, 167,
　168, 169, 172, 173, 175, 176, 177, 178, 179,
　180, 182, 184

G

Galtung, Johan 113
Geertz, Clifford 139
Gervinus, Georg Gottfried 64, 86
Goethe, Johann Wolfgang 199
Goldhagen, Daniel 183
Groethuysen, Bernard 41
Guerre, Martin 139
Guicciardini 42, 43

H

Handke, Peter 163
Hao, Chang 112
Hegel 154, 155, 195
Herder, J.G. 1
Herodotus 17, 120
Hinze, Otto 90
Horkheimer 181
Humboldt, Wilhelm von 63

J

Johnson, Samuel 22

K

Kant, Immanuel 147
Kluge, Alexander 93
Kohlberg, L. 18, 27, 34
Konfuzius 77
Koselleck, Reinhart 17
Kuhn, Thomas S. 132

L

Lamprecht, Karl 65
Lukian of Samosata 61

M

Machiavelli 16
Meier, Christian 109, 163
Macaulay, Thomas B. 46
Marx, Karl 11, 32, 85
Meinecke, Friedrich 199
Menocchio 139
Michelet, Jules 46, 163
Mitscherlich, Alexander 200
Mitscherlich, Margarete 200
Mommsen, Theodor 16, 46

N

Negt, Oskar 93
Nietzsche, Friedrich 1, 12, 32, 86, 119, 189

P

Piaget, Jean 18, 27, 35

R

Ranke, Leopold von 3, 16, 41, 42, 43, 44, 45, 46, 47, 48, 49, 50, 51, 52, 53, 54, 60, 62, 136, 138, 154

S

Shakespeare 9, 10, 11
Sybel, Heinrich von 64

V

Voltaire 16, 17

W

Weber, Max 15, 59, 65, 69, 90, 96, 100, 103, 123, 137, 151
White, Hayden 9, 10, 12, 86, 119